TEACH THEM TO
CHALLENGE
AUTHORITY

Lauren Kline
Merry Christmas 2008
uncle Walter & Sasha

TEACH THEM TO
CHALLENGE
AUTHORITY

Educating for
Healthy Societies

GREGORY S. PRINCE, JR.

continuum

NEW YORK • LONDON

2008

The Continuum International Publishing Group Inc
80 Maiden Lane, New York, NY 10038

The Continuum International Publishing Group Ltd
The Tower Building, 11 York Road, London SE1 7NX

www.continuumbooks.com

Continuum is a member of Green Press Initiative, a nonprofit program dedicated to supporting publishers in their efforts to reduce their use of fiber obtained from endangered forests. We have elected to print this title on 50% postconsumer waste recycled paper. For more information, go to www.greenpressinitiative.org.

Printed in the United States of America

Library of Congress Cataloging-in-Publication Data

Prince, Gregory S.
Teach them to challenge authority : educating for healthy societies / Gregory S. Prince, Jr.
    p. cm.
Includes bibliographical references and index.
ISBN-13: 978-0-8264-9138-1 (hardcover : alk. paper)
ISBN-10: 0-8264-9138-3 (hardcover : alk. paper)
1. Education—Aims and objectives. 2. Education, Humanistic. I. Title.

LB41.P7657 2008
378'.015—dc22

                          2007047137

To teachers everywhere who seek to build healthy societies and

especially

William Sloan Coffin,

Toni Brewer Prince,

Gregory Smith Prince, III,

Tara Prince Chace,

Jameson Fales Chace

—all of whom have shown me what it means to be an exceptional

teacher.

Contents

Acknowledgments

Just as a book has many origins, it has many debts. Among the many to whom I owe a significant debt are:

- Exceptional educators for whom I had the privilege of working directly in my career: Preston Schoyer, A. Baker Duncan, William Davis, Leonard M. Rieser, John Kemeny, and the trustees of Hampshire College, under whom I served as president for sixteen years.
- Those who chaired the Hampshire board while I was president: John Watts, Henry Morgan, Blair Brown, Charles Taylor, and Jerry Nunnally. They and their trustee colleagues accepted and actively supported the premise that a college should model the behavior it expected of its students, even when doing so generated strong criticism of the college or when they personally were uncomfortable with certain activities.
- My presidential predecessors at Hampshire College—Franklin Patterson, Charles Longsworth, and Adele Simmons—who created the culture that made activist behavior an imperative. Their leadership made it clear that being a moral institution took precedence when choices had to be made, no matter what the cost of those choices.
- The educational leaders of the institutions profiled in this book—European Humanities University, the University Natal (now KwaZulu-Natal University), the Asian University for Women, Singapore Management University, and the American University in Bulgaria—who themselves have modeled, or are

modeling, so inspiringly the values they seek to impart in their students and who have done so in conditions that are so much more difficult than are likely to be found in the United States.

- The educators with whom I had direct contact, who spoke so openly and insightfully about education and who are mentioned by name in the text.
- The students with whom I had formal meetings and interviews and who spoke frankly about themselves and their education, including the Belarus students at the European Humanities University: Ihar Stankevich, Dmitry Boichenko, Artyom Anisimov, Olga Gerochynskaya, Iryna Checkanova, Tatsiana Babich, Daria Krapchilo, Olga Mishyna, Polina Pliashchenko, Anastasiya Matchanka, Ales Patapenka, Palina Mahilina, Valeria Paliakova, and Alesia Tsitova; and the multinational students at the American University in Bulgaria: Maria Amelicheva (Kazakhstan), Kastriol Fazliu (Kosovo), Mladen Petrov (Bulgaria), Lorena Baric (Serbia), Bela Geneva (Bulgaria), Sergiu Luca (Bulgaria), Victor Genev (Bulgaria), Spasimir Dinev (Bulgaria), Georgi Tsvetkov (Bulgaria), and Anna Stoeva (Russia and Bulgaria).
- Faculty who met with me at the European Humanities University: Ala Pigalskaya, Andrei Stepanov, Alexaner Filoctov, and Vladzimur Ronda; and at the American University in Bulgaria: Andrew White, Aernout Van Lynden, David Durst, Nedyalko Delchev, Dimitar Christozov, and Cosmina Tanasoiu.
- Administrators and supporters of education who helped me meet those who were so critical to my understanding of the international dimension of liberal education—at the European Humanities University: Anna Geramosiva and Juste Tolvaisaite; at the American University of Bulgaria: Michael Easton, President; Ann Ferren, Provost; and Lydia Krise, Dean of Students; at the Christian A. Johnson Foundation: Julie Kidd, President, who first introduced me to the Artis Liberalis movement in Europe and who later hired a Hampshire alumna, Susan Kassouf, who made valuable suggestions during the evolution of this work; William Newton-Smith, a trustee of the America University in Bulgaria, who introduced me both to the European Humanities University and

to the Asian University for Women; and Nancy Roth Remington, formerly Executive Director of International Programs at the Goizueta Business School of Emory University, who is now doing research on a project on the impact of liberal arts colleges founded in the late twentieth century outside of the United States, and who introduced me to contacts at Singapore Management University. In providing me assistance, they added their own insights and invaluable suggestions for my work.

- Colleagues who read this text and contributed their own suggestions, including Adele Simmons, former president of Hampshire College; Artemis Joukowsky, trustee and alumnus of Hampshire College; David Scott, former Chancellor of the University of Massachusetts; Penina Glazer and Marlene Fried, professors at Hampshire College; Myron Glazer, Professor at Smith College; Christopher Nelson, President of St. John's College, Annapolis, Maryland; Andrea Leskes, former Vice President of the American Association of Colleges and Universities and currently president of the Institute for American Universities in Aix en Province, France; Andrew Sigler, former CEO of Champion International and trustee of Dartmouth College; and Donald Hense, President of Friendship Public Charter Schools, Washington, D.C. (and someone who, by example, has taught me much about challenging authority). I benefited immensely from their comments and the generous gift of their time.
- Wilhelm Lindstrom from Helsinki, Finland, who served as an intern in the President's office at Hampshire in the summer of 2004 and who developed background material about educational developments in Europe and especially about the development of the Bologna Accords—work that proved valuable in my understanding the context in which the European Humanities University and the American University in Bulgaria function.
- Nardi Reeder Campion, who read early versions of parts of the text and encouraged me with trenchant, but sympathetic, criticism, and who passed away just one month before the manuscript was finished.
- The editors at Continuum Press: Anthony Hanes who made the first contact and Alexandra Webster who nurtured its

beginnings both in the London Office and David Barker, Katie Gallof, and Gabriella Page-Fort in the New York office, who saw it to conclusion, and especially the insightful suggestions from Michael Sandlin in the final process of editing.

- Eugene Land, who has encouraged educators in the United States to embrace the importance of community engagement and who helped me understand the importance of getting boards to make explicit commitments to engagement.

In the end, my greatest debt is to Nancy Kelly, who served as Counselor to the President and Secretary to the Board of Trustees at Hampshire College while I was president. Having studied at public and private universities, having taught in the English Department of the University of Massachusetts Boston, and having served as presidential advisor both at the University of Massachusetts, Boston, and at Hampshire, she used her wealth of experience to challenge narrow, self-congratulatory, and provincial views. She blended courage and wit in telling her colleagues when "the emperor"—or anyone else for that matter—"had no clothes," and had the judgment to know how to do it in a way that lessened, not intensified, the problem. She modeled tirelessly and with courage what it means to be an educator. She used all of those skills in assisting me with this manuscript and, as always, worked to lessen my stylistic failings. What is left is simply a statement that there is only so much one person can do.

○ ○ ○

The dedication of this book extends these acknowledgments and deserves some explanation. William Sloan Coffin contributed to my education for years, as well as to the formulation of the ideas expressed here. He not only helped to lead the freedom rides and build a bridge between generations, he was also my college chaplain at Yale University. For me personally he became in those years, and remained so for my entire career, a living conscience— a place where I could measure the rigor and courage, or lack thereof, in my own thinking, analysis, and actions. Sometimes from afar, sometimes in person, he was always gentle and tough at the same time. In person or in public, he never avoided saying what needed to be said no matter what the consequences, but he had the art of speaking in a way that strengthened one's best instincts. He was extraordinary in how he could disarm the resistance, even the hostility, of a listener. His life was a vibrant, ever-present model of what a great teacher should be. I could never match his wisdom or his rigor, but he was still willing to keep teaching and to spend time with me. I hope I returned the respect by continuing to learn.

In the course of considering the title for this book, I had a conversation with Coffin in early 2006. The working title at that point was *Challenging Authority: The Lost Art of Liberal Arts Education*. He suggested that I use the phrase "challenging convention," which he felt spoke to the power and inertia of culture; for him, "challenging authority" did not capture the spirit of the endeavor. In the end I did not use this suggestion because I felt it did not capture the courage of the North Carolina Agricultural and Technical Students who challenged the authority of the state, not just convention and custom. That authority, embodied in the shameful "Jim Crow" laws of the United States, constituted far more than custom and convention. I had a date to visit with Coffin for a second discussion about the title on Easter Saturday in 2006. He died of a heart attack three days before we met, so I will never know what his verdict would have been.

In dedicating this book to teachers, I am acknowledging my good fortune to have known so many exceptional teachers, who modeled far better than I ever could what great teaching means and its value for a society. There were not just one or two but dozens, and hundreds if I think of all of those with whom I have had the privilege to be a colleague over a career in education.

My greatest pleasure and learning have come from my immediate family, all educators and acknowledged in the dedication; but others in my extended family who also are or have been educators—working as trustees, administrators, teachers, and coaches—have added to that pleasure and learning and read and/or commented on this manuscript. In addition to my wife, son, daughter, and son-in-law, they are Cynthia Prince, Mary and Borden Ayers, and Sallie, Steven, Nicholas, and Nina Barker. My brother,

Edward Prince, persistently and patiently advocated, like the lawyer that he is, for the value of the courtroom-like classroom.

Finally, I acknowledge the four young freshmen at North Carolina Agricultural and Technical State University—Jibreel Khazan (Ezell Blair, Jr.), Franklin Eugene McCain, Joseph Alfred McNeil, and David Leinail Richmond, now deceased—who almost a half a century ago defined for me, as explained in the text, the true purpose of a liberal education and gave my generation an example of what all who seek to create healthy societies should want education to produce. My hope is that the content, as well as the title, of this book will respect and further their legacy. Furthering that legacy is needed now more than ever.

Foreword

In January of 2006, *Newsweek* columnist Fareed Zakaria asked Singapore Minister of Education Tharman Shanmugaratnam why Singapore's students led the world in international science and math exam scores but twenty to thirty years later were not leaders in their fields. Shanmugaratnam responded as follows:

> We both have meritocracies. Yours [the United States'] is a talent meritocracy, ours is an exam meritocracy. There are some parts of the intellect that we are not able to test well—like creativity, curiosity, a sense of adventure, ambition. Most of all, America has a culture of learning that challenges conventional wisdom—even if it means challenging authority. These are the areas where Singapore must learn from America.[1]

In the same month, half a world away in the United States, the Pennsylvania legislature was holding hearings on the state of academic freedom in its public universities. A group of academics was describing how the liberal bias of faculty in the United States was compromising the ability of universities to teach the art of critical thinking, which is so essential to challenging conventional wisdom and authority. These scholars argued that the proper role of liberal arts faculties and universities was to maintain an institutional posture of neutrality in the face of major intellectual and social issues: having presented a particular issue's main points, the faculty members would then let the students form their own opinions on the subject under discussion.

If these advocates of "neutralism"—in and of itself a nonneutral position—succeed in transforming universities into neutral institutions, they will undermine the critical thinking they seek to support. They will damage the core values of the American educational system that the rest of the world admires and increasingly attempts to emulate, such as American institutions' capacity to encourage creativity and risk taking and to equip students with the courage to challenge authority and convention in constructive ways. Equally important is the idea that neutrality makes it impossible for universities committed to promoting civic engagement to become models of the behavior they seek to instill in their students. This book, equal parts argument and memoir, is motivated by a concern that challenging convention and authority is becoming a lost art in liberal arts education in the United States. American universities are failing to exhibit the values and behaviors that their rhetorical goals and mission statements affirm. Engagement, as opposed to neutrality, is not a distraction—or as the advocates of neutrality argue, a barrier—to the "proper" role of education; engagement plays a central, critical role in all facets of a liberal education, especially in helping build healthy societies. To silence the university is to silence the citizenry. Our country and the rest of the world require commitment, engagement, and action from our educational institutions—not neutrality.

Academic leaders outside the United States (some of whom are profiled in this book) have inspired me to speak out against this silence. Far from being neutral, these inspirational individuals, often working in extremely difficult political, economic, and/or cultural contexts, have demonstrated the values of liberal education. Each day, they demonstrate with their courage and vision why the art of challenging authority is important to the long-term health of a society. These leaders could not assume a neutral stance even if they wanted to.

Students I have worked with for over forty years also have inspired me to speak out against this silence, primarily by demonstrating how responsibly they can act when given the chance to do so. As they educated me, I became fascinated by the polarity and conflict between those who see students as the objects of education and those who recognize students' creative potential to participate in their own educations. The former worry that students are at risk of manipulation by teachers; the latter feel that students are perfectly capable of defying those who might try to manipulate them.

As both a memoir and an argument, this book weaves together themes derived from what I have learned from students about education, educators, and those being educated. It draws most heavily on my role as president of Hampshire College, a small liberal arts college in Amherst, Massachusetts. Hampshire College was designed by educators at Amherst, Mount Holyoke, and Smith Colleges and the University of Massachusetts and opened in 1970 to offer a liberal arts education in which students engage in shaping their own education by negotiating with faculty a series of contracts that spell out the goals of each individual student's education plan and how his or her goals will be pursued and evaluated.

Part I explores the four principles that underlie my central convictions about the purpose of education:

1. The goal of education should be to build well-rounded, free-thinking individuals and communities that are economically productive, culturally creative, socially equitable, and supportive of human rights.
2. Essential for building healthy communities is the capacity and willingness of citizens to challenge authority and convention in constructive and appropriate ways. These citizens will generate the innovations and changes in their communities that help to limit exploitation, authoritarianism, environmental degradation, racism, or simple selfishness. Their creativity drives economic growth, promotes a vibrant culture, and is a critical source of the courage that allows students to resist inappropriate pressure from peers, the culture at large, or even from governments.
3. Democracy and freedom facilitate critical activities that bind healthy societies together. But these principles alone are not enough.
4. A liberal education is the final critical component to a strong society. An educator's emphasis on developing a capacity for critical thinking—rather than simply introducing students to

different forms of knowledge—is the most effective way to educate students to act responsibly and effectively when challenging authority and convention.

The educators I challenge in this book share my commitment to both the importance of a liberal education and the importance of nurturing critical thinking. But our similarities end there, as they argue that students cannot be taught to think for themselves by individuals who constantly assert their own strong personal opinions. The responsibility of teachers, they argue, is to simply present all sides of an issue and remain neutral, leaving students to make up their own minds.

Part II of this book draws on examples of liberal education outside of the United States to illuminate the importance of choosing engagement over neutrality. These international examples demonstrate for American academics the obligations, power, purpose, and consequences of liberal education. These models from abroad also point to an unusual irony: the student-activist form of liberal arts education that originated in the United States may be better understood in other parts of the world. The original purpose of this type of liberal education was to develop habits of mind that lead to principled action and not simply reflection or inert critical thinking.

Part III of the book explores issues raised throughout the book concerning the nature of students and how best to educate them. I argue that students want to be engaged—they often demand to be engaged, in my experience—and that they are far less vulnerable than my proneutrality opponents assert. Students do not fear advocacy; they seek teachers who speak in authentic voices and both advocate and listen while encouraging students to challenge ideas put forth by faculty members. Absorbing knowledge is an appropriate part of the educational process. But when students are treated only as the objects of education, they learn far less than when they are purposefully engaged in seeking their own answers to questions, rather than relying on a mentor to approve their ideas.

Theodore and Nancy Sizer, leading educators in the United States, have eloquently explained in *The Students Are Watching* that students learn far more by observing adults than by listening to what they say.[2] I believe, however, that adults can learn more by listening to what the *students* say. In the United States and in the international institutions profiled here, students watch closely to see if adults' actions and policies embody the values they try to teach. Furthermore, students want to be know whether faculty and administrators will listen to and engage them in meaningful ways. Educators need to listen, not because students are always right, but because listening is the first step toward engagement, and engagement is the foundation for teaching students how to challenge authority in constructive and appropriate ways.

PART  1

Two Views of Education

CHAPTER

Origins: Educating a College President

Every book has a multitude of origins. The beginning of my understanding of the purposes of education lies in my years as an undergraduate. Around that time, four African American students from North Carolina Agricultural and Technical College (A&T) began to take their studies in philosophy and the contemporary world seriously. They began to ask a series of critical questions that eventually became one simple and profound question: Why could they not eat lunch at the same counter as whites in Greensboro, North Carolina? Their straightforward answer in 1960, my junior year at Yale University, effectively began the civil rights sit-in movements in the United States. This activism connected a younger generation to what an older generation had begun with the bus boycott in Montgomery, Alabama, several years earlier.

As college freshmen, these four students asked questions—in this case about race and the nature of society—analyzed possible answers, made judgments, and then acted in a creative, constructive, appropriate, and courageous way. Their simple act of sitting at a whites-only lunch counter, asking to be served, and when refused refusing to leave until forced to by closing or police, and the dignity with which they undertook it, drew from many sources—family, church, community, and school. But what affected me deeply was that they were students my age, much like me in some ways; but in other ways they were so much further ahead of me at that moment in their ability to connect what they were studying to their society and to understand where authority needed to be challenged and having the courage to do so.

Their act came at a time of quiet ferment and questioning in the United States. At the end of the 1950s, college students were beginning to wonder about the purposes of education. Helping to stimulate these questions were images and articles about the courage and determination of students, such as those who took stands against immoral authoritarian governments in Hungary and South Africa. Some of those students, forced to live in exile, ended up on various American campuses, including Yale. Their presence and their stories represented a level of student purposefulness that, at the end of the 1950s, was not a part of college life at Yale or any other campus in the United States, for that matter. The events in North Carolina changed all of that.

The North Carolina A&T students answered our question about the purpose of education. Their answer was identical to what those of us at Yale had been hearing from the exiled students, but we had yet to realize that their brand of activism also applied to our situation. Education has multiple purposes, but learning how to ask essential questions and how to challenge dogma, tradition, and injustice in appropriate and constructive ways is its highest purpose. Preparing citizens to act thoughtfully to create a more just, open, and creative society gives form, substance, and meaning to the often abstract concepts of freedom and democracy.

Constructively challenging authority requires the basic habits of mind a liberal education seeks to instill: the ability to frame the essential questions; to think critically, analytically, and ethically about the problems those questions identify; and to respond effectively, creatively, and wisely to the implications of the analysis. It requires not only an ability to appreciate the complexity of a problem but also to identify its essence in order to reach effective, just, and fair conclusions.

The answer the four North Carolina A&T students provided about the purpose of education exemplified all of the aforementioned qualities and yet was replete with irony. The irony stemmed from the fact that these students came from a technical university, not a liberal arts university, nor was the university listed among the country's "elite" institutions. As the students' actions played out, commentators of the day noted the visual images of neatly dressed, polite African American students sitting at lunch counters while white thugs and police threatened them. Those images underscored the critical relationship between "means" and "ends." The students set an example with the rigor of their analysis and with the dignity of the means they chose to respond to the situation. They understood that no matter how worthy the end, the means were equally important.

The second point of origin came much later, in conversations with my wife, Toni Prince, about conversations that were not taking place. In the 1980s she began commenting to me about the students with whom she worked. She coached skiing and horseback riding and was increasingly perplexed that the kids she coached rarely seemed to discuss the major issues of the day in their schools. When they arrived after school, she would ask them if they had talked about an impending foreign intervention, a political campaign, affirmative action, or whatever the "front page" controversy of the day might be locally, nationally, or internationally. More often than not, there had been no discussions of these important matters in school. She became increasingly concerned that teachers were becoming so fearful of the anger that controversial topics might generate and of the litigiousness of U.S. society that they simply avoided controversy whenever possible.

She had alerted me to a trend that was nonexistent during our youth and one I would never have noticed, since I was working exclusively with college students. We had both attended primary schools where such substantial conversations about important current affairs were standard: she was at Sidwell Friends School and I attended St. Albans School, both in Washington, D.C. Those conversations opened for us a whole range of educational experiences that we valued deeply, and we despaired that the current generation of children had lost a critical source of information and insight. We worried that children were caught in a growing bubble of silence, increasingly oblivious to the world around them. They seemed unable to ask meaningful questions and did not know how to have a debate or disagreement with someone, yet still be friends.

The third point of origin again related to conversations, but ones that took place during my years as president of Hampshire College, a liberal arts college in Amherst, Massachusetts. With only four or five exceptions, every Monday morning from 1989 through 2005, when classes were in session, I had breakfast in the college dining hall from 7:30 a.m. to 9:00 a.m. so I could talk with students about any subject they wanted to discuss. Breakfast was in their space, so no appointment was needed.

The students probed, complained, questioned, and explored. They shared concerns and pressed me for opinions. The normal whining that can characterize any group of students in a university did occur, although not as much as I had originally expected. Early on, one student assured me there would not be too many whiners: "They don't like to get up at seven-thirty." The students who came to breakfast were anything but silent.

The concerns voiced at these breakfasts were wide-ranging ones: appointments and reappointments of faculty and staff; curriculum, college regulations, and discipline cases; there were conversations about resources for academic programs and extracurricular organizations such as the student Emergency Medical Technicians, and about national and international current events. During this period, the Berlin Wall fell, the USSR splintered apart, China became a major economic power, the United States fought the first Gulf War and started the second, 9/11 took place, and the economy went twice from expansion, to recession, and then to recovery. Through all the conversations, profound and petty alike, the students delivered one consistent message: what mattered most to them was whether the college and I, as its president, were acting in ways that were consistent with what they perceived to be the values and goals embodied in the college's mission. They had two common, strongly held expectations: the college should exhibit the behavior it expected of students and hold true to its espoused values. Students measured almost every decision the administration made against these standards.

Reflecting both the cynicism of youth and of the culture as a whole, many did not believe there was much chance that the college, its president and administration, or the board would live up to those expectations. At times they treated those breakfasts like a contest or a sport. They prepared, practiced, and often arrived as a team. They sought to confront me with an issue about which they felt they held a clear ethical position—a position they felt I might not support because of "practical" pressures. How I reacted would reveal whether or not the college was committed to its ideals. They were doing what all young adults will do at some point with their elders: test them.

Their "tactic" was to challenge me to assess the real purpose of what education should be about; they felt that education should offer serious examination of issues and values in a context that was real, not artificial. The college administrators, faculty, and publications constantly told the students that they had to learn how to think critically and to ask the essential questions; they had to take, defend, and develop positions; they had to be engaged and involved in their work and their community while being ethical, just, and fair. Conversely, they wanted the college to be engaged, to take outspoken positions on social and political issues, and forcefully to lead its students. The administration, collectively and individually, attempted to respond. I often responded that although the college did not take a position on every issue, the one stance the college could never take was that the college and its president should not take positions.

In those sixteen years of breakfast conversations, the students affirmed the most important lessons any educator, and certainly any college president, needs to learn:

1. Listen to students. They speak more frankly than their elders, and they ask good questions, although the questions sometimes come in the form of demands.
2. Respect students enough to engage them with real problems and encourage them to ask real questions. Expect the best, and they will give their best.
3. Model for students the same behavior and values that the institution would like to instill in them. Anything less will generate cynicism.

4. Enjoy students. Although they can be frustratingly immature at times, the same can be said of every other constituency with which an educator works. At least in the case of students, their behavior is likely to be age appropriate. Most of the time, they are fun; they care about the things you want them to care about and have a sense of humor.

If you invite students to speak, if you listen to them, take them seriously, and are not dismissive (even when you disagree with them or they are not as well informed as they might be) they will give back even more of value to you and the institution. They will give you faith and hope that there can and will be a better world in the future.

My experiences teaching at the Chinese University of Hong Kong, working as a guidance counselor and history teacher in a secondary school, as a graduate student, and as an administrator and adjunct professor at Dartmouth College (before I arrived at Hampshire) convinced me that, given the chance, students will be creative, stimulating, and responsible beyond their years. If educators expect the best, they will get the best. For that potential to be realized, however, educators must respect and listen to students. When I did listen, time and again students provided me some of the most meaningful knowledge I received as a college president.

In graduate school, I worked with undergraduates in the Ulysses S. Grant Foundation, which was an independent organization founded in 1954 by Yale undergraduates to assist inner-city students in New Haven, Connecticut, to prepare for college. The program had started working with first-graders in 1954 as the landmark U.S. Supreme Court *Brown vs. Board of Education* decision began to transform the U.S. educational environment. Yale undergraduates were working with their first senior class in 1966 when I entered graduate school. When they discovered there was a graduate student at Yale who had done college placement, they sought me out and asked if I would advise them and the high school seniors. For four years I worked with an extraordinary group of high school and college students during the turmoil associated with the end of the 1960s. I learned from them that 90 percent of education is expectation and that expectations are a critical factor in making a youngster's education successful. Moreover, students often set higher expectations than their elders.

At Dartmouth College in the 1970s and the 1980s I served as faculty advisor to the Native American students, who helped me gain a more nuanced understanding of diversity. These students, representing many different Native American nations, organized themselves imaginatively and effectively to interact with a majority culture that thought of them as a single homogeneous group. They operated on the principle that no one would speak for the Native Americans at Dartmouth until they, the students, had reached a consensus on a position. Failing to achieve that consensus, they agreed there would be no "Native American position," just individuals giving their opinions. This student community faced many complex conflicts with the majority community over issues such as the college's use of a stereotypical and depersonalized image of an Indian as its symbol, while still learning to live with the differences between multiple Indian nations. In response, the students demonstrated courage, patience, perseverance, a willingness to listen, and an uncommon wisdom in their individual and collective responses.

Individual students were also critical advisors in my education. When I arrived at Dartmouth in June 1970 to be dean of the summer programs, I was just out of graduate school. To support my orientation I hired Paul Gambaccini, a recent graduate who had been General Manager of WDCR, Dartmouth's AM radio station. Besides advising the radio station for the summer term, his main responsibility was to spend a few hours each week telling me stories about Dartmouth and his own experiences with the college. Among many lessons I learned were that if you want to know what really goes on at a college, ask the students. Not surprisingly, Paul later became world famous as a music and cultural commentator for the BBC and continues to enlighten audiences with his trenchant cultural observations and commentary.

Another Dartmouth student, Dean Esserman, whom I taught as a freshman, quickly showed me that undergrads could possess a level of creativity, commitment, and follow-through I had never imagined. (Dean would later have an important impact on my time at Hampshire, as I explain in Chapter 8.) During his four years as an undergraduate, Dean helped establish the first emergency medical response team for the New York Transit Police and also helped create a Spanish-language training program at Dartmouth for the transit police. Also through his efforts, Dartmouth would be among the first colleges to host a Chinese delegation after the normalization of relations between the United States and China. He then arranged one of the first student trips to China, which laid the foundation for the college's first study-abroad programs in that country. When he proposed an idea, even if it seemed improbable, I learned to listen.

I created the Monday breakfasts at Hampshire as a way of continuing my own education. These breakfasts confirmed over and over again how much students can tell you about what is happening at a university and were an equally valuable reality check on how our society viewed students. I was often startled by the contrast between what I was seeing and what some outside commentators were saying. In fact, this book found its origins in the very different conclusions others reached while observing the same generation of students, especially Robert J. Bork and his strong criticism (in *Slouching Toward Gomorrah: Modern Liberalism and American Decline*) of the student generation with which I was working. He, and conservative commentators like him, saw wild, irresponsible, hedonistic students attacking tradition and challenging authority in confrontational and inappropriate ways. To be sure, I noticed some of that behavior but never felt it came close to outweighing the students' positive aspects. The conflicts and controversy arising from this dualistic view of students became a central part of the "culture wars" in the United States and remain so today.

The pressure to create the neutral university that this book is responding to has it roots in the culture wars—a term used to describe an ongoing conflict in the United States between conservatives and liberals over what should be most valued in our culture. Conservatives like Bork were concerned most with preserving traditional values, the canon of great books in Western civilization, and what they called the "principle of intellectual meritocracy." The liberals favored more inclusiveness and openness in education, from who attended college to what was taught. The nature and potential of youth was a central point of disagreement.

Indeed, the nature of attitudes toward students defines many of the positions taken on education in the United States, and the positions I take in this book cannot be understood without understanding the intensity of those attitudes. Because I argue that educators should begin by listening to students, my argument must begin with the students. Those with opposing views, such as Bork, represent the cultural context that shapes the debate about the purposes of education.

Bork, a distinguished American legal scholar, provided one of the most exhaustive intellectual frameworks for this opposing view of students. His very negative portrait of young people, widely applauded in conservative circles, was nothing like my own experience with youth. When Bork's nomination for a position on the U.S. Supreme Court failed, it was the first time a Supreme Court nominee had been rejected in many years. He responded by writing *Slouching Toward Gomorrah*, a personal, albeit shrill, commentary on the causes and meaning of that failed nomination. In doing so, he wove together the multiple themes of the conservative critique of tertiary education in the United States, of the professoriate, and of youth. His portrait of students reveals much about the historical and intellectual roots of the concern about bias in the academy and why so many want to impose a posture of neutrality on it. Bork's extreme viewpoints on American youth are echoed today by right-leaning public intellectuals such as Dinesh D'Souza, William F. Buckley, William Bennett, and E.D. Hirsch, and also conservative pundits such as Don Imus, Laura Ingraham, and Rush Limbaugh.

In what was effectively a diatribe against the younger generation and their university teachers, Bork began with a trenchant observation:

> The complexity of institutions and relationships in our society was never well understood, and the freedom and power of those institutions and relationships rested in no small measure on an unreasoned, awed acceptance of them. The spread of education, particularly universal education, has served to decrease that awe without increasing, in the same proportion, the reality of understanding. We are left unhappily in between. Respect founded on ignorance is lost but is not fully replaced with respect founded on sophistication.[1]

Bork's thesis is straightforward. American civilization is in decline because modern liberalism and its powerful ally, American education, have continually led the younger generation astray. The cumulative results over decades, says Bork, have been a decline in moral values, less civic responsibility, and more irresponsible behavior. Modern liberalism, in his view, combines radical egalitarianism and radical individualism into a "corrosive" force in which "the former favors outcomes rather than opportunities, and the latter limits itself to personal gratification." He goes on to argue that when "egalitarianism reinforces individualism, it denies the possibility that one culture or moral view can be superior and the result of such a position is moral chaos." Finally, he concludes that this kind of egalitarianism will push us toward a powerful state oriented to suppressing the differences that freedom produces, thus creating the paradoxical possibility that radical individualism will become the "handmaiden of state tyranny."[2]

Bork regards students just beginning their education as savages who need to be acculturated and civilized. In the conservative tradition, he sees human nature as something to be reined in, so that chaos and hedonism cannot triumph. Liberalism fails for Bork because it places too great a faith in the potential of the individual to be morally responsible. The intensity of the critique of U.S. society that erupted in the 1960s undermined the acculturation process and offered nothing to replace what was being destroyed. For Bork, students were not able to grasp the complexity of the issues at stake and were not active agents in the process of analysis and evaluation. They were the prize that faculty members fought over, and in the 1960s liberals were claiming the prize and having an undue influence on these young people. The result, he believed, was a self-referential morality that allowed the individual's own pleasure to triumph over community responsibility.[3]

What most disturbs Bork is the idealism of intellectuals and their faith that a more perfect world can be created. Bork feels that ivory-towered intellectuals have extended the faith and optimism of religion into politics and into the classroom, generating an unrealistic, unsophisticated, and simplistic view of the perfectibility of society. When that simplistic expectation runs into reality, it supposedly generates cynicism and a resulting inward turn that is selfish and hedonistic: in short, Bork views the intellectual as a dreamer, out of touch with reality and having nothing useful to say. As an example of the problem, Bork cites Hillary Rodham Clinton's commencement address at Wellesley College in 1992: "For too long our leaders have used politics as the art of the possible. And the challenge now is to practice politics as the art of making what appears to be impossible possible."[4] He then cites journalist Michael Kelly, who notes that the Wellesley speech and one given in Texas share all the same traits:

> vaulting ambition, didactic moralizing, intellectual incoherence, and adolescent assumption that the past does not exist and the present needs only your guiding hand to create the glorious future.[5]

A second characteristic of modern liberalism for Bork is its hostility to "bourgeois culture and society"—his word choice here sounding oddly similar to the way some liberals would describe conservative culture. He delineates all of the criticisms academics in the United States have levied against Western Civilization, concluding that the intellectual is sustained by his or her hatred of the West. With this negativism, Bork insists, the academics have destroyed the students' naïve faith in their own culture but did not replace this lost faith with a sophisticated appreciation for any culture. For him, this unwinding of the values of Western Civilization surfaces in all parts of society; and, by implication, the dominance of the radical liberal view in the classroom will bring about the unraveling of American society.[6]

Furthermore, Bork insists that the liberal agenda's radical individualism inevitably undercuts individual responsibility, equating equality of outcomes with equality of opportunity. Moral values disappear among the "barbarians," leading, among other things, to a rise in illegitimate births in our society that, in turn, leads to the rise of crime and violence and the collapse of moral values.

> The approximate cause of these pathologies is the infatuation of modern liberalism with the individual's right to self-gratification along with the kind of egalitarianism, largely based on guilt, that inhibits judgment and reform.[7]

The ultimate pathology for Bork is the "killing for convenience" advocated by the prochoice movement in the United States as embodied in *Roe vs. Wade*, the U.S. Supreme Court decision that legalized abortion. With respect to race, Bork concludes that the fundamental problem in the United States is the dominance of the radical egalitarian philosophy that leads African Americans to believe "that, absent discrimination, an equality of results in every area of endeavor would be the natural outcome for different ethnic groups. Cultural relativism insists that no culture is superior to any other in preparing individuals to succeed in a complex commercial society."[8]

Bork wants us to believe that all of these failures lie at the feet of academics and their molding of society's value system. His passion for the importance of education and the university would surprise the many academics who dismiss his opinions. Although I disagree with almost all of his positions, I admire his reverence for education and his need to be outspoken on this subject. In his chapter on the intellectual, he begins:

> If, as Brigette Berger has quite plausibly asserted, "the fate of the modern university and the fate of Western civilization are inextricably intertwined," our prospects at the moment do not seem bright. Universities are central cultural institutions. Their preservation of the great works and traditions of Western civilizations, including the tradition of rationality and skepticism, have been crucial to the growth of intellectual freedom, respect for the role of law and scientific progress.[9]

He also asserts that an "egalitarian educational system is necessarily opposed to meritocracy and a reward for achievement."[10] For Bork, liberal professors continue to undermine the core values of society, and professors crossing boundaries and indoctrinating students intensify the process. Alarmed by the evidence he perceived to be everywhere, he feared that the "barbarians" had triumphed. Moral and spiritual regeneration usually come from religious revivals and the revival of public discourse about morality and cataclysmic events.[11] In the 1990s, when he wrote *Slouching Toward Gomorrah*, he saw few signs of such a revival. However, he saw a few signs of hope, such as the rise of gated communities and home schooling.

It is hard to tell whether or not Bork is encouraged by the new-found political power of the religious right since he published *Slouching Toward Gomorrah*. The rise of the religious right is truly a double-edged sword for an intellectual such as himself. However, he should be encouraged by the rising chorus of talk show hosts, news commentators, legislators, policy makers, and parents in the United States who urge, and sometimes demand, that neutrality become the standard for tertiary education when dealing with controversial issues. Neutrality has become the antidote of choice to counter the perceived insidious influence of the liberal faculty. Bork's like-minded peers who advocated for neutrality at the Pennsylvania hearings pointed to the widespread influence of negativism among liberal faculty members toward existing U.S. institutions as one of the reasons the public should care about faculty bias.

Many educators and an even larger number of university trustees accept neutrality's core premise, even if they do not buy into the conservative critique of liberal education. They feel that universities should be neutral with respect to major intellectual or public issues of the day, and faculty in the classroom should not take positions on issues that do not relate specifically to the course's subject matter. The advocates for neutrality argue that if professors, in pursuit of the goal of critical thinking, put forth their own opinions, they would unduly influence, if not intimidate or indoctrinate, their students. By extension, institutions taking one-sided stances would be unfair to the multiple constituencies they represent. Balance, fairness, and neutrality are becoming the new mantras in the field of education.

○ ○ ○

My experiences throughout this period inspired a very different strategy for avoiding the excesses to which Bork was reacting and of which, in a later period, I was the object. Engage the students. Engagement provides opportunities to demonstrate how confrontation can be done both effectively and civilly. Many times I found it very difficult, when confronted by anger, passion, self-righteousness, or arrogance, to separate the substance from the manner of delivery and deal with each separately. To help me do so, I developed a consistent set of standards, first as I threaded my way through the controversies my portfolio of responsibilities at Dartmouth—affirmative action officer, faculty advisor for the Native Americans at Dartmouth, and dean responsible for interdisciplinary programs such as Environmental Studies, Native American Studies, and Women's Studies—generated. They involved many of the culture war issues in the United States focusing on redefinitions of the curriculum, inclusion of new traditions in the literary canon, affirmative action, and political correctness for those whose voices had been silenced in the past. Most were controversial nationally and generated conflict with Dartmouth alumni and students and especially with the ultraconservative student paper, the *Dartmouth Review*.

As I participated in, and worked my way through, these controversies in the 1970s and 1980s, I developed my standards into what I came to call the Principles of Discourse, as a way of separating concerns about "process" from disagreements about "substance." I argued that these principles were as critical to the well being of the academy as free speech was to the society as a whole. But I also stressed that what was good for the academy may not always be good for society at large. The Principles of Discourse include the following tenets:

Value truth and the process of seeking truth as ends in themselves;

Accept responsibility to articulate a position as close to the truth as one can make it, using to the best of one's ability available evidence, and the rules of reason, logic, and relevance;

Listen openly, recognizing always that new information may alter one's position;

Welcome evaluation and accept and encourage disagreement and criticism even to the point of seeking out for ourselves that which will disprove our position;

Refuse to reduce disagreement to personal attacks or attacks on groups or classes of individuals;

Value civility, even in disagreement;

Embrace the premise that ends, no matter how worthy, cannot justify means that violate the Principles.

Although my Principles of Discourse first served as a private guide for sorting through issues that arose in conversations with students, I eventually articulated them publicly in explaining to alumni and the public in general my objections to the *Dartmouth Review*'s stance—such as their propensity to transform their objections to academic programs like Women's Studies or their support of Dartmouth's Indian symbol into personal attacks on the groups and individuals involved.

Everyone, including members of the press and the media, would do well to abide by these principles, although the important constitutional protections that freedom of speech and freedom of press provide in the United States make it possible to ignore the Principles of Discourse outside of academia. The flourishing of academic freedom, on the other hand, depends on the Principles of Discourse, as does being an engaged university, since these principles are what make engagement educational and constructive rather than destructive and intimidating.

The Principles served me well at Dartmouth and at Hampshire, and they are ultimately what must guide the entire academic process. They are what help make challenging authority and convention appropriate, effective, creative, and constructive, whether it is for the purpose of promoting social change, for resisting inappropriate peer pressure, or restraining the excesses that Bork appropriately condemns. They embody the essence of civility and underscore that disagreement taking place in the academy is just as important as the substance of the disagreement itself. The Principles can also be a standard for assessing political and social dialogue in the larger society, just as they would be within a single institution.

○ ○ ○

In the United States, debates about whether faculty are too liberal or whether sufficient diversity of opinion exists in the classroom focus on political diversity when the more serious gap comes from a lack of international perspective. The absence of that broader international perspective has crippled America's conversations about education and has, in particular, limited our understanding of the nature of liberal education. The effort to dispel silence, to resist the call for neutrality, and to generate a more nuanced conversation about the purposes of education in the United States must extend beyond our borders and the narrow confines of the U.S. culture wars.

The need for this international or global perspective is ultimately rooted in the multicultural origins of liberal education and its appropriateness and effectiveness across all cultures. This form of education achieved its purest expression in America in the nineteenth century, with the development of small residential liberal arts colleges. But the goals of liberal education have been central to many great universities throughout the world. This universality is not surprising, given that the conceptual origins of liberal arts education followed a path over the centuries that crisscrossed Asia, Africa, Europe, the Americas, and Australia. We are all related through its DNA, just as we are all indebted to those four African American students in North Carolina and to the students who came from Hungary, South Africa, China, and elsewhere seeking a liberal arts education that could nurture their capacity to challenge authority and make positive contributions to society.[12]

The concept of liberal education first emerged during the eighteenth century and the Enlightenment, as scholars, church leaders, and rulers began to argue over the value of reason and experimentation in a world guided by revelation and divine wisdom. Liberal arts emerged as that broad body of knowledge that was needed to support reason in the effort to understand nature, human events, and their relationship to God's will. Content and the affirmation of reason to challenge revelation became one and the same. Knowledge and reason eventually challenged and then replaced revelation as the core of education, and yet the tension between reason and revelation has always remained. It continues to play out in the United States, where the rise of an interest in spirituality and in intuitive as well as rational modes of inquiry have gained a hearing in the academy, and in other parts of the world such as the Middle East, South Asia, East Asia, Africa, and Latin America. That tension is a reminder that even when rationality challenges revelation, there can still be room for both.

In support of reason, liberal education developed over the centuries into a type of education that valued a breadth of knowledge as a means not only for communicating effectively and developing the individual's capacity to think critically, clearly, and creatively but for judging and acting wisely and collaboratively.[13] Although liberal education came to be synonymous with the importance of exposing students to multiform modes of inquiry, at its core a liberal education is about developing a specific set of mental habits. These habits do much to stimulate creativity, innovation, and invention; they also often lead to challenges of orthodoxy, convention, and even authority not rooted in reason and moral and ethical values. Liberal education, unlike general education (a term often used in the United States to describe the requirement that students be exposed to a broad range of fields or modes of inquiry), is about developing a spirit of inquiry, not about acquiring a body of knowledge. Liberal education, with its emphasis on inquiry and critical thinking, inevitably opposes those who seek to create a compliant population, whether for the purpose of creating a competent workforce or for nurturing the blind acceptance of convention, revelation, or authority. Liberal education is not hostile to convention, nor does it reject revelation or authority; it rejects unthinking, uncritical acceptance of these things.

When liberal education succeeds, it creates individuals with the insight to distinguish between that which is ethical, timeless, and profound in their culture and that which is not, and the courage to embrace and advocate for the former. It is an education in the art of knowing oneself and in appreciating the rich potential and complexity of the human mind. It enhances the quality of the conversations we have with ourselves. It celebrates the spirit of individual inquiry, which fact alone makes it invaluable. But a liberal education is also for the communal self. It teaches one how to balance individual and community needs.[14] It generates an ability to handle complexity and change without retreating into simplistic or destructive responses. It develops the art of questioning and of challenging authority and convention. Liberal education frees the individual from tradition for tradition's sake in order to shape a more just, healthy, and creative future. Or as Andrew deRocca, former commissioner for education for the state of Connecticut, defined it succinctly: liberal education exists to develop "skeptical reverence."[15]

When I first heard Andrew deRocca define the goal of liberal education as the development of skeptical reverence, I was attending a conference in Budapest, hosted by the Christian A. Johnson Endeavor Foundation and the Artes Liberalis movement that the foundation has supported. The conference brought together educational leaders from the United States and Central Europe to examine the potential role of liberal arts education in restoring democratic institutions in the formerly authoritarian societies of Central and Eastern Europe.

These European educators clearly understood that liberal arts education stood at the center of the conflicts taking place in many countries over how best to develop human potential and what role that potential, with its capacity for critical thinking, could play in the development of a society. An education that trains students to look at a problem critically and comprehensively must inevitably threaten anyone who wants to build a society based on unchallenged acceptance of authority. These leaders also did not want their new post-Communist societies to mirror the educational systems that existed before Communism. The pre-Communist educational systems had, in fact, made it easier for Communist systems to take root because they discouraged the students from challenging authority or orthodoxy. The conflict they saw was not just one between democratic and authoritarian governments; it was fundamentally about human nature and how education can best develop the human potential.

Freedom allows us the right to be creative or indolent, caring or selfish. Liberal education, on the other hand, is about what we do with our freedom. Liberal education can help individuals use their freedom to better their own lives and the communities where they live and work. As human beings, are we meant to develop as individuals serving only our own needs or also serving the needs of others? Do we aspire to develop as critically thinking, creative, innovative, humane people, or do we just want to think of ourselves as members of a specific nation and culture? Freedom allows choice and liberal education advocates for a specific choice: that the purpose of freedom is to enable creative, critically thinking, caring individuals to build healthy societies that serve universal (not just parochial) ends. In arguing for this communal purpose, I uphold the concept of liberal education as it developed in the United States, where it was most often associated with both a communal and an individual purpose.

Conflicts today in places such as the Middle East, Sudan, or North Korea are as much about an approach to education that will best promote a certain vision of humanity as they are about resources, power, or nationalism. Conflicts about different visions of humanity matter. In some respects, these different visions are what matter most to a society, because they define the type of individuals who will live in any specific culture. Ultimately the conflict within and between these societies is a conflict between those who claim to possess absolute truth through power or revelation and those who claim truth to be the product of critical reasoning. Each position is based on a very different view of humanity and the human potential: the former is absolute and cannot be challenged, while the latter is tentative and seeks to be challenged. Those who support critical reasoning do not necessarily deny that truth exists, but they do accept that the concept of truth is rarely understood and must always be subject to examination and reexamination. Yet they have no need to deny revelation. What they oppose are assertions that revelations cannot be challenged and that their interpretations and meanings are frozen in time.

The effort to eliminate critical thinking and challenges to authority, orthodoxy, or convention can take place in any culture. Critical reasoning has been both supported and suppressed by societies under the influence of Islam, Judaism, and Christianity; freedom and democracy alone do not insure reason will be accepted. That is why demagoguery is so dangerous to democracy. Liberals and conservatives alike have supported and suppressed critical thinking. Dictators fear it. What joins all sides in these conflicts, ironically, is their understanding of the power of education devoted to promoting critical thinking. What differentiates them is the value they place on individual rights. Those who seek to preserve absolute power fully understand the threat of critical thinking and an education that promotes it, just as those who seek to create healthy democratic communities understand its nurturing role.

Every nation has a stake in any one country's stance on the fundamental purposes of education. Both the positive and negative consequences that follow from different answers will affect many countries, not just the one in which such a decision is made. Ironically, peace activists and terrorists alike understand the importance of education. Education matters. If it did not, every authoritarian government in the world would not try so hard to control it. If education matters, then conversations about the purposes of education also matter and are critical to the health of any society. These are not abstract conversations, for the world faces a major divide between those within their respective cultures who celebrate independent critical thinking and those who fear the challenges to authority and convention that come from such thinking. The world today does not face a clash of civilizations. It faces a clash within civilizations about the nature of education, the human spirit, and human development. As every country is beginning to learn, terrorists can come from within and not just from "over there."

○ ○ ○

We need a global conversation about the purposes of education. Educators in the United States should be indebted to a small but growing group of educational leaders throughout the world— some of whom are involved with the Artes Liberalis Movement, such as Serhiy Ivaniouk, Rector of Kiev Mohyla Academy; Jan Sokol, former Minister of Education under Vaclev Havel and then head of the Institute of Fundamental Learning within Charles University in Prague and head of the Center for Studies in Classical Tradition; and Julia Stefanova from Sofia University—who are modeling the fundamental purposes of liberal education with a kind of clarity and immediacy that one rarely sees in the United States. In their respective countries, these leaders are undertaking experiments in liberal education that should instruct and inspire anyone interested in building strong, healthy communities.

From them we can learn the ways in which the art of teaching students to challenge authority appropriately has been reinvigorated. In America, where freedoms are often taken for granted, challenging convention is becoming a lost art. That art desperately needs rediscovery and renewal. Without it, our creativity as a society and the vitality of our democratic civic culture will suffer. A silent, disengaged, and neutral education is even more devastating than a silent spring. We need engagement, even with all of the difficulties that engagement brings. Neutrality, which can breed passivity, is far safer in the short run; but it may also be far more dangerous to our own social, political, and economic stability. As the history of education in pre– and post–World War II Europe demonstrates, any delay in resisting those who would suppress institutions that promote intellectual freedom, democratic processes, and critical thinking quickly makes resistance impossible. As the world fights those who use violence to advance their agenda, engagement, not neutrality, is needed in our educational systems.

CHAPTER 2

The Engaged University vs. the Neutral University

In April 1996, as I departed the courthouse in Northampton, Massachusetts, a large man approached me and said in a quiet but threatening voice, "We know where you live." I had just testified in a defamation suit brought by a prolife activist named John Burt against Hampshire College and Marlene Fried, a Hampshire faculty member and Director of its Civil Liberties and Public Policy Program. Having listened to Burt defend the right to use violence against abortion doctors, I understood all too well the intended threat. Hampshire had already alerted the police about the case and of the potential for some form of violence. Just months before, two medical clinic workers had been assassinated in Brookline, Massachusetts, and a doctor had been shot and killed in the state of New York. In the context of the overall struggle over reproductive rights, my encounter was insignificant; but it reminded me that being president of an educational institution that prided itself on being "engaged" was never simple in theory or in practice.

The events that led Hampshire College, Professor Fried, and me to that courtroom in Northampton began many years before and came to represent an affirmation of the engaged university and the antithesis of the concept of the neutral university. Our Civil Liberties Program had been founded through the generous support of an industrialist, Toni Huber. He had no direct connection with Hampshire but had been attracted to the college by the leadership of my predecessor, Adele Simmons. In particular, he supported the concept that a university should be willing to take stands on social, national, and international issues that affected the students and the institution directly. Seeking to create a civically engaged student required a civically engaged institution. Adele Simmons and Toni Huber, two very different individuals, came together because they believed that the university had an obligation to take public stances on critical issues relevant to students and to the educational mission of the institution and/or the society as a whole. In that context, no issue could be more important for a democratic society than civil liberties.

In the 1980s, when Toni Huber began to support the Civil Liberties and Public Policy Program (CLPP) at Hampshire College, one of the critical civil liberties issues was whether a woman's right to have an abortion would be fully accepted as a civil liberty. That national debate was entering a new phase. And CLPP, as a co-curricular center offering courses and helping students organize activities around specific public policy issues, joined in that debate. It did so because the concept of civil liberties provides a window into the complexity of modernity itself, and because the issue of reproductive rights encompasses many different ethical and social concerns: the responsibilities of science, population growth, religion and cultural customs, and even the growth of the global economy.

As a specific civil liberties case, reproductive rights highlights the tensions that arise when one faction of a society's perceived fundamental rights clashes with another faction's perceived fundamental values and rights. At the same time, the controversy over reproductive rights also offers insight into the complexity of how gender roles shape public policy and how different cultures deal with women's rights and reproductive health. To this day, reproductive rights retain individual, national, and global significance.

The program's stance was that reproductive rights should be viewed as a civil liberty and a human right, and it advocated on behalf of that position. At the same time, the program staff recognized that strong counterarguments existed in the United States and in other cultures. These counterarguments had to be seriously considered, analyzed, and responded to from a variety of perspectives rooted in history, anthropology, ethics, philosophy, and biology. By acknowledging opposing positions while expressing their own views, the program staff modeled how individuals could and should engage in a national and international debate about an important and complex public policy issue.

The program generated internships and research opportunities through different not-for-profit, nongovernmental, or civil society organizations generally referred to as NGOs, where assignments involved issues that looked broadly at women's health and reproductive rights nationally and internationally. The engagement process pursued in organizations such as the Committee on Women, Population and the Environment in Atlanta, the Illinois Caucus for Adolescent Health in Chicago, the National Network of Abortion Funds in Boston, the Native American Women's Health Education Resource Center in Lake Andes, South Dakota, the National Advocates for Pregnant Women and the National Latina Institute for Reproductive Health in New York City, the National Network for Immigrant and Refugee Rights in San Francisco, and Choice USA and the National Asian Pacific American Women's Forum in Washington, D.C., generated intense student interest. In the summer of 2007, in addition to the nine organizations listed above, students held internships in twenty other organizations.

The collective energy created by these experiences led the students to sponsor an annual national conference and workshop for undergraduate students on reproductive rights, women's health issues, and appropriate and constructive ways to advocate and support the issues important to them. As anticipated, the interactions between students and representatives of NGOs and other groups attending these conferences linked reproductive rights to other civil liberty and social justice issues. Over one thousand students and NGO representatives attended the conference in 2006. The conference has become an effective way of encouraging students to promote social change where their analyses indicated a specific need. Perhaps more importantly, it has become effective in linking the Hampshire academic community to a wider national and international community. Overall, the program embraced a broad mission of enhancing understanding of what civil liberties mean to a democracy. By selecting an issue that students cared about and that affected them directly, it engaged, year in and year out, large numbers of students in what was basically a field course on the workings of a democracy.

Unfortunately, Hampshire's communal links beyond its campus led to a lawsuit over a speech given at Hampshire's May 1993 graduation ceremony. Under the school's normal electoral procedures, Hampshire students choose a graduation speaker, often campaigning for specific individuals. The speaker that the graduating students elected that year was Loretta Ross, director of the Atlanta-based Women's Watch, an organization that tracks violence and threats against women's health centers by antiabortion activists. Many in the graduating class were familiar with Ross: a number of students had been interns in her Atlanta clinic and she had spoken at Hampshire in the past. The vote also reflected the widespread respect of the students for CLPP and their pride in its growing national visibility.

In her speech, Ross identified John Burt as one who defended the use of violence against individuals and clinics that supported or performed abortions, and that portion of her speech was included in a CLPP newsletter. The content of that newsletter became the basis for the lawsuit against Hampshire College and Professor Fried, while a separate suit was filed against Loretta Ross in a different venue.

When Burt's lawyer notified Hampshire that I would be called as a witness, I welcomed the news. I wanted to fully support CLPP and Professor Fried. Our attorney may have been a little less enthusiastic. Although his primary defense would refute the slander charges, he planned to assert that the newsletter of a small co-curricular program housed within a small college in western Massachusetts was unlikely to have a large readership. Professor Fried cautioned the lawyer that, in my passion for Hampshire and its mission, I might be reluctant to accept that reasoning. They were right, but I swallowed my pride and promised that I would not challenge our own defense. They still worried.

When I was called to testify, the opposing lawyer wanted to explore how a not-for-profit, tax-exempt institution could justify having a program that so clearly supported a single partisan, prochoice position. I had expected that line of questioning to be only one of many: but this was the only question the opposing attorney pursued. In fact, he tried several different versions of the same question. Each time, as I opened my mouth to defend the educational legitimacy of such a program, our lawyer objected to the question on the grounds of its relevance to a defamation suit. Each time the judge upheld the objection. Finally, the opposing lawyer gave up, then the judged turned to me, thanked me for my time, and apologized for making me show up for no reason.

At the end of the four-day trial, the jury deliberated for less than an hour before they dismissed the major claims. The verdict did not really matter to the complainant. I suspect he never expected to win and that his goal was to focus attention on the program as a potential target for antiabortion protesters. Independent of their efforts, the Civil Liberties and Public Policy Program was gaining a national reputation, and the veiled threat against me outside the courthouse suggested that the antichoice advocates had succeeded, to some extent, in achieving their goal.

Although pleased with the outcome of the case, I was disappointed that I was not allowed to respond directly to Burt's lawyer. His question pointed to an issue that eventually could be just as critical to the health of democracy in the United States as the civil liberty issue Burt wanted to attack. Burt's lawyer, I can only guess, felt confident that he would score points with the jury by arguing that Hampshire's Civil Liberties Program, as part of a not-for-profit educational institution, violated the legal standard that such institutions could not engage formally in lobbying and partisan political activity. And he obviously thought he could highlight an educational standard that viewed advocacy as a form of indoctrination antithetical to the development of independent thinking. By doing so, he would have argued, the college's actions recklessly abetted the alleged act of slander.

I wanted to argue, on the contrary, that advocacy was an appropriate, even central feature of a liberal education. It was legitimate for Hampshire to engage in such a national debate as long as the school was not directly supporting specific political candidates and/or parties (which it was not). Neither Burt's lawyer nor I got a chance to debate that issue in or outside of court. The contest over whether the university should be "neutral" or "engaged" was not a hot topic at the time of the trial.

By the time I retired as Hampshire's president in 2005, America was more politically conservative, and the debate over whether the university should be neutral or actively engaged in public policy issues was heating up. In states such as Georgia, Florida, Ohio, Arizona, and Pennsylvania, legislatures had considered, or were considering, whether the "assumed to be liberal-leaning faculty" was indoctrinating students and violating their academic freedom. In 2005 the American Council on Education, in response to these initiatives, issued its own statement about the responsibilities of institutions and the rights of students, and the Pennsylvania legislature launched a set of hearings on the subject. The prominence of the issue continues to grow as legislatures in states such as Arizona consider legislation not only mandating a pluralism of viewpoints but forbidding the expression of political views in the classroom.

Of all of the legislative actions taken, Pennsylvania's response was the most extensive and offered valuable insight into the issue I wanted to address in 1995 had the judge in that courtroom allowed me the chance. The hearings attracted many of the major spokespeople in the debate, thus becoming representative of the national debate. The genesis of the Pennsylvania hearings was at a picnic in the summer of 2004, where Gibson Armstrong, Republican member of the Pennsylvania House of Representatives, met Jennie Mae Brown, a student attending the York campus of Pennsylvania State University. She complained to him about a physics professor she had who routinely used class time to criticize President George W. Bush's Iraq policies. As a U.S. Air Force veteran, she felt her professor was abusing his position. Her comments struck a familiar chord with Representative Armstrong, who had heard about the liberal bias of faculty and how that bias led to a discriminatory silencing of conservative students. He decided to act.

In 2005 Armstrong and a group of legislative colleagues placed House Resolution (HR) 177 before the House of Representatives of the Commonwealth of Pennsylvania to create a Select Committee on Academic Freedom in Higher Education. The resolution read as follows:

> WHEREAS, Academic freedom and intellectual diversity are values indispensable to American colleges and universities; and
> WHEREAS, From its first formulation in the General Report of the Committee on Academic Freedom and Tenure of the American Association of University Professors, the concept of academic freedom has been premised on the idea that human knowledge is a never-ending pursuit of the truth, that there is no humanly accessible truth that is not, in principle, open to challenge, and that no party or intellectual faction has a monopoly on wisdom; and
> WHEREAS, Academic freedom is likely to thrive in an environment of intellectual diversity that protects and fosters independence of thought and speech; and
> WHEREAS, Students and faculty should be protected from the imposition of ideological orthodoxy, and faculty members have the responsibility to not take advantage of their authority position to introduce inappropriate or irrelevant subject matter outside of their field of study; therefore be it
> RESOLVED, That a select committee ... examine, study and inform the House of Representatives on matters relating to the academic atmosphere and the degree to which faculty have the opportunity to instruct and students have the opportunity to learn in an environment conducive to the pursuit of knowledge and truth and the expression of independent thought at State-related and State-owned colleges, universities, community colleges including, but not limited to, whether:
>
> 1. Faculty are hired, fired, promoted and granted tenure based on their professional competence and subject matter knowledge and with a view of helping students explore and understand various methodologies and perspectives;
> 2. Students have an academic environment, quality of life on campus and reasonable access to course materials that create an environment conducive to learning, the development

of critical thinking and the exploration and expression of
independent thought and that students are evaluated based
on their subject knowledge; and

3. That students are graded based on academic merit, without
   regard for ideological views, and that academic freedom and
   the right to explore and express independent thought is
   available to and practiced freely by faculty and students. [1]

The Pennsylvania legislature considered House Resolution 177 in
an atmosphere of sharp partisanship. At a critical moment in the
debate, the chief sponsor of HR 177, Representative Gibson C.
Armstrong, told the legislature about a biology professor showing
Michael Moore's film *Fahrenheit 9/11* during class time—an incident that had never actually taken place. Nonetheless, the ac-
cusation energized and inflamed attitudes within the legislature.
Professors in the Pennsylvania system, in turn, were anxious about
what they felt could be a prelude to interference in academic curricular matters by the legislature and even McCarthy-like accusations and charges. They launched a strong counterattack on the
motives and purposes of the Select Committee. It was an inauspi-
cious beginning for a conversation about education.

Against significant odds, the Select Committee, under the able
leadership of its two chairs, Representatives Thomas L. Stevenson,
majority chairman, and Lawrence H. Curry, minority chairman, created an informative and intellectually substantive conversation about
education. The public hearings focused only on a narrow range of
subjects, all related to academic freedom and the real and perceived
political bias in the classroom. The hearing took place in four two-
day sessions, held on four different campuses of the Pennsylvania
public tertiary education system between November 2005 and May
2006. The Select Committee found almost no cases of students' academic freedoms being violated.[2] By bringing to the same table educators from all over the United States who represented many different
organizations and perspectives (and whose testimony covered far
more than just academic freedom), the committee produced intense,
well-reasoned conversations about the purposes of education. In
effect, these hearings turned out to be wonderful theater representing the battle for education in the larger culture wars.

Whatever the underlying motives and assumptions that led to this resolution, or one's position on the resolution itself, Representative Armstrong deserves credit for creating a truly teachable moment—a powerful opportunity that was not fully utilized but still valuable—to educate legislators, teachers and administrators, and the public as a whole about the purposes of education. Some educators traveled from all over the United States at their own expense to testify because they saw an opportunity to address real issues. As the hearings unfolded they (sometimes unintentionally) explored at great length the implications of the question that I wanted to answer in Northampton ten years before: Was it appropriate for any university to include advocacy in its educational program?

The first individual to testify, Stephen H. Balch, president of the National Association of Scholars (NAS), emphatically argued no to that question.[3] Balch, who earned his PhD in political science at the University of California at Berkeley in the 1960s and then taught for fourteen years at the City University of New York's John Jay College of Criminal Justice, argued in precise terms that education and advocacy were contradictory terms and that educators and institutions had a responsibility to be "balanced." Indeed, he considered the drift toward advocacy and activism in U.S. education to be the most serious threat to academic freedom.

He began his testimony by defining the words *educate*, *advocate*, and *activism*:

> *Educate*: to train or develop the knowledge, skill, mind, or character, especially by formal schooling or study.
> *Advocate*: to speak or write in support of, to be in favor of. Advocacy is a process whereby one seeks to persuade someone of something other than [what] they originally believe; to convert, to change opinion.
> *Activism*: the doctrine or policy of taking positive, direct action to achieve an end, especially a political or social end. A term that obviously should be familiar to everyone on this panel. It's a term of politics, essentially a term of getting out and influencing the political world.[4]

For Balch, advocating and activism undercut education's central goal of developing a student's capacity for critical analysis and thinking—goals that had been supported through the ages from Socrates to the most recent 2005 pronouncement by the American Council on Education. He explained that in dealing with controversial issues, the "faculty member is expected to be of a fair and judicial mind and to set forth justly, without suppression or innuendo, the divergent opinions of other investigators.... The faculty member is expected to train students to think for themselves and to provide them access to those materials, which they need if they are to think independently."[5] Throughout his testimony, Balch insisted that these were not his ideas alone—they also had the support of a broad consensus in higher education.

Balch argued that advocacy and activism do not seek to open minds and encourage independent thought but, on the contrary, try to "persuade and convert." Under the guise of higher education, he insisted, many teachers presented material in a manner that was clearly out to "persuade and convert." These acts of advocacy appeared as mission statements in programs embodying what he called "programmatic tendentiousness"—an open espousal of a specific viewpoint or persuasion. If he had known about Hampshire's Civil Liberties and Public Policy Program, he probably would have cited it as an example of "programmatic tendentiousness" and, given his definitions, he would have been correct.

Balch worried about "programmatic tendentiousness" because he also concluded that many academic fields were marked by a liberal slant, and that bias inevitably limited students' exposure to ideas and shielded them from the consensus thinking of the wider society. This imbalance goes against what he argued was a widely held educational principle: that intellectual pluralism is an essential value in education and closely allied with the concept of academic freedom. He concluded by noting the American Council on Education's own statement about academic freedom, which argued that "intellectual pluralism and academic freedom are central principles of American higher education."[6]

As examples of "programmatic tendentiousness," Balch referred to several Pennsylvania institutions. He cited the mission statement of the University of Pittsburgh's School of Social Work, which explicitly expressed its commitment to promoting the values of social and economic justice—words that Balch believes carry a lot of "ideological freight." The mission statement explains that the program seeks to develop students' understanding about the nature of social diversity and oppression with respect to race, sex, sexual orientations, age, marital status, political beliefs, religion, and mental and physical disability. Balch continued: "Obviously they think there's a lot of oppression going on according to these categories.... They clearly have a theory of society that they expect students to embrace as part of their work as social workers: it's not a theory to be questioned and discussed as to whether it is true. The student is supposed to end up believing that they are true. And that is how the program promotes social and economic justice."[7]

Balch argued that these mission statements were a form of advocacy; and to that extent they probably violated the law or state policy because, he argued, U.S. Supreme Court rulings hold that political advocacy cannot be a requirement for public office. Balch felt that the school's mission statement also suggested the limiting of intellectual diversity and, in the realm of the student affairs, could even be interpreted as coercive. He pointed to the Office of Multi-Cultural Affairs at East Stroudsburg University, its purpose being "to promote, plan and monitor social justice in the university community"—what Balch thought to be a chillingly totalitarian turn of phrase. He noted that Penn State's goals maintain that individuals should not just tolerate differences but should also value differences. The purpose of these goals, he noted, "is not tolerance, that is in fact the opposite. If you are required to value things that you don't believe, you are now talking about coercing of opinion."[8]

Balch argued that during most of the twentieth century, the goal of the university was to develop critical thought—the capacity for analytical, probing inquiry that often challenged the students even as it made them uncomfortable. And yet now, he decried, much of the rhetoric is about affirming certain worldviews:

> Why then, when looking at traditional cultural values at established institutional arrangements, is the attitude suddenly critical? And when, looking at other cultures and life-styles, is the attitude celebratory?... There is a culture of advocacy and activism deeply entrenched

in many institutions—what I think can fairly be called a political project celebration of social change through critical view of traditional practices.[9]

Having given examples of "programmatic tendentiousness," Balch explained, "the problem of intellectual tendentiousness arises when faculties seek to restrict the ideas to which their students are exposed, or sometimes, when a faculty just grows so one-sided, so inbred, it fails to recognize that there are other points of view and it becomes completely parochial, and that can happen."[10] Balch is absolutely correct about the danger of parochialism. That danger always exists. All institutions and individuals develop a certain level of parochialism.

Balch went on to explain that this parochialism could lead to another problem reflected in the research of University of Chicago law professor Cass Sunstein, who described how groups with similar ideas will develop extremist positions if there is no counterweight to the development of one viewpoint. A tendency toward extremism can occur with any political faction, whether it is liberal, conservative, or other.[11]

Balch's testimony presents the core intellectual justification for the neutralist case. He argues that neutrality was pedagogically necessary, not just a question of fairness. His argument would have provided valuable material for the plaintiff's attorney in Northampton, had it been available and had the judge allowed the questions. Responding to Stephen Balch's interpretation of the goals of education provides me a chance to say what I would have said ten years ago in Northampton and to place my response in a broader national context than I would have then. Balch defines the verb "educate" as "to train or develop the knowledge, skill, mind, or character especially by formal schooling or study." I define "educate" as the act of purposefully engaging someone through the use of knowledge, experience, or values. You can engage yourself or you can engage others. Whatever the purposes and whatever material is used, engagement is the constant. You can engage someone without educating, but you cannot educate without engaging.

As noted in the Preamble, the purpose of education is to build healthy communities. Although many definitions of "healthy community" exist within and among different cultures, one feature is common to all. A community will not become healthy and cannot remain healthy unless its citizens are prepared to ask the "essential questions." And the people in these communities must have the courage and skill to challenge authority, orthodoxy, and convention in appropriate and constructive ways when required to do so.[12] Appropriate and constructive ways of challenging authority result from clear-headed reflection, the ability to listen well, the courage to change one's mind in the face of new evidence, a willingness to admit mistakes, and a capacity to challenge authority without necessarily disrespecting it.

A community's health, whether defined in terms of social justice, artistic, or human development terms, ultimately depends on its capacity to change, adapt, and correct itself. These qualities, in turn, require the leavening effect of citizens who have the ability and courage to listen to internal values, to ask essential questions, and to constructively confront outside powers and forces. Without that capacity, no community can adjust to the inevitable changes and challenges that it will face. It is equally important that individuals who learn how to challenge authority in progressive ways also will learn how to respond correctly when they are challenged. The capacity for a given society's metamorphosis through dialogue, constructive conflict, and democratic processes, as opposed to destructive conflict and force, depends on its citizens learning these lessons. As I have previously mentioned, the lunch-counter sit-ins by the students at North Carolina A&T is a model of this behavior.

Educators must seek to engage students in complex intellectual reflections in order to strengthen the quality of the students' intellect and to strengthen the sensitivity and quality of their engagement with the world around them. In turn, the students expect, like any member of a family, that the educators and their educational institutions will model the behaviors they seek to instill. Authentic engagement, not neutrality, generates the kind of critical thinking that healthy communities and democratic cultures require. Therefore, the liberal arts university, by definition, must be an engaged university.

If a university's mission includes the nurturing of critical thinking, creativity, and civic engagement (as the missions of most liberal arts institutions do), then those universities have an obligation to model that behavior. Insisting on neutrality and refusing to take positions and avoiding any advocacy would be tantamount to saying to the students, "Do as I say, not as I do." Every parent knows that this tack reduces a child's respect for authority and often breeds cynicism and invites rebellion.

If I had been able to testify fully in the 1996 court proceeding, I would have argued that Hampshire's CLPP exemplified the kind of "tendentiousness" that must exist in order to provide students opportunities for authentic engagement. Its activist structure provides a setting for the social science students analogous to what a laboratory provides for science students. It is a place where the hypothesis that a woman's reproductive rights should be a protected civil liberty can be tested within the crucible of a national debate. Students form and defend positions against real opponents who feel equally passionately about their positions. The process seeks reflection, refinement, adjustment, and change. It is a powerful way to promote civic engagement and to produce leaders with the skills and knowledge to become constructively engaged in the democratic process. It produces graduates who become thoughtful and constructive activists able to grapple with complex, multi-faceted issues; thus helping to fulfill the civic engagement part of the mission of a liberal arts college.

I would have stopped there if I had been in court. If it had been Stephen Balch examining me, he probably would have asked an "essential" question. Why was it necessary and more effective to base engagement on taking a position rather than on being neutral? The goals of a liberal arts education, as defined above, can be nurtured in a context where the faculty remains neutral, offering a broad range of opinions and positions so students can come to their own conclusions about a particular subject.

My response then and now has two parts. One of the college's core purposes is to train students to become constructive and creative contributors to society. Training students to take a position on any subject, intellectual or policy-related, is a critical part of one of the most effective pedagogical approaches for promoting the goals of liberal education. The Hampshire program leaders tell the students that reproductive rights is a crucial issue about which responsible citizens should take a stand, although many will avoid it. By extension, professors, in order to provide authentic engagement, have to model the same qualities they expect the students to exhibit, and the quality of knowledge and engagement determines the quality of education. The more active, personal, and connected the engagement, the more the students will experience significant personal growth. The concept that professors and institutions should strive to be neutral limits the richness of that engagement and will inhibit young people's contributions to the health of their communities.

Independent of the modeling argument, the activism of the program represents a sound pedagogical strategy. Activism is not a negative educational force, as Balch argues; nor is it just a political term—"the doctrine or policy of taking positive, direct action to achieve an end, especially a political or social end."[13] That definition ignores the body of literature and research that compares active and passive learning. Activism in learning—getting students, for example, to engage in scientific experiments rather than have them passively learn about science—has become a major part of education reform in the United States and is a central feature of the educational philosophy of Hampshire College.[14] Students will learn more, in greater depth, and with greater retention if they are engaged in asking real questions. Inquiry-based teaching and learning engages the student in solving real problems, and it inevitably makes education active.

Activism, on the other hand, has its dangers, as the neutralists appropriately point out. The neutralists fear that no matter how open professors are to challenges from their students and no matter how even-handedly they present problems, taking a position will, to some degree, reduce the incentive for students to examine their chosen positions critically. In the worst-case situation, this consensus between professor and pupil will lead to a student's unwillingness to listen to conflicting arguments. Such a risk does exist.

The real risk of intimidating the student, or allowing bias to close down debate, should always be taken seriously—but with the recognition that disengagement creates deeper problems. Disengagement does reduce the risk of bias, but it also increases the risk of undermining democratic civic culture by closing off opportunities for students to engage in real debates. That risk leads to serious consequences in our society.

Having defined this broad educational context for the plaintiff's attorney, and most importantly for the jury, I would have explained that when a program such as CLPP advocates a position, the students who run the greatest risk for failing to develop critical thinking skills are those who agree with the program's position, not those who oppose it.

On the other hand, engagement offers an alternative approach to challenging those students who happen to agree with the consensus view on campus; it encourages students to interact with actual individuals and institutions off campus who oppose their position. In the Civil Liberties program students not only have to know the opposing arguments but they are also encouraged to engage those groups directly through internships and involvement with organizations and individuals active in the debate. They learn what it means to follow the Principles of Discourse and how you must comprehend what the opposition is saying in order to develop creditable responses. They come to understand that being an effective advocate means that one must know the other's position better than one's own, and they must be open to why the opposing argument might be stronger. Even in a class where there is no applied activity, they still understand that an inability to empathize with their opponents and to know them thoroughly can have serious consequences.

The best antidote to keeping students from becoming closed minded, true believers is to enable them to engage with those who hold opposing views—an argument that also supports conservatives' pleas for more nonliberal speakers on college campuses. Although I support those pleas and believe that exposure to a multitude of texts and speakers is valuable, this sort of activism is not as effective as the kind of program CLPP can offer. The sort of activism practiced by CLPP creates a more intense engagement. It is a very different experience for a student to work as an intern in an NGO that is engaged in the practice of advocacy, responding to opponents, organizing supporters, planning public presentations, and working with actual individuals affected by and living day to day with the policies and issues that are debated in college lecture halls. What takes place in those lecture halls when speakers with diverse views come to speak is important. What takes place in the service learning environments created by structured internships that require activity, reflection, and assessment is more intense and has a deeper and more lasting educational impact. One advantage of the emphasis on speakers lies in the larger number of students who may be exposed to the visitor. CLPP worked intensively at creating situations where returning interns could share their experiences with other students formally in courses and informally in public presentations. Those efforts were one of the factors that stimulated the evolution of the student-organized national conference.

In concluding my case before the court and in emphasizing the educational value of advocacy, I would have noted that one of CLPP's critical strategies for broadening perspectives has been to place the U.S. abortion debate in the context of international reproductive rights issues. Examining problems in other cultures concerning issues such as women's rights or the value of human life reduces the implicit assumption that the only debate that matters is in the United States. This global context helps CLPP introduce students to a richer set of perspectives than either Balch or Horowitz would have required, since the CLPP perspective embodies cultural, as well as political, differences.

Those advocating for the neutral university have done a service to education by challenging whether enough care is being given to how faculty and universities engage with the students in the classroom. They, too, are modeling the behavior that liberal education should seek to instill in all students. The concerns raised should always be considered important because teaching always incurs the risk of offending students and closing down their willingness to learn. Active learning and engaged learning incur greater risks in some areas than the neutrality model, but engagement also reduces risks in other areas—such as the risk of losing students because of a lack of interest.

At the same time, this pedagogical argument gives added importance to Dr. Balch's standards and principles. Whether CLPP's advocacy is legitimate and appropriate within a liberal arts educational context ultimately depends on the openness and reflection with which the program uses its activism and advocacy to engage the students; also important is the range of views presented. These are standards that Balch appropriately sets out in his overview of education.

If students can only agree with one position, or if their disagreement subjects them to ridicule, the program would be incompatible with Balch's *and* Hampshire's educational goals. The program is not illegitimate just because it would require self-confidence, a spirit of independence and contrariness, and a certain tolerance for discomfort to disagree openly with a strongly argued position. Quite the opposite is true. Institutions have a responsibility to provide "learning" situations in which students can practice how to handle disagreement within the bounds of the Principles of Discourse in just these kinds of circumstances.

Students must be treated with respect, and they must understand the full complexity of the problems before them. This requires receiving information from all sides. Concerning the question of reproductive rights and a woman's right to an abortion, providing comprehensive information is a formidable task that involves more than just letting students read statements from prolife and prochoice groups. Students need to understand the historical, economic, and cultural contexts for those positions; they should also be exposed to the ways different cultures around the world handle the issue. Whatever side one takes on the abortion issue in the United States, any position will look different if viewed from another culture's point of view. When the goal of presenting all sides is taken seriously, the issue of whether CLPP advocates a position or remains neutral has less significance when juxtaposed with the challenge of placing it in a global context, where there are endless perspectives. Meeting the standards of openness, respect, and full disclosure is surely more difficult when advocacy and activism are involved; but there can be immeasurable gains for students who choose a more intense level of engagement.

Engagement, advocacy, and activism involve risks, as do almost any tools used to achieve a grand purpose. Faculty and institutions can abuse their position and power just as any group with authoritative power can. On the other hand, if the Principles of Discourse are followed, it is possible to engage in active advocacy without abusing that power. As a result, students have the right to expect that colleges or universities "practice what they profess." If educators want to develop independent, critical thinkers who will use those skills positively and constructively, and who will integrate knowledge and experience into a socially viable whole, then tertiary education must model that behavior itself. The leaders of universities cannot tell their students that the institution itself will choose neutrality and still expect their students to practice outspoken advocacy. Institutions need not take a stand on every issue; but they cannot refuse, as a matter of principle, to take a stand. By following the Principles of Discourse, they can take a stand and also respect the pluralism of views and interpretations that are essential for a liberal education.

Here CLPP shares a common ground with mission-based educational institutions promoting opposing interpretations of reproductive rights as a civil liberty. Catholic universities, for example, appropriately urge a similar activism in defense of the opposing view that the sanctity of life, as they define it, preempts reproductive freedom as a civil liberty. And these institutions educate in the best sense of the word, just as CLPP does.

Balch and I represent two visions of education that differ in one important respect—his vision embodies reflective engagement, while mine embraces activist engagement. We share a common commitment to liberal education and its goal of enhancing the capacity for critical and independent thinking. We share an understanding that liberal education seeks to develop a student's capacity for purposeful critical thought and to enrich the inner-self while producing a constructive, engaged citizen or communal self. We have markedly different ideas on the most effective way to achieve these goals. The neutralists believe that educational institutions and faculty should operate like referees: they should insure that students have all the information they need and play by the rules with clear writing and rigorous analysis. In their view, the institution should let students reach conclusions on their own.

Those who support the vision of an engaged university see the university and faculty as coaches or players in the game, not referees. The coaches have a responsibility to model the values and behavior they seek to instill in students. In fact, as disseminators of knowledge, they see themselves as player/coaches who believe that their actions are just as essential to engaged learning principles as the efforts of their students. They believe that students learn better when they are actively engaged and not just reflective. Critical thought about poetry, literature, or history that is never publicly shared and never subject to outside criticism will not enrich the inner self or the communal self to the same extent as that which is shared. Silent reflection about a subject rarely evokes the same rigor and quality as open expression subject to challenge. To become independent and valuable contributors to society, students need experience and practice developing their critical and analytical abilities. Teachers in an engaged university play a critical role in helping students become responsible adults by creating classroom environments where students learn to press one another's judgments in appropriate and constructive ways and in a variety of contexts. Furthermore, students should not be afraid to challenge those with more experience and knowledge, such as their professors.

In the engaged university, the essence of liberal education lies in asking essential questions and pursuing answers to the extent that authority and convention may need to be challenged. These critical answers cannot be achieved if pursued in an abstract or theoretical context where judgments are never scrutinized. From my experience, students do not look for neutrality in the faculty. They look for faculty who respect and care for them independent of any specific position taken. They want the faculty to treat them as if, with the faculty's help, they could become their intellectual equals.

The differences between these two views on the potentialities of education have consequences far beyond the academy. Neutralists see danger in the model of engagement, arguing that advocacy will create closed-minded individuals who do not acknowledge all sides of an issue. This is a fair concern. At best, they believe that faculty bias will limit the students' ability to truly understand "reality"; at worst, it will allow for the indoctrination of young people and, by eliminating their ability to think critically, will weaken, if not destroy, democracy.

Activists see the danger of unintended consequences. Presenting all sides of a specific controversy, letting students assess the different arguments and draw their own conclusions is a valuable and effective way of teaching critical thinking, as is having faculty present balanced explanations of major controversies. If neutralism were to become the dominant paradigm, it would eliminate an effective way for students to learn how to craft their own perspectives and opinions and to challenge authority responsibly and practically. The willingness to act energizes democratic cultures to escape the inevitable concentration of power that will incur if those challengers and challenges do not exist. It is an art that neither liberal education nor democracies can afford to lose. Education must be about engagement and about teaching students how to confront advocates, neutralists, partisans, and anyone else with whom they may have an argument. Neutrality cannot be the only, or even the preferred, approach to teaching critical thinking. If it becomes the only approach, the students will see it as a form of disengagement and a denial of the very mission of civic engagement that most liberal arts universities embrace.

The Pennsylvania hearings, while ostensibly limited to examining whether academic freedom was at risk, did provide a forum, however imperfect, for examining the purposes of education. Nonetheless, the real elephant in the room was the Students for Academic Freedom, an organization founded by David Horowitz to promote in every state the adoption of a student bill of rights. The Pennsylvania Select Committee repeatedly reminded the public at the hearings that the committee's purpose was to determine if the students' academic freedom was at risk, not to consider a specific remedy. Some committee members even characterized the hearings as a solution in search of problem. David Horowitz testified at the committee's session held at Temple University in January 2006. Expanding on the themes developed by Professor Balch, the testimony of Horowitz and other neutralists is the subject of the next chapter.

CHAPTER 3

Protecting vs. Challenging Students

Stephen Balch was testifying in Pennsylvania partly because of activities undertaken by David Horowitz and his Students for Academic Freedom (SAF).[1] Like the National Association of Scholars that Stephen Balch represents, SAF had been working since 2003 to organize student groups on campuses. The SAF also encourages the general public to persuade state legislatures to enact its proposed bill of rights to protect students from professors' liberal bias and from the drift toward "program tendentiousness." The SAF focuses on how instruction should take place. The goals of liberal education are taken as a given, as the preamble to the SAF's proposed bill of rights states:

> The central purposes of a university are the pursuit of truth, the discovery of new knowledge through scholarship and research, the study and reasoned criticism of intellectual and cultural traditions, the teaching and general development of students to help them become creative individuals and productive citizens of a pluralistic democracy, and the transmission of knowledge and learning to a society at large. Free inquiry and free speech within the academic

community are indispensable to the achievement of these goals. The freedoms to teach and to learn depend upon the creation of appropriate conditions and opportunities on the campus as a whole, as well as in the classrooms and lecture halls. These purposes reflect the values—pluralism, diversity, opportunity, critical intelligence, openness and fairness—that are the cornerstones of American society.[2]

In pursuit of these goals, the SAF's bill of rights sets forth the following principles or "appropriate conditions":

1. Students will be graded solely on the basis of their reasoned answers and appropriate knowledge of the subjects and disciplines they study, not on the basis of their political or religious beliefs.
2. Curricula and reading lists in the humanities and social sciences should reflect the uncertainty and unsettled character of all human knowledge in these areas by providing students with dissenting sources and viewpoints where appropriate. While teachers are and should be free to pursue their own findings and perspectives in presenting their views, they should consider and make their students aware of other viewpoints. Academic disciplines should welcome a diversity of approaches to unsettled questions.
3. Exposing students to the spectrum of significant scholarly viewpoints on the subjects examined in their courses is a major responsibility of faculty. Faculty will not use their courses for the purpose of political, ideological, religious or anti-religious indoctrination.
4. Selection of speakers, allocation of funds for speakers' programs and other student activities will observe the principles of academic freedom and promote intellectual pluralism.
5. An environment conducive to the civil exchange of ideas being an essential component of a free university, the obstruction of invited campus speakers, destruction of campus literature or other effort to obstruct this exchange will not be tolerated.
6. Knowledge advances when individual scholars are left free to reach their own conclusions about which methods, facts, and theories have been validated by research. Academic institutions and professional societies formed to advance knowledge

within an area of research, maintain the integrity of the research process, and organize the professional lives of related researchers serve as indispensable venues within which scholars circulate research findings and debate their interpretation. To perform these functions adequately, academic institutions and professional societies should maintain a posture of organizational neutrality with respect to the substantive disagreements that divide researchers on questions within, or outside, their fields of inquiry.[3]

David Horowitz testified ostensibly about the problem of liberal bias among faculty members and the resulting damage to students, not about the bill of rights per se, although he did reference it and defend it in his testimony. Its content had helped shape the Pennsylvania House Resolution 177 in 2004. Horowitz began his testimony by criticizing those who said the hearings were a waste of time, a sentiment that even some of the committee members expressed in the hearing I attended. He asserted that no institution in the Pennsylvania state university system informs its students of their rights and that it was not a waste of time to examine this inaction. He cited Steven Balch's argument that departments substituted indoctrination for education and used a political test for hiring faculty. He also noted that university hiring profiles sought faculty who advocated for "social justice," which is generally recognized as code for "socialism."[4]

He then delineated what faculty would be expected to do under his bill of rights. Those who claimed the bill of rights would require that all sides of an issue be taught were simply wrong. That expectation was not part of the text. The document only required that faculty present the significant scholarly debates relative to the subject matter and that college courses should not be used for ideological, religious, or antireligious indoctrination. The goal of having multiple views presented is to make sure students understand that no faculty member's position is gospel.

Unfortunately, much of the concern about Horowitz's bill of rights related to the document's clarity, because the actual wording is not as straightforward as Dr. Horowitz assumes. The statement that curricula should reflect the "unsettled character of all human knowledge" is vague enough to be unsettling to the academy. In particular, who determines what questions are "unsettled" is not specified. Moreover, although Horowitz's bill states only that humanities and social science curricula reflect this "unsettled character," it implies that all human knowledge is subject to debate, leaving open the interpretation, for example, that intelligent design must be included in science classes and Holocaust denial theories included in history classes. Whether Horowitz intended to leave that door open or not is less important than the unsettled question about who gets to deem these questions "unsettled."

Horowitz dismissed the concern about who would determine what the unsettled questions were. He did include the phrase "where appropriate," just as I use it in arguing that students should learn to challenge authority in constructive and *appropriate* ways. Every field has unsettled questions, and students should be exposed to the serious and *appropriate* issues. On the other hand, Horowitz could have worded the paragraph in a less inflammatory manner. Emphasizing that every field enters a period when its knowledge is unsettled would have made the same point. There was no point in raising the far more complicated postmodernist argument that all knowledge is permanently unsettled and uncertain, which is what the paragraph now implies. Independent of that issue, educators *do* carry a responsibility to inform students of the major issues in dispute with respect to the themes and arguments of a specific course.

In his testimony, however, Horowitz's central and very appropriate concern was with actual abuses and, more important, with whether or not students knew their rights when such abuses occurred. Horowitz went on to provide an extensive list of Temple University curricular failings and the biased practices of faculty members, concluding that the issue is not about whether these biases occur but is actually about students being ignorant of their rights and academic freedoms. The Pennsylvania Select Committee's final November 2006 report did not concur with Horowitz's analysis of the problem; and furthermore, the report noted that when an abuse did occur, appropriate remedies were in place.[5]

Independent of how many instances of faculty bias actually occurred, the principle that students should be aware of their rights is a sound one—as essential to the case for the engaged university as it is for the neutral university. In fact, schools have an obligation to make those rights more explicit for every student, and the academy should recognize SAF's contribution to making that case. Making students aware of their rights will help restrain the inevitable excesses that occur if professors stray too far from the core subject matter of a particular course. The Pennsylvania hearing found precious few instances like this, but they do occur. For the most part, students know how to handle these situations; but making sure they are aware of their formal rights is still important.

Opposing the concept of the neutral university does not imply indifference to the excesses faculty members occasionally inflict on students, and, as Chapter 6 explores, insuring the quality of teaching is a never-ending task. On the other hand, having professors speak about prominent current issues, even if they are not specifically related to the course material, can serve a meaningful pedagogical purpose. Taking notice of the world outside the classroom can reduce the sense that knowledge is compartmentalized. How professors present their opinions to the class is the important thing. When faculty members make comments that pertain to subjects outside the core curriculum, they should be able to justify these digressions.

Balch and Horowitz do not condemn professors' extraneous comments categorically. They imply there is a rule of reason for what is appropriate and egregious. Whether egregious actions represent aberrations or a persistent problem is a serious issue, but the main issue remains the assertion that neutrality is the only appropriate means of conveying a liberal education. That issue separates the neutralists from the activists.

Horowitz's case for neutrality has the following major flaws:

- it offers a one-size-fits-all approach to the mission of American education;
- it ignores the value of active learning;

- it assumes that advocacy must be synonymous with indoctrination;
- it patronizes students by exaggerating their vulnerability in the face of a faculty member who advocates a position in the classroom.

Although these issues have been touched on already, they bear repeating when addressing Horowitz's very concrete proposal. The diversity of missions embraced by over 3,500 tertiary institutions represents one of the greatest strengths of U.S. education and marks the first flaw in his case. Horowitz applies his principle of neutrality to all educational institutions, disregarding their purpose, origin, or mission. His one-size-fits-all approach has never been practical within the diverse realm of U.S. tertiary education and would eliminate-church related institutions, progressive institutions with a focus on areas such as the environment, and possibly even single-sex universities.

The United States does not need all universities to be either neutral or engaged. Countries need institutions with different attitudes, values, and missions while sharing a common commitment to education. Countries benefit when different institutions represent varying schools of thought and can challenge each other and accepted norms. What all educational institutions share (as opposed to being centers for indoctrination) is their willingness to encourage their students and others to challenge the school's missions and question its values in appropriate ways. Horowitz is correct that a bill of rights should address what methods should be deemed "appropriate." I disagree with what he seeks to eliminate, not with what he includes.

The necessity of having a tertiary education system composed of different institutions representing a multitude of educational philosophies, rather than requiring institutions to present all issues in the same way, is comparable to another debate in tertiary education in the United States. That debate has focused on the following questions: Is it better to have a) a student body composed of well-rounded individuals; b) a student body chosen by one criteria alone, such as grades or national exam results; or c) a student body comprising singular individuals with very different life experiences, competencies, and creative drives?

A second flaw in Horowitz's argument is that he ignores evidence that active learning offers an equally if not more effective alternative to teaching critical thinking than SAF's assumption in its bill of rights that learning can only happen in a neutral environment. Although balance is important as a pedagogical device, it is insufficient as the only or even the preferred means of developing critical thinkers.

The third flaw in Horowitz's argument is that he assumes advocacy automatically leads to indoctrination. This assumption denies the capacity of individuals to advocate for a certain position and simultaneously to keep an open mind. Yet these are traits that liberal education tries to develop in its citizens. Not everyone is naturally capable of successfully embracing seemingly opposite qualities, and faculty members are no different than anyone else in that respect. The ideal faculty member can model this complex behavior by expressing their opinions, occasionally advocating for certain positions but still welcoming challenges from the students. Exposing students to this model is critical.

Finally, Horowitz's Bill of Rights patronizes students by assuming they are incapable of absorbing the advocacy of faculty members and developing opposing positions. Every student is different, and some will be more impressionable than others. On the other hand, the students with whom I have worked and the students who testified at the Pennsylvania hearings and who are presented in Chapter 8 suggest that, as a group, they are not easily intimidated by power, advocacy, or even arrogance in the classroom.

In spite of these flaws, it is important to understand the widespread support the neutralist views of David Horowitz and Robert J. Bork do have. Acknowledging that such neutralist views exist and are important (even if I disagree with them) underscores the critical relationship between democracy and liberal education. This debate does matter, and the Pennsylvania hearings fortunately provided a platform for prominent neutralist proponents.

Anne D. Neal, president of the American Council of Trustees and Alumni, has been a leading nonacademic public advocate for the issue of bias in the academy. The organization she leads has given voice to widespread concern among trustees and alumni that faculty bias and political correctness are damaging education in the

United States. Whether or not one agrees that a real problem with institutional bias exists, there is no doubt about the existence of real concerns on the subject. These perceptions are an important reality.

When testifying at the Temple University hearing, Dr. Neal focused on the importance of creating a multiplicity of views; and in a brief conversation with me, she had no hesitation in telling me directly that education should not be about social change. Her defense of pluralism and her unhappiness with contemporary education's emphasis on social change were intertwined. This underscored her concern about bias, which combined both unhappiness with the content of the faculty's arguments as well as support for what she considered a fundamental academic principle.

In her formal testimony she argued that the real problem facing higher education in the United States was orthodoxy and the lack of intellectual diversity. Initially, she did not focus on the issue of political bias, but she began by noting that former Yale University president Benno Schmidt warned as early as 1991 that "the most serious problems of freedom of expression in our society today exist on campuses. The assumption seems to be that the purpose of education is to induce correct opinion rather than search for wisdom and liberate the mind."[6]

The phrase "as early as 1991" is interesting because the charge that orthodoxies dominate campuses is a perennial issue within tertiary education. Indeed, the nature of the pursuit of truth is constantly one of breakthroughs followed by the reemergence of consensus and orthodoxy, inertia, and then new breakthroughs. She also was ignoring the history of the development of universities and colleges in the United States where many institutions were founded by breakaway faculty who despaired about the doctrinal tilt of their original home institution.

Dr. Neal did eventually get to the liberal-bias-of-the-faculty theme, citing specific studies in which data provided a broader, if not overwhelming, case for the political dominance of Democrats in college faculty; but her argument then added a new twist. She acknowledged that such a distribution would be "irrelevant" if it were not for the intellectual environment those liberal faculty members worked in—an environment dominated by "postmodern philosophy."

Neal concluded that because postmodernists argue that truth and objectivity are outdated, that all knowledge is political and socially constructed, and that the university should produce "change" agents, the political orientation of the faculty becomes dangerous. As an example, she noted that the University of California had "abandoned the provision on academic freedom that cautioned against using the classroom as a 'platform for propaganda.' The president of the university argued in a letter to the Academic Senate that the regulation was outdated."[7] She stressed the same theme as Horowitz and Balch: a "lack of intellectual diversity is undermining the education of students as well as the free exchange of ideas central to the mission of the university." The typical neutralist position is that if developing critical thinking is part of the stated mission, then presenting a range of material unfettered by faculty bias should be required. But according to Dr. Neal, the university should not have a social mission at all.

Like Balch and Horowitz, Neal has accepted the broad assumptions articulated so forcefully by Bork. Students must become acculturated before they become active. They are passive recipients of knowledge, not active participants in creating knowledge; and that passivity makes the issue of bias, balance, and all the other concerns expressed by these advocates of neutrality more urgent. Passive students require more protection and have a greater need to have information presented in a totally disinterested and unbiased fashion. Because she rejects what she calls the postmodernist assumption that the university should produce "change agents," she does not need to see students as activists. She condemns today's liberal arts curriculum as hostile toward U.S. institutions, and she believes this liberal negativism has generated cynicism and a lack of interest in voting.

Equating postmodernism with social change presents an interesting argument, but the idea that the university should be engaged in social change predates postmodernism. John Dewey and the founders of U.S. land grant universities believed education existed to help generate positive social change, yet would have been appalled by postmodernist theory. Postmodernist ideas about how realities are constructed are not critical to the arguments for social change. The two are equated in the neutralist argument. For them, social change is the enemy.

Another nonacademic witness, Admiral Mike Ratliff, U.S. Navy (retired), director of the Intercollegiate Studies Institute, spoke about one theme Dr. Neal raised: that negativism in the academy toward U.S. institutions and history were developing a cynicism that had reduced young people's participation in the democratic process. Admiral Ratliff related stories about how individuals never heard a kind word about the United States from faculty members, but they heard plenty about "the evils of imperialism, about the need to be skeptical about all institutions and traditional values; and about the stupidity and mendacity of prominent politicians."[8] In describing the cost of academic negativism, he quoted Jon Naisbitt's analysis in *Megatrends*: in the 1950s, 75 percent of newspaper column inches were taken up by positive stories about different branches or offices of the government; but by the 1970s and 1980s, 75 percent were negative.[9]

Admiral Ratliff then cited former Harvard president Derek Bok's 2005 book, *Our Underachieving Colleges*, which argued that education is key to a healthy democracy.

> Bok goes on to describe the tight connection between studying our institutions, our history, and participating in voting, participating in the public life of our nation. If students study, they tend to vote . . . We are finding ourselves in the research we're conducting on the close relationship on those campuses where students are more likely to take courses in history and economics and political science and the likelihood that they will vote, that they will participate in elections, that they will register.
>
> And Mr. Bok talks about that relationship. And yet despite that close relationship between the health of our democracy and studying our heritage in our classrooms, Mr. Bok observes that oddly faculty have paid little attention to this need and that the president of the Association of American Colleges and Universities, Carol Schneider, has reported that after "five years of active discussion on dozens of campuses, I have been persuaded there is not just a neglect of but a resistance to college-level studies of United States democratic principles.

Let me be sure that you understand that Carol Schneider is not someone on one side or the other of the spectrum. She is the head of the main street association of American Colleges and Universities. If there is a spokesman for higher education, Carol Schneider is probably that person.[10]

Contrary to Admiral Ratliff's characterization, I am not sure there can be a single spokesperson for the diversity of U.S. tertiary education. Ratliff was concerned that the investment society makes in education is one of the largest and most crucial investments we make in our country's future and that "educating the student on our campuses in our institutions and values as a nation is important because they must be prepared to preserve those institutions and values."[11]

Dr. Neal and Admiral Ratliff argue that the leftward political leanings of faculty members lead to anti-American propaganda in the classroom that, among other things, discourages young people from voting. Bok argues that failure to study the country's history and institutions leads to fewer young people involved in the political process. He did not argue that the actual content being taught in those courses caused fewer young people to vote. My experience at Hampshire pointed to a third conclusion. If college courses encouraged an active engagement with a specific problem and moved the students to be activists within a particular field, there was a carryover effect that *did* lead to a more politically engaged student body. Students who worked as interns in NGOs came away seeing voting as necessary even if they were cynical about issues such as the role of money in selecting candidates—the most often expressed concern of students about the political process. They learned how to avoid making the best the enemy of the good.

More to the point, Dr. Neal and Admiral Ratliff, along with Stephen Balch and David Horowitz, exemplify a central facet of the neutralists. They presumptuously speak for the average student, but they do not seem willing to let students speak for themselves. In that respect, these neutralists represent a common failing in U.S. education: an unwillingness to engage students with real questions and listen to their answers. Nowhere is this failing more obvious than many academicians' views on the issue of why young people (especially college students) do not vote in larger numbers.

True, the lack of political participation among the young is a serious issue. In the United States over the past four decades, many politicians, commentators, academicians, and the public in general have become increasingly concerned about the decline in voter participation, especially among eligible youth. At the end of the 1990s, as the country approached the millennial divide, that concern seemed to intensify. I attended three meetings on the subject hosted by organizations such as the American Council on Education and Campus Compact. As I sat in one such meeting, organized by the American Council on Education, I was struck by the irony of the scene. Approximately twenty very diverse individuals representing a number of universities and colleges were at the table while no one in the room looked under the age of fifty. We talked about why so few eighteen- to twenty-two-year-olds voted. I finally asked why we did not invite the students to tell us themselves why they did not vote. Heads nodded affirmatively, but at the next conference organized by Campus Compact, an organization committed to promoting community service in U.S. universities, there still were no young people present.

When I received a third invitation to attend a conference on civic engagement hosted by some of the same aforementioned groups in Aspen, Colorado, I accepted it with little hope that students would be included. Approximately fifty college presidents attended—but again, no students. Part of the purpose of the conference was to adopt a millennium-themed statement on voting and civic engagement. After the conference organizers presented a draft declaration and asked if there were any responses or questions, a long period of silence followed. To break the ice, I raised my hand. I know those who recognized me knew what was coming, but I guess they had little choice, since only one hand was up. I explained that I had no problem with the statement; but I also said that we had missed an important opportunity by not asking the students for their voice in this student-related matter. I explained my frustration at the continuing absence of students and acknowledged that because I felt student participation was important, I had a responsibility to do something about it. Therefore, I invited each institution to send two students to Hampshire College to have such a conversation with the commitment that Hampshire would pay full expenses for the trip, not including the plane ticket. I apologized that Hampshire was not wealthy enough to pay the plane fares.

To their credit, the presidents at the conference agreed, and the Hampshire conference took place. The institutions represented were highly diverse, as were the students who attended. The format was simple. My Hampshire colleagues and I, being the organizers, simply asked the students to prepare a statement or statements about why they did or did not vote. When the weekend was over, Hampshire would provide an audience of legislators, community leaders, and others who wanted to hear their conclusions.

All we had to do for the students was feed them and provide a place for them to sleep. They organized themselves and worked nonstop from Friday evening through Sunday morning. Sunday morning they presented their conclusions to a group of local and state elected officials who formed a "panel" of listeners rather than presenters. Two themes dominated the student reports: the candidates chosen were determined by the money primaries, while no one listened to the students. They explained that they only got to vote for those who survived the money primaries and that process represented a real constraint on their choice and led to a degree of homogeneity in the remaining candidates. The second theme pertained to students not being wealthy enough to participate in the money primaries.

Many factors influence why young people do not vote—a subject that goes far beyond what I can cover in this work—but none of the adults listening to the analysis of the students presenting their reports that Sunday morning concluded that the problem was the negative information faculty were feeding to students or the courses the students were taking. The students came from state universities, religious colleges, small liberal arts colleges with conservative and liberal reputations. All agreed that party affiliation and liberal or conservative self-identification did not determine who supported the conclusions presented.

While I am disagreeing with the characterization of students and the analysis that Neal, Ratliff, Balch, and Horowitz provide, I still agree that asserting the rights of students is important. Out of respect for their effort, it is only fair that I should offer an alternative bill of rights. Surely, students do have rights within the academic enterprise. As with the Principles of Discourse, I developed my student bill of rights as a way of responding to a serious issue. In creating my alternative, I focused on encouraging engagement and "liberating" (rather than protecting) student minds. It represents an amalgam of many ideas about the purposes of education and is rooted in the movement to define what represents a healthy society. It draws on such texts as Robert Bellah's *Habits of the Heart* and *The Good Society* and Richard Florida's *The Rise of the Creative Class*. It also incorporates many of the accrediting standards developed by the New England Association of Schools and Colleges (NEASC). For six years I served on the board of NEASC, an organization responsible for accrediting all schools and colleges in New England. My bill is written here in the form of a statement to which universities and colleges can subscribe:

> A Bill of Rights for the Engaged University
> WHEREAS all civic organizations—political, social, educational, and economic—exist to support the development of a healthy society and the individuals who live within it;
> WHEREAS human creativity is the greatest economic and social resource that exists to promote that goal;
> WHEREAS educational institutions at all levels and in all of their great diversity and distinctive educational missions have as their central goal the nurturing of that human creativity;
> And WHEREAS the students of these educational institutions inevitably become the determinants of the future health of our society;
> We, the signers, affirm the following rights and responsibilities of students and our institutions;
>
> Students have the right to:
>
> • compete equally for access to diverse educational institutions representing distinctive educational missions;

- be treated with respect as individuals and to be encouraged to develop and defend their values, ideas and positions.
- have access to faculty competent to advance the stated goals and mission of the institution they attend;
- be free of demeaning or harassing behavior designed to silence them inside the classroom or within the academic community, even while they are being challenged and even made to feel uncomfortable;
- have their academic work be evaluated fairly and equitably against the stated outcomes sought by the institution and in a form that will promote the students' achievement of those outcomes as well as their overall growth as humane individuals;
- have their role as citizens and their behavior within their respective academic communities be evaluated against publicly stated norms of community behavior and be judged by means of publicly stated processes.

Students have a responsibility to:

- observe the Principles of Discourse;
- value the spirit of inquiry and learning;
- treat others with respect and integrity.

Our respective universities have a responsibility to:

- state clearly and publicly their respective missions and the outcomes they strive to accomplish in pursuit of those goals and missions;
- provide programs and pedagogy that intentionally advance the stated goals;
- create a safe intellectual environment in which they encourage students to evaluate and defend critically and creatively their own work and the work of others, to communicate effectively and to measure themselves against the values that they want to incorporate into their lives;
- comply with the Principles of Discourse that guide the work of all academic enterprises;
- provide faculty who will model in their teaching and research the values of critical inquiry that they seek to instill in the students themselves—taking positions based on review and

consideration of all the available evidence and to defend those positions clearly and in compliance with the accepted principles in the fields of their academic discourse;

- grow, within the context of their mission, the capacity of their students to create a healthy society in which people live together well;

- model, as an institution, the behavior it seeks to instill in its students.

The SAF and my student's bill of rights share a common vision: that education should develop critical thinkers who have open minds and a capacity for rigorous analysis; and, furthermore, these goals should be pursued in a way that enables students to make a positive contribution to the health of society. The SAF's philosophy differs with mine over how to achieve this goal. As I've said before, the neutralists feel that simply exposing the student to a diversity of views is enough. My activist bill of rights assumes that it is important to create a context in which the student can also learn how to handle the consequences of critical thinking—consequences that will often involve confronting authority and/or challenging convention.

Conservatives in the United States fear that liberal bias in the universities is compromising that ability for independent thought. These fears should be taken seriously. If what they fear is actually true, then it is important we acknowledge that threat. Conversely, conservatives should consider the argument that creating the neutral university will prevent students from learning how to constructively use their acquired critical-thinking skills. We must remember that the greatest threats to democracy almost always come from within, and especially from an undermining of the confidence and the laws that allow authority and convention to be challenged. Terrorism and outside threats reduce the tolerance for those who question policy and authority; but more subtle threats also erode our freedoms, such as the increasing tendency to personalize disagreements in political discourse—thus making it more discomforting to disagree with opponents.

Balch and Horowitz argue for balance, and they highlight the dangers of imbalance. I do not dismiss their concerns. I have heard too many faculty members make off-handed but outrageous comments such as "Republicans are evil" or all U.S. foreign policy is "imperialistic"; and from the other end of the political spectrum, I have heard, "Martin Luther King deserved to die" or that the "poor are poor because they choose to be." These egregious examples of professorial "insight" may be protected by the principles of free speech and academic freedom, but those same freedoms allow me or any one else to challenge their appropriateness in academic discourse. They violate general rules of civility and mutual respect that should be the foundation of all educational institutions as well as the Principles of Discourse. These kinds of inappropriate remarks do not model any of the values that liberal education seeks to instill in students, mainly because they generalize or personalize issues in a distorted and irresponsible manner.

As Balch and Horowitz further argue, faculty behavior in the classroom is critical. If professors are not always conscious of how certain actions and approaches can affect different students, they will accomplish less and may even harm some particularly impressionable students. Arguing on behalf of engagement and advocacy elevates the importance of the Principles of Discourse and the quality of faculty-student interaction. Faculty who are so enthralled with their own wisdom and message ultimately will fail to meaningfully interact with their students. Advocacy without genuine engagement is as detrimental as the neutralists say it is.

If the goal of liberal education is to create a free and ordered space, as A. Bartlett Giamatti, another former president of Yale, eloquently argued, the central question then becomes whether allowing opinionated or tendentious programs presents a greater threat than insisting on neutrality. Insisting on neutrality is safer but sacrifices the opportunity for students to challenge authority and to understand what it means to assess the appropriateness of their actions (or for that matter, someone else's actions). Students must learn how to engage in robust debate by absorbing the attitude of mind captured in the Principles of Discourse. They must learn how to use those principles to make valuable that free and ordered space for which Giamatti argues and that Balch and Horowitz and I all seek to create. They need to practice discourse, absorb the principles by which it should take place, and make sure the discourse is about real issues where real emotions and people are involved. They must test themselves by confronting people who hold strong opposing views and are not just take opposing sides for the purpose of debate.

Democracy and liberal education are the double helix of a free society. Democracy makes possible, but does not insure, the participation of all citizens. Liberal education strives to provide the skills and instill the responsibility to use that opportunity well. With passivity and inaction, democratic institutions will decline as power accumulates and rights erode. Power does inexorably accumulate when passivity dominates; the only antidote is the existence of a broad base of citizens with the preparation, know-how, and willingness to resist authority constructively and responsibly. America's founders wrote a constitution based on that premise. The capacity to question is also the primary source for the self-reflection, creativity, inventiveness, and entrepreneurial spirit that generate the cultural, economic, social, political, and spiritual well being of society.

○ ○ ○

Societies committed to democratic principles create educational systems that encourage critical thinking and independent judgment. The liberal arts curriculum as a form of education could not have emerged in an authoritarian society such as that of Nazi Germany in the 1930s and 1940s. By limiting critical thinking, a society weighs the odds against creative responses to complex social problems and creates conditions that can easily erode democratic principles.

The educational leaders in central Europe who are active in the Artes Liberalis movement mentioned earlier (see page 22) are turning to the liberal arts model rather than the pre-Communist Germanic university tradition because they understand how essential that type of education is for creating a democratic civic culture. Democratic cultures need an education that stimulates questioning and active engagement of the student.

Understanding how liberal arts education is evolving worldwide creates a deeper appreciation of its power and a practical framework to help guide those who are undertaking the establishment of such institutions—sometimes at the risk of their own lives. The concepts of the old and new worlds may even be in the process of becoming reversed, for the New Europe and emerging democracies have important lessons to teach the United States. The power of those lessons, opened up to me initially by the series of European conferences organized by the Christian A. Johnson Endeavor Foundation of New York City, certainly inspired me during my tenure as president of Hampshire. The individuals I met at those conferences showed me how important it is, however complicated, to ensure that institutions, along with their administrators and faculty, should model the behavior they expect of their students. In education, there is no greater challenge.

The five institutions introduced in the following section not only illustrate many of the challenges confronting liberal arts colleges and universities in the United States but also show how academic leaders in other countries have adapted a uniquely American form of education. In these dynamic and diverse institutions, students and faculty members are using (or have used) the activist model to build or rebuild their societies. Collectively they provide a valuable example by which U.S. educators can examine and evaluate both the challenges and the consequences of promoting engaged rather than neutral universities.

PART

Mirrors for America

CHAPTER 4

The University of Natal: Modeling the Behavior We Expect from Students

Although institutions of higher education around the world are characterized by a rich diversity of missions and aspirations, all have a responsibility to model the behaviors they seek to instill in students. Meeting that expectation can be the most difficult task that any university faces, whether it is preparing students for a specific career or imparting the goals of a liberal education. In 1948, when the pro-apartheid Nationalist Party took over the government of South Africa, the University of Natal in South Africa discovered just how difficult this task of being an "engaged" university would be.

Faced with a government founded upon immoral concepts that violated the essence of a liberal education, the University of Natal, known since 2004 as the University of KwaZulu-Natal after its merger with the University of Durban-Westville, charted a course that exemplified the axiom that universities should model the values and qualities they seek to instill in their students. It also revealed the pain and the difficulty that can come from accepting and carrying out that principle.

Founded in 1910 as the Natal University College in Pietermaritzburg, the University of Natal became an independent university in 1949 and was considering establishing a medical school when apartheid was introduced. The new government informed the university that it could continue its plans to establish a medical school but the school could not serve both blacks and Caucasians. Much to the surprise of the Nationalist Party, the university established a medical school for blacks—a response that echoed what too few colleges and universities did in the American South when Jim Crow segregation laws were introduced in the 1890s.

That controversial choice generated within the University of Natal a sense of pride about its mission and its responsibility to all citizens that has shaped the university ever since. The medical school was situated on a separate campus adjacent to a hospital that did not serve the black community. A residence for the medical students was acquired in an area zoned for use by black people. But more than these obvious separations, medical students suffered indignities from a range of petty regulations to major limitations on their status as university members. Some of these limitations were forced on the university by the government and some were the product of the university trying to retain its independence through accommodation or compromise. Some of these limitations, in retrospect, seem completely unnecessary, but were probably a reflection of the social mores of the time: the black medical students could not enter the main campus, and they could not wear the university blazer. Socially they were separate from whites, but received what was thought to be an education equal to that of white medical students—a small victory under the circumstances. But the racial divisions, nevertheless, created real pain. Most of these graduates chose not to attend graduation ceremonies as a way of protesting the indignities they faced, but they left with a University of Natal degree and made important medical contributions to South Africa and other countries around the world.

When apartheid ended in 1994, the university's vice chancellor and principal, Brenda Gourley (now vice chancellor and principal of the U.K.'s Open University), held a reconciliation graduation to which all past medical graduates were invited. Hundreds came from all over the world. At that ceremony, she apologized for the incompleteness of their university experience and the injustices they had suffered. At the same time, all who were present understood what the university had done for them by taking a courageous stand under apartheid. This reconciliation ceremony for the university started a process that still continues because the institution had the courage to admit its wrongs without excuses.

Although the medical school operated in a way that inflicted hurtful indignities upon its students, it had also created an unusual space within the university, a space that could not be replicated under government regulations but was an ongoing and visible challenge to the status quo. By embracing the obligation of offering education to all students, the university modeled the values it expected of the students, even when it meant the university had to challenge the state. As an engaged university they could have chosen to curse the darkness that had befallen their land (to paraphrase a quote that Martin Luther King often used), but instead they chose to light a candle. The choice of engagement over rhetorical protest involved far greater risks for all involved and accomplished far more. The university could never light enough candles, but the first candle lit may have been as important as all of the rest.

As the government implemented apartheid, several of the university staff, in opposition to the government, created what came to be called the University of Natal Non-European Section—a name with which no one in the administration was comfortable but that underscored the university's commitment to serve all students. The program, widely supported by faculty, staff, and students, was a cooperative effort with the University of Durban-Westville that had been established in the 1960s as University College for Indians. Since the students never officially appeared in government enrollment counts, the faculty worked without a state subsidy while teaching a substantial range of evening and weekend courses in Durban. Through these extraordinary efforts, nonwhite students could earn University of Natal degrees.

Even before the collapse of apartheid, nonwhite students were permitted on the university's campus and could be found taking courses and even living in dormitories. The government allowed nonwhite students to enroll in a course at a white university if the course was not offered at any of the designated universities they were allowed to attend. The University of Natal's faculty surveyed the offerings of those universities and then constructed unique titles for courses even if occasionally the subject matter might not have been much different from courses offered in the nonwhite universities. As Professor Gourley stated in a conversation, "our efforts had to be quite modest; if not, it all could become unstuck." But however modest their efforts may have been, they did set an example for students and contributed in a small way to the resistance that eventually ended apartheid.

As part of its resistance movement, the university also gave sanctuary to nongovernmental organizations, many of which were harassed by the government because of their opposition to apartheid. By the time apartheid collapsed, the university was providing the headquarters for eighty-four NGOs. Their staff was listed as university personnel and often had overlapping positions. However organized, the value of this sanctuary was clear and direct. To attack or directly confront these institutions, many of which were small and without large-scale resources, the government would have had to take on the much larger and better-resourced University of Natal. This arrangement placed a significant strain on the university, which often acted as a last-resort source of administrative, political, and even financial support.

At the same time, Professor Gourley explained that the university was significantly enriched by the NGO presence, changing the quality of the conversation on campus in many different but positive ways. Their presence shaped course material, deliberations in classes, the research agenda of the university, and the quality of its engagement with the local community—in short, the school was fulfilling its mission. Before the term "service-learning"—the practice of incorporating practical community service work into formal classroom study—had even been conceived of in the United States, the University of Natal was engaged in a service-learning experiment of unprecedented scale and consequence. It helped create the concept of "strategic engagement," whereby the university engaged in serious and open conversation with the outside community in order to plan how it could most effectively help that community.

By the end of the apartheid period, the concept of "strategic engagement" was so deeply ingrained in the university that community discussions represented a key component in the development of the university's strategic plan for the postapartheid period. Sixty-seven separate iterations of its priority implementation plan created a powerful example of democratic decision making that itself was very valuable in the transition from apartheid to the new South Africa. There was nothing token about the process; community development became a central part of the mission statement of the institution. Conversations in the United States about "civic engagement" would do well to include the history of this university and its successes and failures with respect to strategic engagement.

Prior to 1994, strategic engagement posed real personal and institutional risks. The police routinely tapped the phones of senior staff (including the vice chancellor), followed certain personnel, and periodically threatened their personal safety. The authorities raided student residences (in particular the residences of the medical school), often arresting students on various pretexts. One staff member was assassinated. There were mysterious fires and other troublesome incidents involving harassment.

Professor Gourley and her predecessors considered that two of the vice chancellor's primary tasks were keeping the police off campus and "policing" the freedom the university was creating on campus. On several occasions she and other staff members stood with students in front of police vehicles and refused to move, so as to stop the authorities' advance on the campus. The university had to deal with students hired by the authorities to act as provocateurs and informers. At every campus demonstration, university officials were well aware that the activities could be directed by student provocateurs; yet in spite of these potential dangers, they had to exhibit how free speech on campus worked. Constantly modeling the behavior expected of their students incurred risks that could even lead to the "disappearance" of individuals.

During all that time they tested the boundaries, the university officials always had the sense that what they were doing was, according to Professor Gourley, simply not enough. Keeping an engaged university required continual reflection and reassessment on what could be done to move free speech on campus forward. Giving in and giving up were never options.

The university's effort to model behavior expected of students could never have been completely successful under the circumstances, but it *was* visible. The university's commitment, however imperfect, was recognized at least tacitly when the African National Congress selected five white members from the university staff to be part of the ANC's slate of candidates running in South Africa's first free election after the end of apartheid.

As I interviewed Professor Gourley, I could only marvel at what she and her colleagues had done both before and after 1994. The post-1994 period presented a whole series of new challenges as the university attempted to implement its strategic engagement policy with the community. Most notable was a widely inclusive expansion in which the student body was transformed from 10 percent nonwhite to 75 percent nonwhite in the span of five years. In the process, the university had to renegotiate with the students all of the university regulations. This was a massive task to be sure, but it was one that allowed the entire university community to experience democratic decision making firsthand. It was an unparalleled opportunity for education about democracy and about education itself.

From apartheid's beginnings, the University of Natal attempted to model the behavior that it expected of students. Its courageous actions highlighted and answered a question that today is often ignored in the United States: If an institution promotes, through its curricular and extracurricular programs, the value of civic engagement for its students, what obligations does the institution have with respect to that goal? In its commitment to strategic engagement, the University of Natal graduated hundreds of citizens who absorbed its lessons in the art of nonviolent, creative confrontation, contributing, at least in a small way, to the final peaceful transformation of South Africa's political system. The students of the university owe an immense debt to the courage of Professor Gourley and her predecessors, staff, and colleagues for their willingness to advocate for human dignity through positive activism and not just rhetoric. And the staff recognized that they owed an immense debt to those students who took the risk of supporting them. Anyone who cares about education should feel indebted. At the very least, the University of Natal's example dismantles the case for neutrality and replaces it with a difficult question: When is the level of engagement enough?

O O O

From the scores of instances in which universities took similar stands—the University of Cape Town had resisted apartheid equally vigorously—I picked this example for three related reasons.[1] As an undergraduate I came to know about South Africa through a classmate who had left South Africa because of his opposition to apartheid. Before I became president of Hampshire, the existence of apartheid in South Africa itself had played a critical role in shaping the character of the college. And while I was president of Hampshire, the college developed an exchange agreement with what was then the University of Natal.

As an undergraduate at Yale, my personal association with a classmate, Heinrich von Staden, was both inspiring and disturbing. Von Staden made the decision to leave his country because of its immoral policies. The sense of character, the analytical sharpness of his mind, and his courage was inspiring. The disturbing part was being unable to imagine how I might have handled some of the same situations he had been in; besides, he seemed much more mature and intellectually sophisticated than me. If it had not been for him, I would not have read Alan Paton's *Cry the Beloved Country*; and if I had not read that book, I might have not have so quickly understood what the actions of those black students in North Carolina meant in 1960.

My first direct association with the University of Natal came when I attended the World Congress Against Racism in Durban, South Africa, in August of 2001. I was representing the American Bar Association's Council on Ethnic and Racial Justice, serving as a lay nonlawyer, member, and its vice chair. In order to attend the congress and personally welcome the new students to Hampshire, I asked the University of Natal if they would provide a studio and direct-TV link to the Hampshire gymnasium where the new students and their parents gathered the first day of the term; then I asked if I could recruit some of their students to join me in welcoming the Hampshire newcomers. The university agreed, suggesting a simple-but-effective low-tech solution: a video signal sent over a phone line from their studio. Thanks to the technical ingenuity of both institutions' staff members, what I thought would be very expensive cost no more than a phone call, albeit a long one.

Two Hampshire faculty members who were in Durban at that time, Jay Pillay, whose family was from Durban, and Stephanie Levin, who taught periodically as a visiting faculty member in the law faculty at the university, arranged for me to meet with faculty and students at the university via TV link. Our primary purpose was to talk about a possible exchange program, but I also used the occasion to ask students if they would be available and willing to join me as I welcomed the new students at Hampshire College two days later. The South African students joined us for an informal late supper, followed by an informal conversation with a comparable group of students sitting on a stage at Hampshire College ten thousand miles and seven hours away, where another four hundred newly arrived students (and many of their parents) were listening and watching.

In return for the South African students' participation and the university's help, we proposed that Hampshire sponsor a group of students from the University of Natal to visit Hampshire for two weeks later in the year. The students understood that there would be a "competitive" selection process for that visit—participating in the transatlantic video conference would not ensure the chance to visit Hampshire. Twenty students appeared for dinner.

As we began planning for the ensuing conversation, I asked them how they would welcome new students to their university. They responded instantly: "With music." That became our plan. Natal students were all strangers to each other as well as to Hampshire, since they came from departments in different schools at a university with over twenty-five thousand students. They represented a cross-section of the country's population as a whole. They quickly agreed to sing South Africa's national anthem but soon realized that only a couple of them knew all three verses—one verse each in English, Afrikaans, and Zulu. The students quickly set about helping each other learn all three verses. When we opened the program with Hampshire, the Natal students were no longer strangers to each other. Their rendition of the national anthem, accentuated by beautiful harmony and spirit, brought tears to many of those sitting in Amherst, Massachusetts. No one in Amherst had any idea of what had transpired in Durban to produce the emotion they saw and heard in that anthem.

What did come through was how excited these students were to express their collective university spirit to a group of interested foreign students. The conversations between the two student groups that followed the initial "welcome" went well technically and substantively. What those of us sitting in the studio in Durban saw in the South African students was a pride in what their university stood for and in what they were trying to accomplish in building a new postapartheid society. When I returned to Hampshire, students there were also excited to have been part of this video bridge. But many students also made comments to me concerning their embarrassment. South African students seemed to know so much more about the United States than the Hampshire students did about South Africa; and the South Africans seemed to be so much more knowledgeable about world events. I was delighted to learn later that newspaper subscriptions at Hampshire increased that year.

Six months later, the trip having been delayed by the events of 9/11, a diverse Natal student group visited Hampshire. What interested the Hampshire students the most during the visit was watching the South African students interact with each other—none of them had known each other before this trip to the United States. The South Africans ended up forming a very cohesive group. Perhaps the greatest consequence of the visit was the Hampshire students' new understanding of what it means to live together harmoniously. They saw immediate examples of how to respect someone while disagreeing with them and how differences are celebrated. It was a modeling of behavior the Hampshire students never envisioned when the visit was planned originally.

These connections evolved into a formal exchange agreement between the two institutions. That visit's success owed everything to the visiting students, but the visit also benefited from Hampshire's strong antiapartheid position that had shaped Hampshire's own culture. In response to student demands, Hampshire became the first college in the United States to divest its investments in companies doing business in South Africa. When Nelson Mandela spoke in Boston on his first visit to the United States after being released from prison, he relayed how pleased he was to be speaking in the cradle of American democracy. He listed the seminal events in American history that had taken place in Massachusetts, beginning with Boston Tea Party and concluding by pointing out that Massachusetts was the home of Hampshire College, the first college in the United States to rescind its investments from apartheid-era South Africa. I understand from visitors that my letter to Nelson Mandela about his visit to the United States can be found in a book in his home, which, as a historic site, is open to the public.

Hampshire's decision to divest its investments from apartheid-era South Africa laid the foundation for a culture of both student and institutional activism and a community pride, similar to that felt by students at the University of Kwazulu-Natal. Hampshire College was conceived by educators at Amherst, Mount Holyoke, and Smith Colleges as well as the University of Massachusetts as a liberal arts college where students would shape their own education by negotiating with a faculty committee a contract that defined students' educational goals, plans for achieving them, and the standards for evaluating their achievement. Negotiating one's own education teaches students how to frame questions and gives them the self-confidence to pursue their own unique ambitions. It is an entrepreneurial education that encourages students to design or invent their education—not just receive it. It certainly is one that encourages students to challenge authority and convention in appropriate and constructive ways. Given that design, it was natural that Hampshire College would espouse, as part of its mission, the idea that a college should model the behavior it expects of its students. The divestment decision gave substance to that principle. For a college with almost no endowment, divestment from wealthy companies supporting immoral governments was a symbolic act, but one that had a major role in creating an activist campus culture.

Symbolic as it may have been and important as it proved to be in shaping the culture of Hampshire, the divestment decision did not come easily.[2] Students and faculty spent weeks gathering information and discussing details. The meeting of the board of trustees took place at the end of the academic year in an atmosphere of tension and confrontation: students, faculty, and trustees argued with one another, and there was heated debate among the trustees themselves. Without being disruptive, students, faculty, and staff gathered outside the board meeting and made a very visible show of strength in support of the divestment question.

Some board members felt intimidated and did not want to discuss the issue in such a confrontational atmosphere. But the board as a whole moved past that concern. The board accepted the idea that the students were rightfully expressing concern about issues of social justice and equity; therefore, as the college's governing body, the trustees felt they had to accept this challenge to their authority. As campus authority figures, they knew they had a responsibility to listen to students, even if the board was uncomfortable with the tone of the voices echoing from outside of the boardroom.

The trustees concluded that a nondisruptive demonstration, even if confrontational, was an appropriate example of community activism. In an atmosphere that continued to be emotionally charged (and sometimes painful), the board addressed the issue of whether the college should take a specific stand or whether it should represent a multiplicity of views. If the school took firm stands on certain issues, would this lead to a fracturing of the institution? The debate was intense. While many might have liked to remain neutral about the particular issue at hand, the majority was not willing to adopt the principle of neutrality. The board accepted that an educational institution that encouraged its students to be engaged with world issues could not ignore its own responsibility to engage with society in the same way. There was no reason to take a stand on every issue, but the school could not set forth, as a principle, that it could not take stands, period.

Having decided that the institution, in principle, should take stands, the board then had to address the substance of divestment itself. Was apartheid in South Africa an appropriate issue for the institution to address. If so, was divestment an appropriate strategy to pursue? The board concluded that divestment was appropriate because it related to the college's mission to respect and advance human dignity and social justice. Whatever the complexity of the response, the students were asking the kind of questions that critical thinking required and were doing exactly what the college's mission statement said it was preparing them to do. The board, in effect, accepted that what was transpiring was a responsible and ethical challenge to them to use their authority responsibly, not simply a challenge of their authority. The board accepted the challenge and addressed the divestment issue at hand.

The debate then focused on whether divestment was the most effective policy to address the evil of apartheid, a fascinating and complex question; some questioned whether disengagement was the best way to be engaged, seeing the obvious irony in such a seemingly contradictory policy. However, what was important for the history of the college was that a substantive debate occurred and was not avoided on procedural terms. The debate continued in a charged and often confusing atmosphere and was not as ordered as this description suggests. Motives were questioned; anger and frustration expressed. At the conclusion of debate, the board decided on divestment.

The divestment debate provided an extraordinary opportunity for education. If the board had decided that this act of divestment was not an effective means of engagement, the clarity of the message that engagement was appropriate would have been lost. At least some board members understood that more was at stake than just the issue of what was the most effective response to apartheid. They understood that their actions would have a far greater impact on Hampshire than on South Africa. They knew it was important for their young institution to send a clear signal to its community: Hampshire had to model the behavior that it expected of its students. They wanted to acknowledge that the challenge students were presenting should be celebrated and applauded, not simply tolerated. The students, faculty, and staff had sent a message, which was perceived as shrill by some board members but still within the bounds of appropriate discourse.

The board listened and ultimately chose to focus on the message and not just the manner of delivery; and they responded with the care and respect a serious question deserved. This sort of productive, vigorous dialogue continues to shape the culture of Hampshire and enrich its education. Since that first divestment decision was made, there have been periodic debates, confrontations, and subsequent controversial decisions about Hampshire's investment policy; but, in the end, the college came away with a strong socially responsible and evolving investment policy.

As president, I was fortunate to inherit the tradition that these passionate debates created. For sixteen years, I struggled with how to live up to the expectations such a mission generates. More important, I learned from that expectation. Before arriving at Hampshire, I had argued that higher education institutions, independent of what their graduates accomplish, have a responsibility to try and make a difference in society as a whole. Educational institutions contribute to their respective societies through the quality of the education they provide and through the accomplishments of those who receive that education. But because of the special status that colleges and universities enjoy within the society, they also have an obligation to make a positive difference as institutions independent of what their graduates accomplish.

While at Hampshire College I began to recognize that the responsibility to make a difference was based on an even more profound obligation: an institution dedicated to critical thinking, civic engagement, and the advancement of social justice had to model that behavior for its students, not just assert it as a goal of their education. Fulfilling that expectation afforded a pathway for the college, as an institution, to make a difference. Ignoring that expectation would undermine any other contribution the college might make to the education of its students. A university might contribute a new method of teaching or establish a new research center, but everything must be judged ultimately against its willingness to be true to its mission. That realization was the most significant challenge I experienced as president. It was both liberating and frightening.

Because of Hampshire's actions, expectations, and its national reputation as an "activist" college, it attracts students who expect the institution to live up to its activist standards.

With the enthusiasm that can only come from young adults and adolescents who relish challenging parents and other authority figures, students energetically looked for situations where they could push perceived moral imperatives against the "practical" challenges of operating any institution, particularly a college. It was a rich educational environment for everyone involved— including the faculty, the staff, the trustees, and myself. Trying to meet the school's expectations and challenges generated the most demanding, exciting, and dangerous experiences I encountered as president—including threats to the college and to me personally. But in a sense, these experiences were also the most rewarding, educational, enjoyable, amusing, and proud moments I had during my time at Hampshire.

My experience at Hampshire taught me that whatever difficulties I faced as president, they were not as extreme as what many American educators dealt with. Hampshire's board members did not always agree with me, but they never expected me to be silent because some other constituency or part of the larger society might object to my wishes. I was blessed with a board that was fully aligned with the college's mission—by design, not accident, I would argue. At the same time, I would acknowledge that that alignment was also the result of a certain amount of good fortune, since it is impossible to predict what issues will arise and how individual board members will react to them. I often wondered what I would have done without their support. Choices would have been so much more difficult, as I learned often from the stories related to me by other college and university presidents.

Based on those conversations and what I read in papers and journals, I worry that the manner in which American universities structure their boards, form alliances, and manage dissent is rendering these institutions coconspirators in their own silencing. With important exceptions, such as colleges and universities with religious affiliations, governing boards do not accept the premise that institutions should model the behavior they expect of students, especially when it comes to civic engagement and activism. The moral courage shown by those responsible for the University of Natal's decades-long resistance of apartheid might serve as an ideal model for trustees of U.S. institutions and as an antidote to an inexorable drift toward acceptance of the premise that institutions should be neutral rather than strategically engaged.

Ironically, a growing number of educational leaders and their boards in countries where democratic institutions are a relatively new phenomenon understand more clearly what is at stake than educators in the United States. The academic leaders in these emerging democracies have seen firsthand how silencing of the academy, rejecting its engagement or advocacy role, and adopting the neutrality model for higher education represent significant dangers to a democratic society. At the same time, they have also seen firsthand what can happen when universities are "politicized." Understanding the knife's edge on which liberal education balances is critical for any society, as is the need to perfect that balancing act. To become politicized and to deny independence of critical thinking will kill the university. But adopting a stance of neutrality to avoid politicization and adopting a "do-as-I-say, not-as-I-do" model will implant in young people a level of cynicism that will erode all institutional integrity. Politicization and cynicism both will damage democratic institutions. Neither neutrality nor indoctrination is an answer.

CHAPTER

The European Humanities University: Challenging Authority Abroad and at Home

The boards and the academic leaders of the European Humanities University in Minsk, Belarus (later relocated to Vilnius, Lithuania), have walked a knife's edge since 2002, two years before the university closed operations at its home campus and reopened in Vilnius. They both failed and succeeded. Professor Anatoly Mikhailov, Rector of the European Humanities University (EHU), writes the following in a letter posted on the university's Web page:

> The mission of the European Humanities University is determined primarily by the historical fate of Belarus, which, because of its geographical position was a focal point of the interaction between Western and Eastern cultures. Cultural variety is one of the main goals of the University, founded in a dramatic period of social transformation and called upon to revive a humanistic tradition in education not restricted by national borders.
>
> This new educational institution is based on the national pedagogic heritage, while also seeking to adapt and incorporate European and American educational traditions.[1]

What is not revealed at the beginning of this letter is the reality of that historical fate. As I write this chapter, EHU is based at the University of Vilnius, having been shut down by the autocratic leader of Belarus, Alexander Lukashenko. Lukashenko found the mission of EHU so threatening, despite the rector's letter and its guarded language, that he could not tolerate its presence. Given the mission statement of the university, his fears were justified even if his actions were not. The mission statement threatens authoritarian rule directly and unequivocally:

> The European Humanities University is a non-state educational establishment taking its bearing from the educational standards of the leading European and North-American universities. By taking part in international programs, the European Humanities University aspires to contribute to the formation of a new generation of highly educated professionals in the field of economics, public life, and culture, capable of leading Belarus away from the heritage of totalitarianism toward an open society, based on the values of European civilization.
>
> One of the leaders in creating EHU was the Orthodox Church of Belarus, which aspires to end the domination of official atheistic ideology in education and to develop traditions of Christian humanism as one of the fundamental principles of European culture. Some non-state establishments, private enterprises and famous scholars concerned about the crisis in the traditional system of education, also united to create a new independent model of higher education, open to modern developments in pedagogical thought and culture.
>
> In the field of natural and technical sciences, the Republic of Belarus was a recognized leader in the training of specialists for the entire Soviet Union and many other countries. In the field of the social sciences and humanities, art, economics, and the law, however, the situation was and still remains different. In the period of transition from the communist past to a future founded on the values of an open society, our country needs to assimilate the experience of Western civilization in these fields. The creation of the European Humanities University is a response to the challenges of this transitional period, which revealed the crisis of education and cultural

values in the country, dramatically poised between the totalitarian past and the democratic future.[2]

In the words that Stephen Balch used in his testimony before the House Select Committee in Pennsylvania, EHU is a "tendentious" institution. It exists to advocate for an open and democratic society based on the "values of European civilization." In the context of that mission, the concept of a neutral university has no meaning. To advocate in that context, however, does not mean that the university practices indoctrination. The mission statement makes clear that the university is explicitly committed to the values incorporated in an open democratic society and the European educational tradition. It exists to give voice to values that have been and are being silenced. In the process it has no alternative but to challenge the authority, values, and conventions of the current dictatorial leadership in Belarus.

The EHU mission statement does not mention liberal arts education. It does not mention social justice or critical thinking, nor does it explicitly state what Western Civilization's values are, other than to speak specifically of Christian humanism and the important values of the leading European and North American universities. And yet the EHU mission states that the university is committed to challenging "autocratic authority." It explicitly and actively advocates for the values and rule of law that democratic cultures depend on. In the context of contemporary Belarus, EHU clearly exists to promote social change and its vision and mission capture the essence of the attitude a liberal education seeks to create.

When the university was founded in 1992, initially offering a PhD as well as an undergraduate program, the ministry of education, the Belarus Academy of Science, and other public institutions supported EHU as a vitally important step in reconnecting Belarus to the Western European tradition of education, embodying the foundations of a democratic civic culture. As the university developed, there were high hopes that EHU would help lead Belarus into the Bologna process initiated by the European Union, which was established to harmonize the educational systems of member countries.

As Lukashenko gained power, that hope faded, and Professor Mikhailov, himself a professor of philosophy who never expected to be cast in the role of challenger of the state, and his colleagues faced an increasingly difficult task of fulfilling the university's mission. The faculty, the students, and the public all expected the university to model the values explicit and implicit in its mission. By 2002, the community (and especially the board) had to figure out how they could model those values without doing something that would lead to the university's closing. Each pioneering step EHU took inevitably clashed with Lukashenko's persistent counteractive efforts. The very existence of EHU itself was making a profound statement to the country's citizens, and that alone made the university a threat to an increasingly authoritarian government. In 2003, in a move to increase the state's political control over the students, the regime utilized an abrupt change in policy to sharply curtail academic rights and freedom. The ministry of education announced that all tertiary educational institutions would be recertified in 2003–2004. The shock was meant to isolate Belarusian higher education from outside influence and restore a level of state control reminiscent of the Soviet era.[3]

During that process, on January 21, 2004, Minister of Education Alexander Radkov telephoned Professor Mikhailov. After complimenting him on how much the university had accomplished, he told Professor Mikhailov that it would be best for the university if he resigned. Professor Mikhailov refused, and the board of the university refused to accede to the government's demand. Professor Mikhailov explained to me in an understated and poignant manner, "someone has to take a stand."[4] For an individual to defy the government was indeed a significant example of taking a stand, and the consequences of such actions could be dire. And in some respects, there already have been serious consequences for Professor Mikhailov, as it is unlikely he can return to his country now—certainly not as the head of an operating university. As rector, he did have the full support of the board and the university community. The students, faculty, and staff understood all too well what was at stake and willingly put themselves at risk as well. In twelve short years the university had been able to establish a strong sense of the values of academic freedom, and the students as well as the entire community "stood up courageously for the Rector, the university's mission and the fundamental values of academic culture."[5] On February 9, 2004, professor Mikhailov informed the minister of education that he was declining the minister's invitation to resign.

Following this effort to intimidate EHU, the ministry began to subject it to intensive and repeated inspections, but no problem or violation was ever found. In April of 2004, with no explanation, the ministry delayed renewing the university's license to run an educational enterprise. Professor Mikhailov surmises that the government had hoped to tempt the university to keep operating during this delay, thereby creating a situation where the university could be closed for a bureaucratic violation—operating without a license. Mikhailov responded, in what he said was one of the hardest decisions he had ever made, by shutting down the university. The resulting student protests and activism led to the issuing of a five-year license on May 7, 2004.

However, the conflict between the government and EHU did not end there. It just became more direct. On July 19, 2004, the minister of education sent an ultimatum to the university demanding the immediate resignation of its rector, otherwise serious repercussions would follow. The board refused. The ministry then took a new approach. It ordered the university to vacate its government-owned building on July 21, 2004, and then "several days later, [July 27, 2004] the Ministry of Education revoked the University's license for academic activity due to deficiency of classroom and office space."[6] During this period the students actively supported both the rector and the university. With a certain awkwardness but a definite sense of pride, they described their own role:

> When a wave of licensing and attestation checks hit EHU, each student did his/her best not to stain the University's good name with low grades. After several months of tenacious efforts, hard work, and sleepless nights, the students defeated the endeavors of various authorities to censure EHU for a low standard of instruction. The students gave steady and confident answers during tests and examinations. We had been thrown a challenge and we met it with dignity.[7]

In July the students started public protests, and in August they began a series of "flash demonstrations," assembling for fifteen minutes in a public place and then disappearing before the authorities could assemble. However, authorities still were able to detain students because riot police were always stationed nearby.

In September 2004, speaking to students in the Brest region of Belarus, Lukashenko finally admitted that the university was closed for political reasons, eliminating any pretense about the course of events. With the shutdown of the university, Professor Mikhailov appealed for international help, and the response was immediate. Universities in Europe and the United States took in EHU students for the fall 2004 term, much like universities in the United States took in students when schools in New Orleans had to close because of Hurricane Katrina. The United Nations, the European Union, the European Parliament, and individual countries and NGOs all condemned the actions of the Belarus government. In the United States, Jonathan Fanton, president of the John D. and Catherine T. MacArthur Foundation, and Vartan Gregorian, president of the Carnegie Corporation, representing donor organizations, wrote letters of protest to Alexander Lukashenko. Gregorian expressed concern and noted the importance of having a diversity of institutions:

> The closure of the university affected its faculty and students and undermined the belief of both Belarusian and Western individuals in the primacy of higher education in your country. It sent a signal to those of us in the West who believe in the importance of promoting cross-national academic networks that the government of Belarus favors parochialism over progress in international cooperation. As a former president of one of America's oldest and leading private universities (Brown University) I am particularly mindful of the benefits to a society of having a diverse educational environment. The United States has been able to advance scholarly research and scientific innovation largely due to the existence of both private and public institutions. Those of us concerned about the future of post-Soviet states hoped that these countries would gain similar benefits by adopting an open-minded approach to education and scholarship.

The government's position with respect to EHU put into question the commitment of Belarus to free and open education.

The Carnegie Corporation remains dedicated to strengthening educational institutions internationally. We join the Council of Europe's Committee of Ministers, who stated that the closure of EHU represents a violation of the basic principles of the European Cultural Convention, to which Belarus is a signatory. We also applaud the resolve of EHU faculty, staff and students to retain their rightful position in the Belarusian society.[8]

With this support and with the courage and commitment of the board of trustees, the EHU community, the international advisory board, and especially the Lithuanian government, EHU was able to open in Vilnius as a "network" university in June 2005. Through the support of the European Union and Lithuania, EHU became formally recognized and accredited as a new university in March of 2006, just one year after its forced closure in Belarus. The transition institution, EHU-International, still exists and offers Web-based distance-learning courses. The new university plan includes on-campus education in Vilnius, the remote use of courses and materials through cooperative agreements with other universities, and the offering of courses to citizens of Belarus through the Internet.

The great irony in this story was that Alexander Lukashenko had the same expectation about how the university would model the values incorporated in the university's mission as did the university community. He was terrified by the prospect of a liberal arts–oriented university operating within the state, so he shut it down before any of its specific actions could challenge his authority. In a perverse way, his fear of the university was an intense form of respect for its power and its mission.

Professors Gourley and Mikhailov and their respective academic communities confronted challenges far beyond what any U.S. academic leaders and communities have had to face in recent decades. I admire what their respective communities did and what they are trying to accomplish, and I salute the leadership of those communities. In an elemental way, they represent what liberal arts education means for a democratic society, and they set a standard that all liberal education institutions should consider. Their stories illustrate the ultimate complexity that comes from living up to the expectations that must remain at the core of any liberal arts institution.

○ ○ ○

Modeling the goals and values defined in a mission creates complex challenges, even in the less dramatic context of education in the United States. Less elemental cases in some ways provide a better test of principles. It is in that context that I use my own experiences at Hampshire. Being more mundane, those experiences are easier to relate to, and yet they still provide insight into the relevance of modeling behavior and challenging authority.

On October 7, 2001, three days before Hampshire College's annual Family and Friends weekend, and a month after the September 11 terrorist attacks in the United States, the Senior Counselor to the President, Nancy Kelly, came into my office with a look that I had come to recognize after ten years of working with a gifted educator and wise advisor. It was about to become one of those long days that college presidents know all too well, especially in a community where students accept the responsibility to challenge authority figures when they feel circumstances require it. In fact, it was about to become a very long fall *term*, not just a long day. Yet, this also became one of those times when I was most proud of the Hampshire College community.

Ms. Kelly reported to me that the college press office had just received a call from its counterpart at Amherst College, a partner college in the Five Colleges consortium. Colleagues at Amherst alerted us that a group of students from "other campuses," all but one of whom had refused to give their names, had just held a counterdemonstration following a rally at Amherst College that had been advertised as "patriotic" rally in support of the victims of the 9/11 attacks. The students did not disrupt the rally, but rather waited until it ended, and then they immediately launched their own loud chanting of slogans, accompanied with the burning of an American flag. The one student who had given his name was a student at Hampshire.

The students participating in the counterdemonstration knew there would be significant press presence, since patriotic rallies on college campuses in the United States, especially in New England, are quite rare. The protesters were opposed to the growing likelihood of U.S. military action abroad and decided to use the Amherst College rally as a backdrop to advance their views. They got the attention they wanted, and the flag burning made the front page of the *Boston Globe* the next day. Since the only student who provided a name was enrolled at Hampshire, Amherst let us know that the press might be calling. On hearing the report, I groaned, understanding the seriousness of what was about to unfold. Neither Nancy Kelly nor I doubted that most, if not all, the counterdemonstration students were Hampshire students. Hampshire's curriculum had a strong anti-imperial theme that provided background for a case for restraint in the U.S. retaliation. And they were concerned that the response to 9/11 would be far more complicated and drastic than necessary, including expansion into the Middle East to protect American oil interests.

Emotions were raw after 9/11, and understandably there would be little public patience with "protests" questioning U.S. policies that had any relationship to 9/11. I was not pleased, to say the least, that our students had intruded on and taken advantage of another college's event to make their protest statement, just because they knew the press would be there. I was even more dismayed that they had burned the flag—not because they should not have the right to do this, but because I did not think this action was appropriate or effective in those circumstances. As I was to write later, it was an extreme statement that was unwarranted by the circumstances and not tactically smart at the time.

My staff and I began to think through all that we would face. Hampshire does not volunteer information about its students, but it will confirm whether or not a given individual is a Hampshire student, since the college directory is a public document. We knew the press would call each member institution of Five Colleges to see if the one name they had was a student there. They did call, and we confirmed that a student by that name was registered at Hampshire. We knew that the story would be in the news that night and the next day, and it was. But on that Wednesday

afternoon we could only guess at what would unfold. We suspected that we would have to respond to the public, to the respective communities of the Five Colleges, Amherst College, Hampshire,
and especially to family and friends who would be visiting the
college in the next two days. We talked briefly, alerted other staff
that we would have to be prepared to both react and act; for the
moment, we would gather more information and wait to see what
the press reported.

The next morning we breathed a sigh of relief, even as we
pondered an even more difficult problem. Everyone in the immediate area knew that most of the counterdemonstrators were
Hampshire students. But the *Globe* article, without being explicit,
left the impression that it was an Amherst College story, since the
event had taken place on the Amherst College campus. The story
noted that the only name provided matched that of a Hampshire
College and also of a University of Massachusetts student who
had been enrolled at U. Mass at the beginning of the fall but was
no longer a student there. When speaking to the press, the
university simply could have said that no student by that name
was enrolled, leaving the finger pointing to Hampshire; but
knowing there was a name in common with Hampshire, U. Mass
merely denied there was a student enrolled by that name, thus
making it impossible for the reporter to know what school the
student was from. To the reporter's credit, all that was reported
was the double match. Hampshire escaped the initial difficult
publicity.

I could have left the issue at that, but Hampshire was responsible for the actions of its students. The college should not have
left Amherst or the University of Massachusetts to deal with the
flag-burning incident. Equally important, the Hampshire community would expect me to "make a comment." Students would
want to know what I thought about the underlying issue as well
as the protest itself. In short, it was an opportunity for education
to take place.

Within a day, I had enough information to know that almost
all of the protestors were from Hampshire. Although I respected
that the students were challenging the community to think more
deeply about America's response to 9/11, I felt that I had to

challenge the means they had used to pursue that goal. I also knew that many questions would be directed to me about the incident at Family and Friends weekend and my own daughter, who herself was living in an academic community and happened to be in town with her family, also was urging that I respond publicly and immediately. I decided to write a letter to the protestors. To confront the issue head on, I chose to read that letter to the opening assembly for Family and Friends weekend, and I would also release it to the surrounding community and the public at large.

Open Letter to the Students Protesting on the Amherst College campus, on October 18, 2001.

I have just written a common letter to those who are writing to me or to Hampshire College condemning you collectively or individually for the protest you conducted on the Amherst College campus on October 18. Having defended your right to protest the current policies in Afghanistan and having defended Hampshire's encouragement of student activism in the pursuit of constructive social change, I am writing to you to express my deep disappointment in the means, place, and manner you chose for that protest. As I write, I only know for certain that one of you is part of the Hampshire community, but that does not matter. Whoever you are and from wherever you come, I hope that you might learn something from this experience.

Burning the flag is one of the most extreme means of non-violent protest a citizen of any country can make. As a symbol, the flag belongs to every citizen alike, not to some party or policy, not even to the government. It is an expression of the best of the aspirations and values of the collective culture of the country it represents. Thus, when you burn the flag, you inevitably are rejecting every other citizen categorically. It is, in effect, an extreme form of undifferentiated categorization or stereotyping. I defend your right to protest by that means, but I reject vehemently your inevitable categorization.

Your act is a statement that my support of the flag means that I support all policies of the United States. I do not. I do support the values and aspirations of our society, no matter how imperfectly we achieve them, even when the imperfections are catastrophic, such as they were with slavery or when our government overthrew a democratically elected government in Guatemala. The flag does not belong to a party or the government and certainly should not be seen as the symbol of any specific policy of that government—a point that is important for all parties to remember on all sides of all issues. Those desecrating the flag as an act of protest should recognize whom they are rejecting. Those waving the flag actively as a sign of support have an equal responsibility to recognize that it represents ideals imperfectly realized even while actively and appropriately celebrated.

I object to the place that you chose to make your protest. Those who organized the Amherst forum expressed fully and sensitively this sense that the flag belongs to everyone—this sense that it will mean different things to different people. They wanted to embrace all those meanings simply as a sign of support for each other. They were attempting to reach out to those who are afraid, who feel alone, who simply are concerned and confused, who are for and against various policies, who have suffered loss, who know someone who has suffered loss. And they did all the work to set up the event. You, feeling so strongly about the issue, felt compelled to co-opt their event, to reject their openness to make your case. You simply co-opted their hard work—a time-proven strategy of protest based on the principle that the issue is so critical people must be made to confront it. But if it is so critical to you, why did you not devote the energy and time to developing an event that could be far more effective in getting the society to address your concerns. Or why did you not create an event following the Amherst one that sought the help of those present rather than categorically condemning them. You lost potential supporters and you caused needless pain, especially for those who were present and who had lost family or friends in the September attacks. Your passions are clear, but ends do not justify all means.

Finally, your methods of protest violated several tenets of what I call "the principles of discourse," a set of principles critical to discourse in an academic community. They include principles such as:

- presenting a case that is as close to truth as you can make it;
- taking ownership of and responsibility for the views expressed;

- not distorting or falsifying evidence to make a point;
- not personalizing disagreement and argument;
- not appropriating the work of others without clear attribution;
- not misattributing material or positions;
- you will respect all individuals, even when disagreeing with them and you will not use other people as a means to an end;
- rejecting that premise that the ends, no matter how worthy, can justify any means that pursue those ends.

The principles of discourse are to the academic community what the Bill of Rights is to U.S. society as a whole. They are not identical, but they are equally critical and an academic community cannot survive without them any more than our society can survive without the Bill of Rights.

You violated those principles in one fundamental way—your unwillingness to take responsibility for your acts. Only one person in your group as far as I can tell had the courage to give his name. As much as I disagree with his actions, I respect him for having the courage to stand by his convictions. I cannot respect the rest of you. Your failure to do so suggests that you clearly understood the pain and even anger your acts would generate. If you understood that impact, I would then question the wisdom of your choice of means and methods.

Since I cannot address this letter to you personally, with one exception, I must make it an open letter—a means I would have preferred not to use since it may lessen the chances of this letter having a constructive impact on you. That is my goal, however, and I would welcome the chance to meet with you who were involved to discuss my reactions with you.

Gregory S. Prince, Jr.

I chose to write the letter for many reasons. We sent the letter to the Amherst College community to be used as they saw fit, so they could distance themselves from an act they were not responsible for. Amherst College's then-president, Tom Gerety, never pointed the finger at Hampshire; he treated the incident as just something that inevitably happens within an academic community. Among the many comments I received from students, staff, and faculty, both positive and negative, what touched me the most was the effect my letter had on those who had felt silenced by the events and the prevailing mood on the campus—a point that is directly relevant to the case the neutralists are making about liberal bias on campuses.

Using the neutralist definitions, Hampshire is liberal, politically correct, and biased, and parents continually asked about this imbalance. I consistently responded that it was a challenge, and we would welcome more diversity of opinion. I would ask them to urge conservatively inclined students to consider Hampshire. I would explain that politically conservative students should be ready to engage in debate and should welcome challenges to their points of view; they would get an extraordinary education because of how vigorously they would have to defend their views. I assured them that most students would probably welcome and respect them. I added that I would like their help in challenging the views of those who will be challenging them.

I further explained that what was critical about their choice was not the bias of the college but rather how we evaluate students. Hampshire uses a portfolio system of evaluation rather than grades. I explained that in such a system the evaluations focus on developing the students' strengths while reducing or eliminate their weaknesses. How their son or daughter would be evaluated was transparent and available to the advisor and other faculty with whom the students share their portfolio. Hampshire would provide a safe testing ground where their sons and daughters would learn how to work in a world where all kinds of biases exist.

The challenge for me as president and for the institution first and foremost was to ensure that all students were treated with respect and that they respected each other and those who worked at the college. We did not always succeed. No college or university can, but the goal is clear. A complementary goal was to look for meaningful ways to give space to those students whose views were in the minority over whatever issue was currently roiling the campus. For example, when I first arrived at Hampshire, the college was aggressively secular in ways that I thought reduced the richness of the campus. When I left, the only endowed professorship was in the history of religions, classes were not held on Yom Kippur, and Hampshire and Mount Holyoke College were sharing the costs of a joint Chaplain's office. The advocacy of a small group of students made the difference over and over again.

The task of creating the "free and ordered" space previously referred to by Dr. Neal is never ending. The intensity of the need, however, can be a positive reflection of the intellectual ferment on campus, if it is a sign that students are pushing against whatever orthodoxy exists. In an ironic sense, what disappointed me most about the outcome of the Pennsylvania hearings was that there were not more student complaints about bias. The lack of reported incidents may be the product of the passivity and apathy of students as much as anything else.

With the flag-burning incident I had what I considered a perfect "teachable" moment in which I could take a stand and engage students, faculty, and the outside community simultaneously. I know I succeeded in giving some members of that community space because they told me so specifically. I asked why it took my actions to give them that space, and I suggested they ask themselves whether they really needed my help or just thought they did. I would ask many other students why some of their peers felt silenced and what could be done about it. They were always thoughtful and concerned in responding. Many of these conversations took place at the Monday morning breakfasts with both groups—those who felt silenced and those who had not experienced the problem—present and engaged in the conversation.

Some days later, a group of faculty and students responded with a letter in the school paper challenging my position. Its content and tone were within the bounds of civil discourse and reflected the kind of debate that should characterize an academic community, except for one fatal flaw—the letter was unsigned. Its authors were unprepared to take public responsibility for its content, which was a critical failure when measured against the Principles of Discourse.

I did smile when one faculty member later admitted to signing the letter. She complained that I was the only person silencing debate because I had taken a stance and, as president, I had undue influence. I laughed, noting that no one else at Hampshire seemed to think I had that much power, least of all the rest of the faculty. I probably should have challenged the underlying presumption that college presidents should not take stands. I did not at the time, probably because I still was very disappointed that those who wrote the letter were unwilling to identify themselves.

That unwillingness was a mark of failure in light of the education Hampshire wanted, and claimed, to provide. The fact that other faculty and students were unwilling to sign a letter opposing my position signaled that, overall, Hampshire had not created sufficient intellectual openness nor had a sufficient commitment to the Principles of Discourse. For some, their actions may have even stemmed from an emotional need to assume a posture of risk-taking when there was actually little risk. Whatever the motives, their unwillingness to reveal their identities underscores the difficulties that arise when communities engage with difficult public issues. In this case, I did smile a little that the "fear" of speaking out publicly in this case was coming from the "liberal" faculty.

The next stage of the debate emerged in November as a group of students organized a college-wide referendum condemning the U.S. intervention in Afghanistan. One of their motives was a desire to live up to the ideal embodied in Hampshire's decision to divest from firms doing business in South Africa. It was an expression of school spirit that I never tired of seeing, even when I did not share the same position.

Hampshire's governance protocols state that if a majority of all members of the *community*—faculty, staff, and students—vote for a specific position in a referendum, then the results become an official institutional position. The students organized to make sure they reached the needed level of participation and received the "right" answer. They drafted a statement, and then in a clever but questionable tactic, they went room to room canvassing each individual in the community, checking off their names, and marking how they responded. It was not the normal secret ballot associated with a referendum, but it did create "turnout" and probably influenced the results; after all it was not a secret ballot. The students got their majority, and immediately, before any real questions could be asked by other students, they sent out a press release on the last Thursday of November that Hampshire College had "officially" denounced the invasion of Afghanistan.

The next two days were quiet. When I arrived at breakfast on Monday, however, there many students present who were incensed about the irregular way the "referendum" had been conducted. They asked *who* should speak for Hampshire and *how* could I have allowed those students to represent the college in such a manner. They wanted to know what I would do to set the record straight. I told them that I was as disappointed as they were with the results of the referendum, independent of how it was conducted. They knew I had spoken out against the referendum process and its content in an open meeting, and they knew I would continue to speak out against the petition. Beyond that, I informed them, I was not going to do anything; but I wondered what they were going to do. I reminded them that if they felt someone had "hijacked" the Hampshire name to be used for what they perceived to be a negative purpose, then they, too, had a right to speak out. If I spoke for them, I would only be compounding the problem of how silenced they felt. I encouraged them to speak out, and they bravely began to do so.

Only after I had left breakfast did I learn that a specific incident had galvanized the students to speak out. On Sunday morning, Fox News, the most conservative network in the United States, had singled out Hampshire's "crazies" for condemning the intervention in Afghanistan. Since no one in the administration regularly watched Fox News or had seen the broadcast (perhaps a problem in itself) I had no warning about what had happened or what was about to happen. The students assumed I knew what Fox had done, so there was a certain sense of "passing of ships in the night" in the breakfast conversation.

Arriving in my office after the breakfast session, I could see immediately that something was drastically wrong. The staff had arrived at 8:30 a.m. to find the voicemail filled with angry messages—some expressing felonious threats, including threats on my life—and hundreds of e-mails condemning Hampshire's position. We had clearly entered the maelstrom. Students at breakfast had known of the Fox News attack and were there because they were concerned that the college's reputation would be damaged. Seeing some of them later, I reassured them that the college would survive the tempest, but I also stressed that such assurance should not lessen their desire to be outspoken.

Later that morning, Fox News called to tell us that a reporter and TV crew wanted to visit the campus. Our press officer, Elaine Thomas, responded that the president would be happy to meet them and would be available whenever they wanted. The network assumed the president would want to be interviewed first. Our feeling was the opposite. Visitors were always impressed with the students, so whether it was donors, applicants, or possibly unflattering press, we always wanted to direct any attention to Hampshire's student body. Ms. Thomas responded that the students had started the petition, so they should be interviewed first. The network was surprised. Fox said it could not set a specific time if the reporter did not start with me. Ms. Thomas replied that I would be available anytime with fifteen minutes notice—about the time it would take to set up the camera in my office. Fox finally agreed and contacted the petitioning students. Those students, at the suggestion of the press officer and to the students' credit, agreed to meet with Fox but only if the network also agreed to interview the students mobilizing opposition to the "official" position.

Fox agreed, and the reporter, Heather Nauert (now at ABC), arrived on a snowy Thursday morning, interviewed students and Fox News filmed on campus until well into the afternoon. She finally arrived in my office around 3 p.m., and even before the cameras were being set up, she asked, "Were Hampshire's students always like this?" I did not know for sure what she meant by "this," but I answered confidently, "Yes." She added that she was impressed with all of them. She then began the formal interview and eventually asked what I had suspected she would: "What did I think of what our students had done?" This was a standard effort to create a win-win situation for the network and a lose-lose situation for the interviewee. If I said I supported the students, then I was one of those "radicals" Fox liked to condemn. If I criticized the students, I would be on record as condemning my own students.

My response caught her off guard. I told her I was proud that the students had been able to get a major network to cover their actions; I mentioned how grateful I was to Fox, since the network was helping us provide an invaluable, real-world education for our students. We wanted our students to take strong positions on important issues, however controversial these stances may be perceived; we wanted them to understand that taking stands like this can have complicated consequences. Having Fox cover the story—no matter whether it condemned or praised the college and its students—would create real consequences and the network, therefore, was helping us create a powerful educational experience. Moreover, I expressed to her how proud I was of the students for getting Fox News to cover the story and that I was grateful for the network's help in advancing our educational goals. She cut the interview, I suspect because she was taken aback by my response. We went on to have a frank and very open conversation about what it meant to teach students to be engaged. The camera crew took a few silent shots of me at my desk and left.

The story aired at 6 p.m. on a Friday evening in December as part of "The Big Story," the network's major evening newscast. The video showed a group of articulate students expressing opposing opinions, along with shots of the campus and a narrative that talked about the debate on campus. The college and its students could not have looked better. The program then cut to the studio where Heather was sitting with the anchor John Gibson. I held my breath and just knew Hampshire would be run through the mill yet again. Almost every day since the first attack there had been a reference to Hampshire, sometimes an extensive one. Gibson began by making disparaging remarks about those "crazies" at Hampshire. Ms. Nauert did not join the feeding frenzy. "John," she responded, "you have to understand that they are students. They are passionate about their positions. It's not the students; it's the faculty who mislead them."[9] I laughed. Blaming the faculty for misleading students was not newsworthy. Everyone was blaming the liberal faculty. Everyone "knew" the faculty was liberal. That was old news.

I suspect Ms. Nauert was impressed enough by the students' seriousness and engagement that she did not to want to condemn them. It did not seem appropriate to write to thank her, but I hope she will read these lines someday. I have great respect for her. She

gave our students a valuable education by the example of her profes-
sionalism: being willing to cover the story and taking all of the students (including those she disagreed with) seriously. She created a
positive example of respect for independent thought even as her network trashed such speaking out and fueled the hate-mail deluge.

The aftermath of that deluge engulfed the college for much of
what remained of the school year, as the college responded to
every e-mail and message that provided us an address. To the more
reasonable letters, we sent a reasonable response. To the passionate but inarticulate, we simply urged them to read what was on
our Web site. We could not respond to the threats because they
never came with a return address. For my part, I had as much to
explain on-campus as I did off-campus; but throughout this
intense period, the institution consistently modeled how debate
and discourse on emotional and difficult issues could and should
take place.

With the exception of those who hid behind anonymity, the
community acted in the spirit of the Principles of Discourse, as did
Ms. Nauert, although the Principles did not bind her. I was proud
of the institution; and most of all, I was proud of the students. We
all learned how difficult it can be to model the behavior we expect
of our students. I was dismayed at the level of hostility the general
public had for that mission. We had intense discussions about
whether we should involve law enforcement authorities, just as we
had with previous threats about positions taken at Hampshire
with respect to reproductive rights. Although we took some
precautions, I decided not to involve the local police or federal
authorities. Since the threats came immediately after specific tele-
vision stimuli, we concluded that they were not well thought out
and that there would be time to react if the level of antagonism
continued to rise. I did not want to divert attention from the substance of the debate and the educational opportunity that was
provided. Thankfully, there were no incidents. I cannot know if
our analysis was correct or if we were just lucky. I do know that
activism, advocacy, and open debate continued and that significant learning took place because of it.

After the Fox News incident, many more students felt embold-
ened to talk about the need for more diversity of opinions on

campus. In this instance, I was not with Hampshire's mainstream, and my position had encouraged others to express their opinions. Creating that space may not have made a lasting difference, but it did lead to discussions about how the college could and should have a strong social justice mission but still create space for those who opposed the mainstream sentiments. Although I certainly would like to have developed more sensitivity toward the silencing that did take place and that could have been avoided in the classroom, it remains a constant topic for consideration, without any sense that the college should be less engaged or public in its positions.

In fairness, while I objected to Fox's use of attack versus editorial rhetoric, I am not aware that anyone at Fox questioned whether an institution should or could take positions. The network anchors were simply apoplectic about the position taken by the protesting Hampshire students. After all, the Fox network itself had an obvious position. And rightfully so. We also received support from other networks. PBS's *The McLaughlin Group* featured the issue, and Eleanor Clift, a well-known, widely respected commentator and a regular on the show (and also a Hampshire parent), called us to get some information. Having been alerted, we watched, holding our breath.

At an appropriate moment in the segment, McLaughlin turned to Eleanor Clift, and with some intended coyness said, "Well, Eleanor, tell us of your connection to this story" as a way of prompting her to reveal the inherent "conflict of interest" being a "Hampshire parent." But before she could speak, another panelist interrupted to make the point that whatever side anyone was on, he was just glad that somebody was debating the issues. That sentiment was scarce over the course of these events.

O O O

While the situations Hampshire College and the European Humanities University faced were very different, one similarity was the fear and hostility the actions of each institution generated. The very existence of EHU struck fear in Lukashenko, and Professor Mikhailov had to face the hostility of an autocratic leader who could use the power of the state without accountability. Hampshire and I personally only faced amorphous, anonymous threats, even if they were difficult to assess. In Hampshire's case, however, the individuals expressing threats seemed as possessed by some undefined fear as Lukashenko was in his actions against Mikhailov. The tolerance of dissent is never in great supply.

The Afghanistan referendum was an important event for Hampshire as much for what did not happen as for what did happen. Such debates look different if viewed from outside the United States and from the perspective of undemocratic societies. Events in those societies and the courageous activities of educators to defend the principles of liberal education have much to teach the United States. Board members, administrators, and faculty who resist the proposition that colleges should model the behavior they expect of their students should carefully consider these case studies.

The examples set by the University of Natal and EHU are a reminder to all citizens that silence is alarming. Liberal education is essential for the health of democratic societies, and such education should never be taken for granted. Silence about critical or difficult issues by colleges and universities and their leaders should be criticized, not welcomed. Educators should also be alarmed at what silence does to student expectations. Expectations are a critical part of education and played a critical role in shaping what happened at the University of Natal and EHU. Mission statements matter because they set expectations, and educational institutions and their administrators have an obligation to defend and take their stated goals seriously. Neutralists understand the importance of mission statements and that is why they focus on them and seek to eliminate what they define as activist- and advocacy-oriented goals. Mission statements matter; and for that reason, along with many others, it is more than likely that the Asian University for Women, profiled in the next chapter, will face challenges every bit as difficult as EHU has faced.

CHAPTER 6

The Asian University for Women: Charting a New Course and Living Up to Expectations

Every society benefits from having educational institutions that represent a diversity of missions. This scenario is certainly more promising than having universities with the same mission that treat all sides of every controversy with "balance." The United States is blessed with that diversity of institutions. It has two of the best tertiary educational systems in the world—its public universities and private, not-for-profit universities.[1]

Immense differentiation of missions in the United States gives it a tremendous competitive advantage because it makes education possible for a broader segment of the population. The American Council on Education's 2005 statement on the value of diverse perspectives, which is quoted frequently by the neutralist proponents includes a paragraph they often ignore:

> American higher education is characterized by a great diversity of institutions, each with its own mission and purpose. This diversity is a central feature and strength of our colleges and universities and must be valued and protected. The particular purpose of each school, as defined by the institution itself, should set the tone for the academic activities undertaken on campus.[2]

Stephen Balch and David Horowitz, in stressing the obligation for neutrality, do not place as high a value on this diversity of missions as I do.

The need for a diversity of missions is often the driving force behind the creation of liberal educational institutions around the globe. This need contributed to the creation of the European Humanities University (EHU) and has been the driving force behind the creation of the Asian University for Women (AUW), slated to open in 2008 in Chittacong, Bangladesh. The university's board of directors is working to create an institution that will be open to women of all classes, castes, nationalities, and religious faiths in Asia (and particularly South Asia) and that will help women gain equal rights in their own cultures and societies.[3] This type of university will be almost unique among Asian institutions of higher learning. Its mission to provide a liberal education to any qualified woman will certainly challenge convention, if not specific authorities. It will be a remarkable case study about the importance of mission, the challenge of meeting expectations, how to be an engaged university, and the impossibility of being a neutral university. Watching it evolve and work to meet the expectations created by its mission will provide invaluable lessons to all universities.

In 2006 when I met with Kamal Ahmad, president of the Asian University for Women Support Foundation, I asked him directly about the motivation for establishing this new university in Bangladesh. His answer was simple and direct: "tolerance." He noted, with a quiet passion, that no university in South Asia sought out students from all religious, ethnic, class, and caste backgrounds. And by focusing on women, they were focusing on a group that, independent of all those divisions, was disadvantaged throughout the region. It is hard to imagine another mission that could challenge more conventions or so many authorities or that could accomplish so much in trying to build healthy communities.[4]

Through his career in international development work in the region, Kamal Ahmad had concluded that the university had to be a force for overcoming the strong sense of the "Other" in the societies of South Asia. Community in many of the cultures of that region was defined by religion, ethnicity, and caste, not by geography and physical place. Thus, the founders felt that this new university had to be residential, not simply institutional and intellectual. People had to learn to live harmoniously in a community—it was not enough just to study and live in proximity to each other.

That it should be a liberal arts university was never in doubt. Indeed, I had to work to focus the conversation on that dimension of the enterprise, partly because it *was* so much a given. Those planning the university understood that the liberal arts focus alone was challenging the preprofessional expectation of those seeking an education. In response, Kamal Ahmad noted somewhat apologetically that they had decided to offer a three-two program with the first three years focusing on a liberal arts curriculum and the last two on a preprofessional curriculum.

Ahmad was eloquent about the importance of the liberal arts curriculum establishing the values of critical thinking and tolerance, but he still felt the need to meet the preprofessional expectation. I commented that in other universities students in similar situations whose options did not include the fifth year or a three-two option often chose double majors in order to get a broader perspective. I did not think he should be defensive. The three-two approach recognized a reality that had to be addressed. The design of the final two years can reinforce the values and themes developed in the first three years, showing how those values had practical application and how liberal education really is about developing an attitude of mind, independent of any specific subject.

Ahmad's passion for the cause was infectious and yet grounded in reality. As interesting as that part of the conversation was for me, the story he told of how he began conceiving the vision of this new university was even more intriguing. When I asked him about what path had brought him to this enterprise, he started relaying a set of observations and conclusions he had reached as his career developed—observations that compelled him to try and remedy what he was seeing. While working in various international development organizations, he concluded that in South Asia, public universities were not acting as a leveling influence within the society as they had done in the United States. He also noted that organizations such as UNESCO and the World Bank were drawing the same conclusions and did not focus on aiding universities in South Asia, since they correctly perceived them as elitist. In the language of development, the gains to the individual were greater than the cumulative gains to the society as a whole, and thus investments in tertiary education were not warranted. Primary education had the reverse ratio and was a focus of aid development.

Rather than focus on tertiary education as a strategy for capacity building, development agencies concentrated on mid-level managers and professional education. They were looking at capacity building in the narrowest of terms. It was problem solving without connecting the problems to larger social issues and complexities. Tertiary education, and particularly liberal arts education, was not a priority for capacity building. Kamal Ahmad found that the international development community usually conceived of education in the language of workforce development, not in the language of liberal arts education.

The unintended consequences of this approach often took years to emerge as specific projects unfolded. Ahmad concluded that the role of the Internet and the globalization of the economy had created challenges a nontertiary education–based approach to capacity building could not possibly meet. The growing need for a science- and technology–based workforce influences all economies and educational systems, but perhaps even more critical is the development of manufacturing and service systems composed of global networks. Societies that do not invest in tertiary education will remain or become centers for the low-end, low-return, low-value nodes on those "global value chains," and as a result these societies will suffer economically and ultimately socially.

What was urgently needed, in Mr. Ahmad's analysis, was tertiary education that places a premium on developing capacity for new learning, invention, and entrepreneurship—a focused definition of a liberal education. This type of education would not only prepare individuals for more sophisticated jobs but also help them to become employers and to create jobs. Development strategies simply could not continue to ignore the need to strengthen tertiary education in these societies and to instill the values and habits of mind created by a liberal education.

Having identified and analyzed a serious problem, Kamal Ahmad set out to remedy it. In 1998, he was part of a group that helped persuade both UNESCO and the World Bank that universities had to play a critical role in capacity building and that these institutions could challenge convention and social custom and be a leveling factor in the society. To be effective, these institutions had to expand access and opportunity; they also had to stimulate social change and technical invention, not simply reinforce existing social stratification.

Kamal Ahmad and the planners for the Asian University for Women were able to persuade UNESCO and other international organizations and foundations to support this new kind of university in South Asia, although Kamal Ahmad is not sure that any of those organizations, even today, can be effectively persuaded of the cost of ignoring tertiary education. In Bangladesh alone, millions of dollars in development money remain unspent because there are too few qualified managers to lead the needed projects. In Africa, over $2 billion has been spent over the past few years on consultants alone. Individuals come from the outside to design or manage a project that cannot be implemented successfully because these outsiders do not really understand the country's culture, customs, and history.

A properly conceived liberal arts university can be an essential tool for capacity building and overcoming the fragmentation and inertia of society. And an institution like this should challenge convention, if not authority. The founders of AUW understand that although they are setting out to challenge social and economic practice and convention in order to build a healthier society in South Asia, political challenges and conflicts with authority would probably arise in the process.

The new university's "plan of operations"—a prelude to what became the university's mission statement—may make those conflicts inevitable:

> We know that effective leadership by women is essential for establishing equality of the sexes in terms of status and opportunity and in reversing social, cultural, political, and institutional barriers to women's progress in society. Fostering that leadership depends on strengthening women's access to high quality higher education. We also know that national and regional development is closely linked to advancement in the education of the population, particularly of women. However, higher education in many Asian countries has suffered from poor quality teaching resulting from outdated and

often irrelevant curricula and methods of instruction, under-funding, inadequate facilities, poor management, poor student preparation, poor job prospects among graduates, and political interference from both within and outside the university. In addition, critical thinking, immersion in basic sciences and the scientific method, facility in language and breadth of mind are underdeveloped in many Asian curricula that emphasize rote learning, in a context divorced from the reality of student's lives, and a focus on narrow technical disciplines from the beginning of university study.[5]

The planners for AUW, drawn primarily from the United States, but also from other countries, have set goals that may lead to political challenges with authorities over social justice issues and that will certainly challenge custom and convention.[6] It is a bold experiment that cannot easily be contained in one sphere, and this plan of operations recognizes the range of issues involved in living up to the university's philosophy and the inherent expectations it generates. The plan also attempts

to provide a vibrant and diverse residential learning community where highly talented women and those with uncommon potential from South, Southeast, and West Asia and from many cultural and religious backgrounds can grow both intellectually and personally;

to create a student-focused learning environment where the humanities and natural and social sciences establish a broad base of inquiry, where disciplinary and independent studies provide learning depth, and where applied studies in both the general studies and majors' curricula require students to link theoretical understanding with contemporary issues and challenges facing Asia and the world;

to focus student learning on the acquisition of intellectual abilities (e.g., developing critical thinking skills applied to multifaceted problems), reflective personal growth (e.g., coming to accept and appreciate persons and cultures different from one's own), leadership abilities (e.g., developing collaborative solutions to complex problems and communicating them well), and a service-oriented outlook (e.g., coming to understand that the life of work and concern for one's community are interdependent).[7]

The focus on educating women with a "service oriented outlook" receives additional attention:

> AUW seeks to be a distinctive and high quality university that graduates women as resources for positive change in addressing the most challenging problems in the region; namely, providing education in economic and community development that will allow for sustainable human development; thoughtfully engaging the global marketplace in ways that are equitable for a greater portion of the Asian workforce; attending to the ecological and environmental factors that permit sustainable use of natural resources; and addressing the ethnic, linguistic, and religious barriers to peaceful collaboration of diverse peoples within and among Asian nations.
>
> Second, AUW seeks to attract talented women students from all economic, cultural, religious, and geographical areas of Asia—though it will focus primarily on South, Southeast, and West Asia. In a diverse region that has experienced frequent and persistent ethnic, religious, and national conflicts, AUW wants to provide a safe and supportive learning environment for a diverse population of students and staff to explore collaborative and creative problem-solving solutions for a more economically equitable, tolerant, and sustainable Asia.
>
> AUW believes that providing a residential campus where diverse students live together is a prerequisite to achieving such lofty learning goals. The educational, social, and physical design of the campus is intended to create an educationally vibrant and ecologically friendly learning environment.
>
> The AUW welcomes women students from urban and rural areas and from backgrounds of material comfort as well as economic need. To provide true economic diversity, a significant portion of students attending AUW will receive full scholarships. To provide cultural diversity, approximately 25% of the entering classes will come from Bangladesh and 75% from South, Southeast, and West Asia. AUW will seek to create a student body that is diverse geographically, culturally, and ethnically. To take advantage of such diversity, educational and residential policies will encourage student and staff interactions that promote mutual respect and learning from the cultural, religious, and other differences present on the campus.

The campus community will seek to balance individual and human rights with collective and community goals.[8]

The Asian University for Women, like the European Humanities University, embodies a "tendentious" mission. It certainly does not embrace David Horowitz's principle of neutrality in the face of the "unsettled" questions of the times, unless you accept that its goals embrace "settled" values. It does represent a valuable case study of the more fundamental premise that the engaged university should model the values it seeks to instill in its students. Meeting that standard is very difficult, especially with a new institution where anything and everything is possible.

The Asian University for Women faces a major dilemma arising from that freedom. Beginning with a blank slate, the university is free, theoretically, to design a system that lives up to its high expectations. On the other hand, if the university is to succeed in its explicit goal of generating a different understanding of the "Other" and a new basis for toleration, it cannot afford to be indifferent to the larger community. The community either may not hear the core message; or, in the worst-case scenario, the community may be so afraid of the message that it tries to destroy the university. At the same time, if the university compromises too much in its alignment of means and ends, it risks losing the respect of its own community and the women it seeks to serve.

Living up to expectations will be difficult for AUW. Kamal Ahmad stressed that the goals of the university must shape the nature of the curriculum. He indicated there was some concern that early drafts of the academic organization did not align resources and program closely enough with the mission. For example, the founders asked themselves whether the traditional departmental course-based curriculum that dominates contemporary tertiary education institutions was best suited to accomplish the goals of AUW; or would a more progressive system in which students helped design their education—thereby, learning to be intellectual entrepreneurs—might better carry out the institution's mission?

Identifying the hypothetical choices its own statement of philosophy creates will illustrate the richness and complexity of the task AUW has set for itself; the statement will also be effective in dealing with the myriad issues its students may raise as the university evolves. And the decisions the university does make will be examined and tested by the students. As a new and untried academic institution, it will likely attract independent, risk-taking, activist students who will insist that the university's actions exemplify the values set forth in its plan of operations. The liberal education community around the world will have a chance to watch a star being born. It should watch carefully; for whatever happens, the results will offer many valuable lessons about the importance of being extremely focused with respect to how resources, pedagogical strategies, and administrative governance structures are aligned to achieve the university's goals.

○ ○ ○

Nowhere in United States tertiary education has the issue of alignment, expectations, and engagement been more thoroughly and imaginatively addressed than by the Association of American Colleges and Universities (AAC&U) and its Greater Expectations program (and the essay by the same name). The Greater Expectations program, created under the leadership of Carol Schneider (president) and Andrea Leskes (vice president), represented a call for reform in liberal education in the United States as well as a defense of its importance for the economic, political, and social health of a democracy. In terms of reform, it stressed the importance of testing programs, resource allocations, and decisions against the stated purposes of the institution.

If an institution talks about the importance of independent work, it should distribute resources in a way that supports that priority. If it emphasizes the importance of developing an international perspective, it should offer students a chance to integrate those perspectives into all of their work and not just give them a chance to spend a term abroad. Greater Expectations argues that universities should model their values and align the allocation of resources in a way that supports a university's mission.[9]

New institutions, having the proverbial blank slate, face the alignment issue with a freedom seldom available to established institutions. That freedom, while creating a challenge, also serves as a new institution's greatest resource. This is certainly the case with Hampshire, and it will likely be the same for AUW. The two situations, while different in most respects, were similar in one important respect: both exist to be a new model. The Asian University for Women will face many of the same choices Hampshire faced, and the question of alignment will be central to every decision AUW makes as a new institution. Comparing some of those questions and answers with the Hampshire experience and understanding how they will force AUW to address controversial topics will underscore the potentially complex principle that all institutions should model the behavior they expect from students. This comparison will also will help put issues that are currently dividing U.S. education in an international context, making some of these issues seem more significant than others.

The AUW mission will inevitably require the university to define the qualities it seeks in its applicants and to determine how they will identify them in a very test-dependent educational culture. Hampshire faced a similar issue. It seeks students who exhibit creativity, intellectual passion, and the potential to channel that passion into creative and constructive academic work and social activity. Faced with the application of a straight-A student, Hampshire has always wanted to know whether conformity and habit or intellectual passion produced that record. Confronted with a student who has a record consisting of both high and low grades, the college wants to know if something excited the student to produce the high grades and if it was boredom or simply a lack of discipline that generated the low grades. In short, Hampshire wanted a comprehensive portrait of their applicants. To help gain that insight, upon its inception, the college decided not to require college board scores. It did require, however, a lot of writing because the overall curriculum requires extensive writing in every field, asking students repeatedly to rewrite work and to assess themselves.

The AUW admissions process will send important signals in an exam-based educational culture. The university will need to consider what to seek from them, how much to depend on quantitative measures, and how much importance to put on the applicant's life stories. The precedents set in the admissions process will generate other alignment issues. For example, will the university use normal grades and exams or seek alternative approaches to assessing the students? Hampshire's founders sought to create an alignment between the method of evaluating candidates for admission and for evaluating academic work by adopting written evaluations and a portfolio instead of grades for assessing all student work, concluding that portfolios have significant advantages over grades: with portfolios, students worry less about how they are doing relative to each other and more about how they are doing relative to their own expectations, strengths, and weaknesses. They have more freedom to experiment, innovate, and think creatively, knowing this approach will not put their class rank in jeopardy—in fact, it could lead to an improved written evaluation. Throughout the years, we found that the portfolio system strengthened the intellectual atmosphere and the motivation for learning.

In evaluating a student body that is highly diverse with respect to cultures, class, ethnicity, race, and religion, the core mission of developing a different way of dealing with the "Other" would be enhanced if students were evaluated through portfolios. Using essay evaluations that identify strengths and weaknesses measured against the goals of the course and of the educational program as a whole, rather than judging a student simply on the basis of grades, creates greater accountability and transparency and reduces the competitive focus on the grade. In a highly diverse community, portfolios also reduce questions about whether grades are the product of something other than competence, since portfolios carry samples of the work evaluated as well as the evaluations themselves. Faculty both within and outside the institution see the narrative evaluations and can judge whether they seem fairly constructed. Kamal Ahmad was interested in the concept of portfolio evaluation, but he noted that it might be hard to convince employers in the region to accept portfolios, especially from an institution that was already challenging convention in such a dramatic way.

In one other area of admissions, AUW offers an interesting point of comparison for the United States. Unchecked by the U.S. Constitution, the university's mission states that as an international university committed to creating a new definition of the "Other" in South Asia, national origin, religious background, and ethnicity will be factors in admission. Moreover, because it is located in Bangladesh and is likely to attract a disproportionate number of Bangladeshi students, it appropriately has set a limit on Bangladeshi students. Although it is uninhibited by any constitutional questions, one can imagine such a decision being questioned and having to be defended in the future. For example, in Malaysia, a quota system for public institutions has contributed to a significant movement of Malaysian Chinese seeking tertiary education opportunities outside of Malaya.

In fact, the university may have to defend its policies in ways very analogous to what the University of Michigan had to do at the beginning of this century in the United States, when it successfully defended its affirmative action policies before the U.S. Supreme Court. Diversity enhances the education of all students and is appropriate and defensible when it supports the core mission of the institution. Looking at disparate universities such as AUW and Michigan with respect to diversity suggests why the argument that universities should be neutral on significant social issues is a meaningless position in the end. How can a university be neutral about the values for which it exists?

The University of Michigan, a public state university, decided that it needed to defend in the courts its affirmative action polices as a means for creating the diversity it sought. In the process, it provided all American universities with an extraordinary example of institutional courage. Led by President Lee Bollinger and his Chief Counsel, Marvin Krislov, and with the support of the board of trustees, the university argued that its educational quality required a diverse student body and that affirmative action was necessary to achieve that goal. As a state university dependent on the legislature, it had many reasons to be neutral on the issue or to let others lead the fight and hope for the best.

The University of Michigan prevailed in the courts, but in 2006 a statewide referendum eliminated the use of race as a factor when considering someone for any public position or any grant by a state organization. Michigan now faces an even more difficult decision as it works to figure out how and whether to respond to this new challenge.[10] Being true to the mission of a university sometimes means going against the expectations of the majority, a difficult position in a democratic society founded on the rule of law. The choices will not be easy; but given the history of the institution, I predict that Michigan will continue to seek a way to achieve the diversity it has consistently championed as an educational necessity.

Although questions about how students will be admitted are important, decisions about academic structure are even more crucial. Kamal Ahmad noted at the time I met with him in 2006 that the board did have questions about how different the academic structures should be. The Statement of Philosophy uses standard phrases about active learning, being interdisciplinary, blending theory with applied problem solving, and focusing on developing skills in critical thinking and communication. The founders of Hampshire College faced these same questions and developed what in the United States would be called a nontraditional approach, although viewed historically it was "traditional" in regard to John Dewey's view of progressive education. As a way of achieving the interdisciplinary-applied, problem-solving goal that engaged the student, they created a curriculum structure in which each student, through a process of negotiation with faculty committees, designed a personal course of study and signed a contract with the committee outlining the central questions being examined, the course, internships, research answering the student's essential questions, and how the project would be evaluated. Finally, each Hampshire student is required to complete an independent, original project before graduation.

Hampshire students initiate the process of defining the question and rarely frame questions in terms of traditional academic disciplines. They recruit faculty to be on the committees and most committees include faculty from very different fields. The committee structure has achieved intended and unintended results—nearly all extremely positive for students and faculty alike. Faculty who may not know each other or each others' specialties serve together on committees and must "learn" more than the student in order to work effectively with each other and the student. The committees have proven to be an effective form of faculty development, especially when students recruit faculty from other universities or outside of academia. Some students use the "outsiders" to build a network to help with future job placements and/or graduate school admission.

The "outsiders" also help broaden the perspective of Hampshire faculty and build understanding of Hampshire's educational approach in the larger academic community and outside the academy.

This negotiated approach represents the core of most honors or special scholar programs used in universities around the world. What is distinctive, even radical, about Hampshire's approach is that the college requires all students to engage in this negotiated education. Although not all students are honors students or produce honors-level work, the process is transformative for more students than a traditional system. Because students help frame the essential questions that guide their work, they almost always care actively about the questions and the answers and become deeply engaged in their own education. The system places faculty in the role of coaches who guide the students in identifying what they need to learn and how to set about acquiring that knowledge. Faculty members are not expected to be experts or to have the answers to all the questions that students frame. However, as they guide students, faculty members are expected to model what intellectual inquiry should represent and how scholarship is pursued.

The emphasis on having students participate actively in designing their own education also encourages an emphasis on inquiry-based learning, in which individual courses focus on creating opportunities for students to work on unanswered scholarly questions. In inquiry-based courses, theory and application easily integrate. The tension between research and teaching that faculty often confront can also be reduced, since faculty can use their research as a focus for courses they teach.

Although I advocate for this approach to education, the purpose of describing some of the choices Hampshire College made as a new college is to underscore the extraordinary range of choices that the Asian University of Women faces. Those choices will have major implications for how AUW aligns its resources, practices, and mission. Since AUW already is challenging major social conceptions of the "Other," it is unlikely, nor necessarily should it, challenge traditional academic approaches. On the other hand, just the process of questioning it has started and the likely risk taking, independent characteristics of its future students will create pressure for further challenges to conventional educational practices. But an intentional and transparent process of evaluating options against the core mission—a process that appears to be taking place—will advance its mission and help set and meet student expectations. Living up to those expectations will be difficult because so many choices exist at an institution's inception. How well the university can align its community norms, living arrangements, resource allocation, and curriculum with its extraordinary mission will have a great deal to do with how well the university can meet the expectations it is creating.

Alignment also will raise questions about the university's relationship to the outside world. Specifically, how far will the institution go in modeling the behavior it seeks to instill in its students through the example of its own relationship with larger communities? It is easy to imagine the questions and emotions that students from different religious backgrounds, nations, castes, or economic classes will have about critical human rights, social, political, and religious issues. Although many cultural differences in attitudes toward authority will exist on campus, it is likely that many students will want to know the opinions of the faculty, the president, and the institution regarding at least some of those issues. The electoral difficulties in Bangladesh at the beginning of 2007 would have generated intense debate had the university been open at that time. Although not all students will be activists and engage with these issues, the pioneering nature of the institution itself is likely to attract students with an inclination to challenge convention and authority. How all parts of the university respond will be critical to the success of its mission, as will its ability to resist the very real pressure it will feel to remain neutral, since any single position the school takes is likely to disappoint a sector of the community.

○ ○ ○

Expecting an institution like AUW, with its regionally ambitious mission, or Hampshire, with its activist mission, to accept the principle that universities should be neutral would deny the missions of these institutions. It would undermine their roles as shapers (as opposed to reflectors) of their respective societies. Neutrality as a pedagogical strategy is not wrong. It simply is not a

universal principle. My concern about the negative impact neutrality would have on meeting student expectations would disappear if the principle of neutrality were embodied in the mission
statement of the institution. If students were then to demand that
the institution take a strong position, the response would be that
doing so would not only violate a fundamental institutional principle but also the contract that mission established with its students. Such a mission statement might read as follows:

> Neutral University believes that the true purpose of education is to
> create a context where all issues are debated openly and where all
> ideas can be expressed. Believing that authority and power tend to
> suppress openness, Neutral University has as a core principle that
> the university and its administrative officers will remain neutral on
> all critical debates and issues in order to create the greatest possible
> openness.

Such a hypothetical institution reinforces the point with which
this chapter began. Rather than embracing neutrality, the United
States (and every other country) should have a diversity of institutions with a diversity of values and missions. And these schools
should all have the courage and commitment to live up to their
professed values and mission statements. Ironically, an imagined
Neutral University might have to advocate for its neutrality in
order to meet the expectations of its students.

After reading an early draft of this manuscript, Christopher
Nelson, the president of St. John's College in Annapolis, Maryland,
another liberal arts college, commented eloquently and succinctly
that he saw liberal arts colleges "as animated by a spirit of inquiry,
not a sense of mission—and this difference may make all of the difference in how one responds to the challenge you and the Neutralists both raise." His point is well made. President Nelson, the neutralists, and I agree that the heart of liberal education is the spirit
of inquiry—the act of what many call "critical thinking." St. John's
College, often described as the antithesis of Hampshire College,
has a very distinctive curriculum focusing on the close reading of a
core group of works—what has come to be called the Great Books
curriculum. Its mission is to promote the spirit of inquiry coupled
with the discipline of rigorous and thoughtful analysis. Its mission

statement does not advocate social change.[11] This attribute will naturally follow if the goals they seek are accomplished.

Although Hampshire and St. John's are very different in their pedagogical approaches, they are similar in their emphasis on a distinctive, coherent approach to learning, coupled with emphasis on an aggressive spirit of inquiry and creative thought. The United States is a healthier society because such different approaches to education exist, and there is nothing in the St. John's approach that requires neutrality nor does it require the advocacy for which I argue. The differences are meaningful, but so are the similarities. And I believe President Nelson would agree about how hard it is to recruit faculty who teach critical thinking effectively. The difficulty of the task is little appreciated. The challenges facing Singapore Management University described in the next chapter highlight the difficulty as well as the importance of the task.

CHAPTER 7

Singapore Management University: Teaching Critical Thinking and Why Teachers Teach

When Singapore's Minister of Education, Tharman Shanmugaratnam, explained to *Newsweek* in 2001 that Singapore needed to look to the United States to learn how to create a talent meritocracy (as opposed to an exam meritocracy), Singapore was already addressing that challenge. It was creating a new university that, through demonstration and competition, would transform Singapore's two existing national universities: the National University of Singapore (NUS) and Nanyang Technical University (NTU). The government had concluded that these two eminent universities focused too much on conveying knowledge and not enough on developing the critical thinking skills that Singapore needed to remain independent and economically viable.

Deputy Prime Minister Dr. Tony Tan first floated the idea of creating a new university in 1997. His proposal started a process that, at least by U.S. standards, quickly led to the creation of an independent private university: Singapore Management University. Dr. Tan picked Mr. Ho Kwan Ping, founder and executive chairman of the Banyan Tree Group, to chair of the board of the new university. As the university's own history describes it, Mr. Ho being a public figure known in Singapore and Asia for his outspoken views was shocked when Dr. Tony Tan asked him in 1998 to help set up the new university. "I wasn't exactly an obvious choice, being a total outsider to education," remarks Mr. Ho, who had strong and critical views of Singapore's education system at the time. "I didn't think there was anything wrong with Singapore's students," he says, "but there were problems with the system. I believed if we changed the way our students were taught and gave them freedom to think, they could be as brilliant as anyone else."[1]

By creating Singapore Management University (SMU), the country was declaring unequivocally that education should be about stimulating creativity and independent critical thought, not just about conveying knowledge. Singapore is gambling that such attitudes can be contained within the existing social structure and can be focused on economic activity, not on social change.[2]

How Singapore would achieve this goal was not clear. Experimentation and intense discussions eventually led to the selection of U.S. liberal arts universities as the appropriate model. In 1999 SMU formed a five-year agreement with the Wharton School of Business at the University of Pennsylvania for "technical assistance." SMU's first president was Professor Janice Bellace from Wharton. The university's own publication suggests the spirit of experimentation existed from the outset:

> Professor Janice Bellace reckons that the government did not know exactly what changes SMU would bring to the education landscape, but one thing was clear, she points out: "If SMU was successful, the others would want to change too. The government was deliberately injecting competition to see what would happen."[3]

SMU determined that the curriculum "should be an American-style university offering a broad-based education that was not overly dependent on examinations." This was in contrast to the university model being followed by Singapore's established universities, which emphasized early specialization and relied on examinations to evaluate student's academic performance.[4] The new university introduced an admission approach that included narrative histories of applicants and did not rely exclusively on exams.

Small classes emphasized class participation, team projects, independent work, and critical thinking.

The founding principles were a remarkable departure from educational institutions in the region, not dissimilar from the reasoning that led Amherst, Mt. Holyoke, Smith, and the University of Massachusetts to create Hampshire College as a catalyst for change. These institutions concluded that radical change was needed in post–World War II U.S. liberal arts education and that educational institutions are inherently conservative in spite of political rhetoric to the contrary. The most effective strategy was to create an entirely new educational institution.

Founding a new institution to become a competitive catalyst for change is easier than retooling an existing faculty that has been dedicated to a less-than-progressive mission. Singapore's decision explicitly recognized that the motivation and actions of faculty are critical and that it would be extraordinarily difficult to reeducate an existing faculty whose established approach was to focus on only conveying knowledge.

Measured by two standards, Singapore Management University is succeeding. In the short time since SMU's founding, the other two national universities have already begun to change. All three now use a common application process and set of standards that are qualitative as well as quantitative. And the Singapore government is giving the two public universities more freedom to manage their own resources and design their curriculums.

The second measure of SMU's success is the impact on the students. Although this is harder to assess, some faculty and administrators feel that employers are beginning to perceive SMU students as more flexible, creative, and independent than those from other universities. Students are becoming more outspoken in and out of class. In one recent public conversation with Lee Kwan Yu, considered the founder of the state of Singapore and its prime minister from 1959 to 1990, the SMU students were clearly beginning to challenge their elders and to raise difficult questions in ways that would never have happened a mere five years before. The experiment has just begun. It remains to be seen how and if this activism among students, visible primarily at SMU, will spread.

SMU's understanding of its challenges is an important mirror for the United States, highlighting first and foremost the lesson of unintended consequences. From its founding, Singapore understood the importance of education and devoted significant resources to it. They used the liberal arts tradition embodied by Oxford and Cambridge and the British system of education as a model. Yet pressured by an increasingly competitive global economy, the emphasis on the importance of education and the respect for China's exam-based culture combined to transform the liberal arts values of the Oxbridge model into a diagnostic test-based form of education. In the end, Singapore lost the very essence of what it was seeking to replicate.

○ ○ ○

Currently in the United States, the Bush administration pushes an education reform model based on explicit standards measured through standardized state and national exams. As it considers implementing the same strategy for universities, the country should pay particular attention to the problem Singapore has identified. It is ironic that, as Singapore works to undo the consequences of an exam culture characterized by high-stakes testing, the United States has adopted an exam-based approach to setting standards and achieving accountability. The United States should be deeply concerned about unintended consequences. Both countries are engaged in important experiments. Singapore does not know whether students will channel their critical thinking into economic activity or whether they will use it to challenge all types of authority (including political authority). The United States is unsure whether its growing emphasis on high-stakes testing will lead to the exam meritocracy that, as Singapore has concluded, stifles innovation, risk-taking, and entrepreneurial spirit—hallmarks of U.S. economic vitality.

Singapore understands the connectedness of liberal education, innovation, economic growth, and prosperity. This understanding offers a second lesson for the United States, where the concept of liberal education is primarily seen as providing a wide breadth of knowledge for students. Singapore understands the connection between liberal education and democracy; it is willing to accept the potential social unrest liberal education may generate in order to gain the economic benefits. Much might be gained from organized conversations between the educators and policymakers of these two countries.

The counterpoint of educational trends in Singapore and the United States puts the American conversation about the neutral university in a different perspective. It is hard to see how the faculty recruited to teach at SMU could be neutral with respect to some of the social issues that will emerge with respect to democracy and human rights. Students will look to the faculty to demonstrate how complex issues can be resolved and how to use the "freedom to think" that was cited by the chair of the board. On the other hand, it is likely that the authoritarian structure of the government will create much pressure for neutrality.

The decision of the university's organizers to select a business school as the model for liberal education offers its own set of lessons. And I suspect the model chosen raises the eyebrows of presidents of liberal arts colleges in the United States. Those presidents, steeped as they are in the environment of the small residential liberal arts college, sometimes forget that since liberal education is about developing an attitude of mind—not acquiring a body of knowledge—its goals can be pursued successfully in almost any educational context. Advancing the goals of liberal education and teaching critical thinking are not the sole prerogative of the small, residential liberal arts college, no matter how solid those institutions might be. Nor is it the domain of any specific set of disciplines.

The goals of liberal education can be advanced in any educational setting, since any problem or body of knowledge can be used to promote critical analysis and thoughtful questioning. Any instructor in any field can encourage freedom of thought and the pursuit of an idea wherever it might lead. Conversely, any instructor can squelch that spirit of inquiry. The most prosaic of subjects can advance the goals of liberal education and can be used to illustrate the scope and interrelatedness of knowledge. Conversely, any given faculty member can take the broadest and most profound subjects and present them in an intellectually parochial manner. Hannah Gray, former president of the University of Chicago and on the board of advisors for the Asian University for Women, once reminded politicians who sometimes ridiculed the esoteric titles of projects supported by the National Science Foundation in the United States that there are no narrow subjects, only narrow minds.

The case-study approach used in business schools, when exploring a breadth of questions beyond technical analysis, can foster all of the attitudes that liberal education seeks to create. That is partly why Singapore selected the Wharton School as its lead U.S. partner in establishing SMU. The early leadership at SMU, in addition to Professor Bellace, included Ronald E. Frank, former dean of the Goizueta Business School at Emory University (the second president) and Howard Hunter, former dean of the law school and provost of Emory University (the current president). The missions of both the Pennsylvania and Emory business schools promote an approach to business education that is consonant with liberal education, and both business schools exist within universities that have a strong liberal arts focus. These early leaders were steeped in the traditions of the liberal arts university and fully understand the importance of developing critical thinking as a core goal for any educational institution.

Perhaps the most important lesson provided by SMU relates to the recruitment of faculty. Singapore's and SMU's recruitment strategies are a reminder that the faculty ultimately lies at the heart of any educational institution's success in achieving its specific mission. Singapore's conscious act of picking liberal arts universities as models and recruiting from them the leaders for SMU was a necessary (but still insufficient) first step in pursuing the goal of creating an alternative, transformative institution. Those leaders understood that what ultimately mattered was recruiting the necessary faculty members to advance the university's path-breaking mission. The greatest challenge facing a blank-slate strategy for creating a completely new institution is how to recruit a faculty that will understand and implement the new mission and model. Adroit faculty recruitment will be key in SMU's ability to create fundamental or even superficial change. The right faculty will also determine whether the university generates a dynamic for gradual social transformation to a more open society, whether it creates an economic engine for growth without changing the political and social structures of the society, or whether it unleashes a set of forces that ultimately destabilize society without strengthening its democratic potential.

In separate conversations with Ron Frank, SMU's second president, and Emory University's Sundhar Bharadwaj, a visiting faculty member at SMU in 2005–2006, one theme was constant: the importance and challenge of recruiting faculty who understand what teaching critical thinking really means. Such a recruiting effort can assume nothing. Just because faculty candidates may have taught at a liberal arts college does not mean they really understand how to teach critical thinking. Ron Frank talked frankly about the difficulty of finding faculty who fully understood the goals of liberal education and the importance of creating a classroom environment that would encourage students to develop critical thinking skills.

Frank explained that although the university had been largely successful in attracting faculty committed to establishing a new educational dynamic, SMU faced an ongoing challenge to establish the desired culture throughout the university. He stressed that difficulties existed in all parts of the university, including the arts and sciences departments, and not just in the professional and technical areas such as business. Humanities professors did not automatically understand all the implications of teaching critical thinking any more than the business faculty did. The leadership of SMU understands it cannot assume that faculty from any one field or even one tradition of education will automatically understand or be committed to the values of a liberal education.

The extent to which SMU's leaders talk openly about the challenge of hiring faculty reveals their awareness that fully understanding why candidates are in the academic professions and why they might want to teach at SMU will be as important as their professional competence in their respective fields. Watching what is happening at SMU is a reminder that focusing on the motives for teaching is a conversation that only seems to take place with explicit intensity when academic institutions are being founded or when they embody distinctive missions. In most other situations, motivation is taken for granted and less explicitly examined. I witnessed that process at Hampshire and have seen it happen at other relatively new institutions. The drift toward assumptions about motivation, in the end, can weaken the execution of the institution's mission.

Perhaps one reason for less focus on the type of teacher desired or the faculty's motivation is the difficulty and complexity of addressing a subject infused with so much subjectivity, intensity, and emotion. If not done with clear and narrow focus on what qualities are sought and how they relate to the academic mission of the institution, the process can and will compromise academic freedom and undermine the quality of the university. Educational leaders everywhere should take heed of what happens at SMU. Liberal arts colleges in the United States may learn much from how SMU probes why candidates teach, why they want to teach in a particular context, and what they see as their professional goals and responsibilities. These colleges may learn even more about the importance of aligning the motivations of a potential faculty member with the goals and expectations of the institution.

SMU's leaders have set out to find faculty members who are committed to a style of teaching that will encourage students to speak out, to take positions, and to think critically. The university understands that many potential faculty members seeking a position at SMU may not be steeped in liberal arts traditions; they realize that even those with experience in liberal arts institutions may not be as aware of core liberal arts principles as they should be. To have taught in a liberal arts college does not mean the individual will have examined thoughtfully or understood fully the nature of that form of education. Understanding is assumed and the core principles of liberal education too infrequently examined with depth and rigor. The competitive pressure young scholars face to find regular faculty appointments anywhere increases the need for such examination. The usual institutional statement that faculty performance will be judged on the basis of "excellence in teaching, research, and community service" provides little guidance for the public, students, and faculty about what all those phrases can and should mean given the purposes of a specific college or university. SMU must overcome this confusion that contributes to why neutralists' views of what should take place in the classroom are more restrictive than mine.

If the neutralists and I were to conduct a debate on the SMU campus, the entire community would probably find it thought provoking—but also amusing or perhaps even unintelligible. The neutralists would urge that the university seek out faculty members who were dedicated to research, had a passion for knowledge, and wanted to instill in students a capacity for rigorous analysis and an ability to think critically—a position that many SMU faculty would probably support. The neutralists would warn against recruiting faculty who also had a proclivity to apply their skills to social questions of equity and justice. Such advocacy, they would agree, would be detrimental to the students and inhibit the development of their critical reasoning—it might even generate unneeded tension with the government. They would urge that faculty recruitment pay particular attention to the capacity of the individual to be balanced, acting like a judge rather than a prosecutor. Neutralists would insist on avoiding faculty whose agenda included the importance of social change.

I would respond that the neutrality that Balch and Horowitz were proposing is probably impossible to achieve; and even if it were possible, it should be avoided as dangerous and even irresponsible. If SMU were to recruit faculty based on the neutralist model, they would run the risk of instilling in students the capacity for critical thinking without allowing them the chance to practice using these skills in meaningful situations. They would run the risk of leaving the students unprepared to handle the consequences of the challenges their critical thinking was likely to set in motion. The cost of this failure is likely to be greater in an authoritarian society than in the United States.

Teaching critical thinking is the equivalent of opening a Pandora's box. Whether the forces unleashed help change the society constructively or destructively will depend on whether those doing the challenging will be sensitive enough to not only the questions about substance but also questions about means. Whether stated in these terms or not, Singapore Management University, as a liberal arts institution, exists to challenge authority and convention. Therefore, all such institutions have a moral responsibility to develop the capacity of their students to respond in appropriate and constructive ways to what these universities are unleashing. Starting the process by stimulating critical thinking and then standing back and saying, in effect, that the university is neutral with respect to the results of this critical thought is irresponsible and unethical. Liberal arts institutions, having armed the student with critical thinking tools, have a professional and moral responsibility to model responsible and constructive uses of that power.

To meet that challenge, Singapore Management University must find faculty who understand that students living in Singapore and many other countries in the region (such as China) will face formidable limiting social and political structures. They will need not only to absorb the attitudes that lead to critical thinking but also to gain experience with how to use those new skills in appropriate and constructive ways. The students cannot have those experiences if their professors remain neutral. The only way students can acquire the capacity to challenge authority responsibly and effectively is by actually having the experience of doing so in an environment that promotes creativity. Having the opportunity to confront faculty members who are also advocates is such an environment. The task faculty members face is immensely challenging. Not all faculty members are up to it, and many need training to accomplish the multiple but blended developmental and intellectual goals incorporated in teaching and learning.

Faculty members who remain advocates but can still create the sort of openness that encourages genuine debate will most often be those who have a balanced passion for both the intellectual and developmental roles of teaching. The developmental and the intellectual motivations for teaching are equally valuable and mutually dependent on each other. Neither is superior, and each can be the prime motivation for inspirational teachers. The way they work together creates the unique signature—or the social DNA—of every teacher. The most effective teachers balance a passion for ideas with a stake in the personal growth of each individual student—this is a balance that fuses intellect, judgment, and values into wisdom. When the passion for ideas drives out the energy and time devoted to the developmental life of the student, teaching can suffer and the intimidation or arrogance that Horowitz and Balch envision can, and probably will, occur. When a teacher's attention to students' individual growth drives out or limits the energy and rigor given to learning and the search for new knowledge, students may feel affirmed, but they will not be stimulated to reach their full intellectual potential.

Whether the neutralists like it or not, the goal of teaching is inherently about social change and social justice. The overwhelming majority of those who teach do so because they believe in the innate potential that exists in each student, and they believe developing that potential will enrich the life of the student and make for a better society. Wherever a teacher stands on the spectrum between the "hard," intellectual, research-driven end and the "soft," caring, developmental end, one factor links them both. Individuals become teachers because they believe that an educated individual leads to an educated community. They are never neutral with respect to their hope for the outcome of their effort. Asking them to become neutral, as the only way to teach independent thought, ignores the reason most people choose to teach in the first place.

Faculty members whose passion depends on research and the intellectual substance of their fields can stimulate rigorous analysis through a variety of means. They do not need to take positions; but given their intellectual commitment, they are likely to have strong opinions on all sorts of issues directly or indirectly related to their field. Since they do not put as much effort into their interactions with students as those more concerned with the developmental role, they must be careful not to intimidate students by advocating a certain position. However, such faculty members should not be discouraged from doing so. Faculty with a more personal connection to students may have more leeway in taking positions and advocating for values in ways that would not intimidate students; but neither "type" ensures a specific outcome. Teaching yields specific results but rarely, if ever, with certainty.

The selection of faculty at SMU has to take into account a complex set of variables affecting the balance of subject matter interests with interest in individual development. They must consider how these factors will contribute to, or inhibit, the achievement of the school's mission. Faculty drawn to teach at

SMU more will likely be advocates for democratic values and open societies. What should be sought is not neutrality but rather a caring for student development that gives the students the space and courage to challenge the professor's authority. What protects the student from rigid arrogance—as opposed to a flexible, open advocacy—is the faculty members' commitment to the personal growth of the students. Any institution accepting SMU's approach should seek professors who are as dedicated to knowing their students as comprehensively as they know their chosen field of study. And they should be as concerned with students' personal developmental issues as they are with their own grasp of intellectual issues.

In recruiting faculty, the essential issue for both SMU and for U.S. institutions is that an institution should encourage and support students—not dismiss students for exercising critical, independent thought. Institutions should ask themselves: Are they open to being challenged and do they encourage this? The ultimate sin on the part of a faculty member, in the classroom of an institution whose purpose is to develop critical thought, is arrogance. The issue is not whether faculty members advocate a position in a particular class, but how they encourage their students to take certain positions and how they react when their students express views that challenge their own.

All "tendentious" institutions such as SMU, the European Humanities University, the Asian University for Women, and the American University in Bulgaria (to be discussed in the next chapter) must look to their faculty recruits to teach in ways that are far more explicit and complex than those used by long-established institutions that do not challenge the status quo. All institutions, however, could benefit if they made their expectations of faculty members more explicit. Having done so in the United States over the past decades might have created a more productive debate about tertiary education in general.

○ ○ ○

I oppose the call for neutrality in David Horowitz's Academic Bill of Rights (discussed in Chapter 3) in part because of what it implies and assumes about teachers and the nature of teaching. Asking a professor to adopt a position of neutrality in a classroom, especially on significant issues facing his or her field or on major social issues, is like asking a doctor to be a Christian Scientist or a Christian Scientist to be a doctor. The advocates of neutrality ignore or misunderstand the complex reasons why individuals teach, the nature of teaching, and the resulting character of the faculty. They want teachers to be impartial like judges, when teachers are actually more like artists. They want teachers to be managers when they should be more like inventors.

The neutralists are compelled to move in this direction because they assume that a faculty with a one-sided political bent consciously works to limit the critical thinking of the students. In the United States today, the neutralists are convinced that there are hundreds, if not thousands, of college faculties full of liberal biases attempting to undermine the purpose of education by indoctrinating instead of stimulating critical thinking. They assume the worst because they do not understand the nature of teaching and because they assume teachers would act as they themselves would.

While debate continues in the United States about the myriad ways in which faculties express liberal bias, I am prepared to accept that such a bias exists somewhere. And I do suspect these accusations from neutralists are accurate for a large number of what might be called the elite institutions, if not all of tertiary education, and especially in certain disciplines within each institution. The faculties of U.S. universities have shown biases in one way or another throughout history. Whatever issue raised passions in a specific historical period, it is not likely the faculties at many prominent institutions were balanced with respect to their attitudes and opinions on it—whether it was evolution in the 1870s, Jim Crow legislation in the 1890s, isolationism in the 1930s, or gender issues in the 1960s. A state of imbalance is more normal than one of balance, whatever the issue. Who knows what the relevant bias or topic will be twenty-five years after a faculty member is hired.

Ultimately, my response to those who feel so much concern about this imbalance is a simple question: Why is it so alarming?

The neutralists seem to assume that because advocacy and passion are there, it will shape everything that happens in the classroom and that the faculty lives to indoctrinate. Neutralists think the classroom is a two-dimensional black-and-white world where advocacy and the encouragement of independent thinking are mutually exclusive.

Most professors are more concerned with getting their students to engage in healthy debate. Mostly, professors are happiest when the students take part in discussions. Whether the students express a liberal or conservative viewpoint is far less important to a faculty member than the number of students who raise their hands or speak out when a question is posed. Without the engagement of the students, it is hard to teach, let alone indoctrinate. Advocacy can be an effective way of getting students to "push back," and pushing back is an effective way of generating engagement. Because the neutralists assume that advocacy and closed-mindedness are inextricably linked, they cannot imagine how one can advocate and still stimulate independent thinking. They take the egregious examples of faculty who cannot advocate without being closed-minded and define them as the norm. Those examples always will exist, but they are not the in the majority. And they certainly are not as dangerous as the proponents of neutrality assume.

The neutralists, having concluded that professors are driven to have their biases shape their teaching methods, must transform them into what they are not—simply conveyors of other people's positions. The neutralists fail to see the diversity of motivations for why individuals teach. Those motivations make it impossible for many faculty members to be neutral. At the same time, the diversity of motives that inspires people to teach also leads them to become engaged with students and open to disagreement.

Great teachers, like great artists, combine a passion for substance with a passion to widen the perception and understanding of another individual. Some will have a passion for creating new knowledge, and some will enjoy transmitting it. Effective teachers have entered the profession because they believe you can change people's lives for the better through education. In a recent conversation, several of my own family members, who are educators, put it simply: "Teachers are the ultimate optimists."

The neutralists' perceptions of the teaching field is to strip the profession of not only its energy but also its capacity to support different missions. Education is about more than teaching critical thinking. It is about teaching students how to use critical thinking to advance constructive and worthy ends through appropriate and effective means. For many drawn to the profession of teaching, critical thinking is an important tool. But an education devoted to critical thinking must also be applied correctly. Confusion about what motivates individuals to teach and about the nature of teaching itself makes this conversation about education urgent.

The decision by the Singapore government to create Singapore Management University as an independent, American-style liberal arts university provides a remarkable case study about the importance of taking into account the motivations for why individuals teach. The fact that the No Child Left Behind strategy in the United States has failed to pay sufficient attention to motivational issues has hampered, if not, crippled, its impact. Most teachers do not teach simply to have their pupils do well on tests. They want the students to do well as a consequence of adopting a broad range of attitudes and values, dealing with respect, integrity, creativity, and leadership—qualities not easily tested but that have much to do with succeeding in college or in life. The efforts to write standards in many states have tried to capture that complexity. The writing of tests has been less successful in doing so. Because policymakers at the federal level do not seem to value those developmental dimensions, teachers feel discouraged before they even begin.

Educators, whether teaching at the Singapore Management University, a small residential liberal arts college like Hampshire, or in K-12 education, face an immense challenge to respond in a constructively critical way to each and every student with whom they work. The challenge comes from a combination of the vast numbers of students taught and the tremendous varieties of personalities, interest levels, skills, cultural and economic backgrounds, and attitudes that can be represented by any group of students. The more inclusive and less selective the institution is, the greater the challenge. No profession outside of those directly serving the public confronts such variety in the raw material it deals with in combination with its mission's diverse goals.

Setting standards and creating accountability in education has proven to be difficult because of the diversity of students to be taught, not because its practitioners are more resistant to creating standards than those in other professions. Legislators, school boards, and the public in general often forget this crucial point and end up blaming the practitioners for the inevitable failures. Conversely, the practitioners rarely get the credit they deserve. In the United States this myopia is most pronounced at the K-12 level, where teachers are often treated like weapons of mass destruction and blamed for everything critics think is wrong with U.S. society. *A Nation at Risk*, a seminal but flawed study of U.S. education in the 1970s, set the tone for blaming teachers. Universities focusing on improving K-12 education often assume the teachers are the problem, and that premise was central in the No Child Left Behind legislation. Teacher improvement should always be a goal, for teachers matter, but they are note the core problem.

It is important to understand that the issue in the United States is not that the quality of education has declined. The test scores of American students on international exams have not declined in most cases. What has happened is that other nations, having seen the importance of education and invested increased resources, are now doing better than the United States. The relative position of the United States has declined. That decline matters, but blaming the teachers is not the solution. Indeed, the negative public attitude toward teachers makes it almost impossible to recruit the best and the brightest into the field.

The broad public attitudes toward K-12 education in the United States are now being extended to the tertiary level as are the specific strategies that stem from those attitudes. The 2006 Spelling's Commission Report on higher education authored by a commission George W. Bush created with the advice of Margaret Spelling, the U.S. Secretary of Education, extends to tertiary education the same assumptions about the efficacy of national testing and the failures of educators upon which the K-12 No Child Left Behind legislation and policies are based—assumptions that have support across both major political parties in the United States. That report stands in stark contrast to the view of tertiary education that motivated the creation of Singapore Management University. Although educators and national leaders in the rest of the world emulate a model that has worked so well in the United States and are accepting of all the complexities and challenges that it presents, some in the United States want to abandon that model. An emphasis on tests and on neutrality is an appealing form of standardization; but it does violence to creativity, innovation, and invention. It is ironic that the current Bush administration, with its emphasis on freedom and democracy, prefers a model that even Lee Kwan Yu's authoritarian government in Singapore found to be inadequate for facing future challenges in the global economy.

Tertiary education will not be able to reverse that trend unless it begins to speak out forcefully and work explicitly and strategically to educate the public about what must take place in the classroom, often under difficult conditions. Liberal education leaders must persuade the public that its fundamental task is actually to develop the capacity of individuals to challenge authority in appropriate and constructive ways. It will be a long time before that message is understood. It will be even longer before the public understands just how difficult that task is. At the same time, tertiary educators should not dismiss the public's concerns about the quality of teaching and teachers at all levels. The goal should be to make the public understand that their voices have been heard, even as educators try openly and forthrightly to explain the difficulties teachers face, how much they actually have accomplished in the face of formidable challenges, and the need to support them given the complexity of the sometimes conflicting demands society makes on them. The problem is more pronounced at the K-12 level in the United States, but tertiary education leaders in the United States should be alarmed at the extent to which the same brush that paints K-12 education in such broad and simplistic strokes is beginning to do the same to tertiary education.

Singapore Management University has confronted many of the same issues the United States and its schools must face. Both may have opened a Pandora's box, with the outcome being far from clear. Nonetheless, teachers emphasizing critical thinking know that the greatest challenge still remains to get students actively engaged in learning. The neutralists have identified the wrong problem. The key problem education must address is how to get students engaged with ideas and issues, not how to protect them from the assumed depravations inflicted by biased faculty. When students are engaged, as the next chapter explores, they have a capacity to know the difference between quality teaching and blatant indoctrination.

CHAPTER 8

The American University in Bulgaria: Speaking to Authority

The proponents of neutrality assume the worst in individuals, whether they be faculty or students. And they limit the pluralism they advocate to politics. I, too, condemn closed-minded faculty and affirm the values of pluralism. My quarrel with the neutralists is rooted in how we view the world around us and not so much in the educational values we espouse. My experience with the American University in Bulgaria, where I am a trustee, underscores the differences.

Ninety percent of education is expectation. If a society expects its students to be vulnerable and passive in the face of authority, that is what their youth will be. If teachers believe all students can learn and set high expectations for them, the students will rise to the occasion. Students can learn how to stand up to authority, question, and challenge in appropriate and constructive ways. And the more opportunity they have to do so, the stronger their powers of critical analysis will be, and they will be more effective advocates for the positions they believe in. The best students are capable of confronting opinionated, obstinate faculty who occasionally act inappropriately. If given the chance, most students can rise to the occasion when necessary, especially if they are coached on how to do so appropriately and are supported in these efforts.

While the proponents of neutrality and I differ in the confidence we have in students, we do agree on the value of diverse opinions and perspectives. Generating diverse perspectives is clearly ideal. That principle is as well established as any in education and represents the most important part of the neutralist argument. The neutralists, however, focus only on political orientation, when there are many other issues related to diversity that should be included in their concern. The difference in perspectives between liberal or conservative, Republican or Democrat within the United States seems far less significant when compared with differences among the political positions of the United States, China, or Russia.

The neutralists are right to be concerned about American students' lack of exposure to diverse perspectives, but they have identified the wrong area of concern with respect to that diversity. In the United States, students are in far greater need of exposure to diverse perspectives rooted in cultural, ethnic, and racial differences than to domestic political differences. American students are far behind their peers in many countries with respect to their knowledge of many cultures, their familiarity with more than one language, and their direct experience interacting with a culture other than their own.

In March 2006, I had the privilege of spending a day interviewing eleven students at the American University of Bulgaria (AUBG). Founded in 1991 through support from the Open Society Institute and US AID, and with the active involvement of the University of Maine at Orono, the American University in Bulgaria adopted a liberal arts educational framework to serve two key goals: to be a foundation for cultivating a democratic culture in a formerly authoritarian state and to promote reconciliation and understanding between the different cultures and nationalities in the historically conflicted region of southern Europe.

The students I interviewed came one each from Kazakhstan, Serbia, Kosovo, Moldova, and the United States, and six from Bulgaria. My discussions with them focused on the themes of this book and affirmed one of the main lessons I had learned at Hampshire: listen to the students. The AUBG students fully understood the complexity of what it meant for a university to model the behavior expected of their students. What is most striking is that they could not imagine that it could be otherwise. Although very polite, some wondered why the "subject" was worthy of a book at all. To them, a university living up to its mission was what universities did, for better or worse. These students had already experienced the worst aspects of authoritarian society; now they were experiencing something better, at least from an educational perspective. They assumed that all universities sought to instill a set of values in their students and that those institutions would explicitly take positions and actions to advance those values.

The students made the point that even in its authoritarian past the universities in Bulgaria and the other formerly Communist countries were very good at modeling the behavior they expected of their students. The universities produced competent professionals who had the appropriate knowledge and skills to serve the perceived needs of the economy and compliant citizens who accepted societal norms. Universities valued the acquisition of knowledge over critical thinking and competence over creativity. Students conformed to defined norms and the leaders of universities did the same.

That judgment may or may not be completely fair, but the students' reading of the situation was part of their motivation to seek out an American-style education. The other part of their motivation, they freely admitted, was the advantage an American-styled education would give them in the job market. They also noted the two points were related. The quality of the education was, in part, what created the career value. Their experience had taught them that every institution modeled the behavior that it expected of its students. They had seen this in their home countries, and they found the same pattern of behavior at the American University of Bulgaria. What excited them about AUBG was how different the expectations were for the students.

The students expected AUBG to model a more permissive and liberal attitude consistent with its mission and goals, and they were excited that their expectations had not been disappointed.

They acknowledged that there were times when they felt the "administration" had not acted democratically enough and that they had not been sufficiently consulted on certain issues; but they felt that, as with any democratic community, there was a commitment to the democratic process, even if imperfectly implemented. Most of all, they felt the university was willing to listen to them and engage them in discussion.

They cared deeply about this topic, the meaning of education. And none left after their thirty-minute sessions ended. For them, this subject was not abstract; it had immediate, direct, and practical consequences for them. When I described to them the concern in the United States about liberal faculties, the fear that professors indoctrinated students, and the desire by some to make the universities neutral, they had a lot of difficulty understanding the problem. The resulting conversation covered many aspects of liberal education and was as thoughtful, well informed, and surprisingly as easygoing as any that I have had with faculty or administrators. As students joined the group, they had very little difficulty picking up the thread and quickly joining the conversation. They did not possess great knowledge of the theories about liberal arts education and certainly could not have recited all of its intellectual antecedents in Western thought. But they understood in poignant and personal ways what critical thinking meant; and they understood the costs, literally and figuratively, of its absence.

In many respects, I ended up having to play devil's advocate to force more depth into the conversation by describing some of the dangers inherent in the position I was advocating. Faculty could end up being so passionate about an idea that they closed off debate and their institutions could lose needed support, or these narrow ideas could become orthodoxies. Many of their responses took me aback. Indoctrination was a concept that was as real to them as that of critical thinking. They completely understood how fundamentally different these concepts were and yet how closely they were related. As one student put it, "We know the difference even when the person trying to indoctrinate us does not."

The students acknowledged that few had direct memories of the Communist governments that had largely been dismantled by the time they were in high school, if not before. Collectively, however, they noted that because of their parents' memories and family conversations, the students felt they had lived in those times. And in many respects they felt their schools still reflected those days under Communism. Indeed, they wondered if the non-critical passivity of their schools was all that different before, during, or after the Communist era. They explained that explicit indoctrination took place during Communist rule. A set of values was imposed on students and an effort was made to insure compliance; however, no effort was made to "persuade" students of the soundness of those values—their integrity was a given.

The students accepted that AUBG was "indoctrinating" them about the rights and responsibilities of citizens living in a society based on democratic principles as well as about the advantages of such a civic culture. The difference was that no one took these values for granted. The concepts had to be examined and analyzed and then accepted or rejected. Neither the students nor their parents found it unusual or troubling that AUBG was trying to persuade them of the merits of democratic values. The issue for them was the content of the intellectual exchange, and what excited them immensely was the institutional assumption that it was worth spending the time to "persuade or educate students about critical thinking and democracy." Education had to persuade, not decree. As one student put it, "I expect teachers to be trying to persuade me of something. What I like here [at AUBG] is that most of them like it when I question them about their views or even argue against them."

They explained that in a community as culturally and internationally diverse as AUBG, all members understand that everyone, including the faculty, would have a personal history that influenced perspectives on almost any issue. The sources of bias could be cultural, nationalistic, religious, ethnic, political, or all of the above. One student raised an interesting question about why the political bias of the faculty dominated other biases. Were faculty members in the United States always politically engaged? Up to that point I had spent more time thinking about levels of faculty bias. Her questions made me realize that I had heard little mention of bias as it pertained, for example, to religion, a topic of concern to many in the Balkans.

As a group, the AUBG students did not believe that being completely impartial, let alone neutral, was possible. For them, impartiality and neutrality were not synonymous terms. For some, the former term implied that an individual had strong opinions but refrained from articulating them forcefully. The latter implied that the individual did not have a position or was indifferent to the answer. These young adults respected impartiality even if they were skeptical about how successful someone could be in achieving it. Some viewed neutrality as a form of amorality; but even that interpretation generated discussion about whether being neutral in a dispute meant precluding judgment and some form of favoritism. The accuracy of the definitions was less important to me than the interest of the students in the nuances of these words and in what it meant to withhold one's opinion. All of these conversations, including the nuanced discussion of vocabulary, were conducted in English without interpreters and underscored the enormous gap in bilingual language competence between these students and many talented American college students.

The AUBG students explained that they did not worry too much about bias, impartiality, or even the occasional effort to indoctrinate them. They expected such efforts to occur every so often. With a certain amount of unintended cockiness, they felt they knew how to compensate for that bias and how to work around it. I asked if I would be describing the process accurately if I said that dealing with bias and the opinions of the faculty was part of learning how to express their opinions and how to cope with authority figures. They all agreed.

I also asked the students if perhaps they were too confident in their ability to speak firmly to authority figures. They responded that at other universities they would not have the same confidence in being outspoken. They appreciated the freedom AUBG provided them. This group's strong confidence in speaking out contrasted somewhat with my earlier conversations with students at AUBG about the durability of their new freedoms. The level of confidence was usually reflective of conditions at the time within their respective countries, with some being confident the freedoms they now enjoyed would last, while others saw these liberties as fragile and in need of nurturing. Still, all the students to whom I spoke valued the mandate to challenge the opinions and analyses of their professors.

During the March conversations, I asked the students if they felt they received a fair evaluation in such a system. All felt they had, although they all thought that problems did arise every so often, more because of cultural misunderstandings than because a faculty member wanted to "punish" them for their opinions. For example, they noted that faculty members often favored the more outspoken students over the introverted students, but this advantage was marginal since writing was so crucial. They expressed little concern about the fairness of grades, and when I probed that subject, most students said grades were less important than in their home-country institutions. They felt that simply graduating from an American-style university would give them a tremendous career advantage.

As they tried to understand why the issue of neutrality in the classroom was so important in the United States, they suggested that a possible difference for them was the highly valued opportunity to pursue an education in a context where so many different positions were held, simply by virtue of the diversity of nationalities and cultures represented in the university. In that respect, AUBG has more of the character of large urban universities in the United States, like the City University of New York or Miami-Dade Community College in Florida. The cultural and age diversity of the student bodies of those institutions add a richness that small liberal arts colleges can rarely match.

At AUBG, there was no dominant culture unless it was a "student" culture. There was only one dominant intellectual position and that was the value of liberal education for creating open, democratic societies. Both within and outside the classroom, AUBG students take pride in questioning and learning how to keep an open mind, even while rejecting certain values and ideas to which they were exposed. Their greatest concern was that international and cultural diversity might decrease as the university grew, with the percentage of international students not keeping pace with the overall growth of the university.

The students clearly valued the opportunity to debate. They argued that silence came from an imposed orthodoxy, not from strongly held opinions of classmates, the faculty, or the institution itself. At the same time, they appreciated the "irony" that AUBG promoted the orthodoxy of liberal education but advocated that orthodoxies be challenged and tested through a process of critical thinking. I asked them directly if they felt the AUBG education was preparing them to challenge convention and authority. They liked the "challenge convention" bit and responded, "Yes, everything is open to challenge." They were learning how to do it. They fully understood the danger of being silenced. Reflecting the self-confidence that is perhaps natural for young people, they felt they would never be silenced again.

The students and alumni of the American University in Bulgaria valued the "tendentiousness" of their institution and their education. Their greatest challenge was not what is most feared by American neutralists: the silencing by overbearing and biased faculty. Instead, the challenge for them was learning to live in harmony with students who came from so many different countries with such conflicting historical and cultural backgrounds. These students are committed and optimistic, but they understood the complexity of the education they were receiving. An alumnus speaking at the fifteenth anniversary celebration in 2006 captured that spirit, born out of the exceptional history that gave birth to the institution:

> Participating in the founding of a university from scratch is [a] once-in-several-lifetimes experience. Imagine applying to a university that only exists on a thirty-page five-year action plan, which, by the way [was] mailed to every applicant in 1990 in lieu of a regular prospectus, come on! You either have to be a great risk taker, true believer, or a totally desperate person, or possibly all of the above. And when the establishment of AUBG takes place as a result of the collapse of Soviet-style Communism, all the hopes vested in this university are vented in its mission to "educate the future leaders of the region"— the stakes are as high as they can get.
>
> As a generation disillusioned by the pervasive fallacies of Communist society we had come to AUBG in search for the TRUTH. Honestly, we sincerely wanted to learn the right answers to all questions about society. However to our gradual astonishment and

dismay we were one too many times taught that we have to learn to first ask the right philosophical and political questions and that there was more than one right answer. Learning to reason tolerantly within the plurality of possible views, answers, opinions, and nuances was one of the significant metaphysical shocks we had to experience coming out of the black-and-white Marxist universe.[1]

The advocates of neutralism fear the liberal bias of faculty and the pressure of political correctness on campuses are creating a similarly one-sided black-and-white view of the country.

○ ○ ○

I arrived at Hampshire in 1984 recognizing that the charges of political correctness that were being leveled against tertiary education in the United States was an issue that should be taken seriously, especially since Hampshire was perceived to be one of the most "politically correct" of all American institutions. Indeed it was highly "politically correct" in the sense of having a broad consensus about human rights, values, and social justice issues.

Notwithstanding the substance of that consensus, the college still lacked the diversity of political perspectives that Balch, Horowitz, the American Council on Education, and I all value as part of the principle that diversity of perspectives enhances liberal education. My colleagues and I had to constantly acknowledge and adjust for that specific lack of diversity—a condition that emerged almost from the day the college opened. The college was founded at the end of the 1960s to create educational reform by giving its students great responsibility for shaping their education. Not surprisingly, it ended up attracting students who were more concerned with asserting their independence and challenging authority than with educational reform. They created their own political and intellectual culture; again not surprisingly, it was liberal and activist.

Hampshire's founders got the intellectual engagement and the results they wanted. In exchange, the college had to learn how to live with the unintended consequences of a less diverse political environment. Having worked in environments where there was greater political diversity and less intellectual engagement. I found it easier to offset a lack of diverse perspectives than it is to generate intellectual curiosity. Without intellectual engagement, the presence of a diversity of perspectives will not lead to a significantly better education.

The process of creating more political diversity began in 1989, the day after it was announced in the paper that I had been selected to be the next president of Hampshire College. Within hours after that announcement, Dean Esserman, the student I had taught and worked with at Dartmouth College, called. In 1989 he was general counsel for the New York City Transit Police. He wanted to know whether Hampshire would be willing to host a series of conferences on the U.S. urban crisis in partnership with the International Association of Chiefs of Police (IACP). He explained that Lee Brown, then commissioner of police in New York City, was about to become the president of the IACP and wanted to use that platform to focus on community policing and the crisis that was emerging in U.S. cities.

The IACP was interested in the partnership with Hampshire for two reasons: to send a signal to the country that the problems of the cities were approaching crisis proportions and because a partnership with Hampshire would attract attention. Since Hampshire was known to be so liberal and thought to be so politically correct, it was the last college in the country anyone would expect to be working with the police. I immediately agreed because I knew the partnership would allow Hampshire to send a signal that it was dedicated to exploring all `qsides of social justice issues and would work for positive social change with anyone who shared a similar commitment. We wanted to show that the college was dedicated to both advocacy and to diversity.

Hosting the first conference did generate politically correct knee-jerk hostility. The day before the conference, an anonymous group or person put up posters on campus protesting the police presence. The posters urged that the conference be shut down and called for a protest rally at the conference opening. In response and on their own, the students who were planning the conference put out a series of announcements reminding the community that concern for social justice required working with those on the front lines. I could not have been more proud of those students and the effectiveness of their message. When it came time for the protest, the only person who showed up was a reporter to cover it. We never knew who put up the posters in the first place, but we had reason to believe it was some alumni living in the area who had heard only part of the story. Their actions, whoever they were, suggested that their capacity for critical—as opposed to rote—thinking was not as developed as we would have wished. On the other hand, they did absorb the message the students sent them.

Other situations offered a little more comic relief with respect to creating an open environment on campus. During one break-fast meeting, representatives of the Young Republicans Club came to complain that their posters announcing a conservative speaker were being taken down. This was an act that we always spoke out against with notices and memos to the community but could not always prevent. Understand that the existence of a Young Republicans Club at Hampshire is akin to an igloo village on a Hawaiian beach. The club members seemed discouraged, not only about the posters, but also about being such a small group among so many liberals. Out of a 1,200-person student body, there were only about a dozen official members of this conservative club.

Before addressing the poster issue, I asked how they were feeling in general. They looked discouraged and expressed frustration. I suggested they should not be. "After all," I explained, "they were the true Hampshire students." They looked quizzically at me, wondering what I meant. "Hampshire is a very contrarian place," I explained. "Hampshire students are always questioning the accepted wisdom, so what could be more contrarian than to be a Republican in such a liberal stronghold." They laughed and seemed immediately encouraged by my comments and even more by the support they received from the "liberals" at the table, students who happened to be there to discuss other issues.

We then went on to talk about the posters. I said that the dean of the college would send out a college-wide announcement condemning the removal of the poster, but I also suggested that the group might want to develop their own strategy. They should keep in mind that at least they were getting someone's attention. As president, I had to be concerned with the inappropriate destruction of the posters. On the other hand, they had an opportunity to make these unfortunate and inappropriate acts work to their advantage. I felt they left encouraged.

A week later, a reinvigorated and excited group of Young Republicans returned to my Monday breakfast. With smiles and obvious pride they laid out on the table the new posters they had been putting up around campus. One read: COME HEAR STAR PARKER WHO SOME STUDENTS ARE AFRAID TO HEAR—a poster that explained why some people were taking down their posters. A second poster headlined as follows: WHY ARE SOME CALLING STAR PARKER AN UNCLE TOM? This was a poster they first cleared with the speaker, who loved it. I loved the posters. They were creating a teachable moment for the entire campus. I asked how they were being received. The students smiled and said the new posters must be working because someone had actually begun putting up the old ones. As I laughed, they said they had one really serious question. I waited with some nervousness, worried that something had gone wrong with the approach they had developed. With a wry sense of humor, they asked, "Why? Do you think they saved the old posters?" I laughed, responding that I had no idea, except that maybe they recognized that someday the Hampshire Young Republicans would be famous and their posters would be really valuable. Indeed they might, so I asked if I could keep the copies they had brought me. They left breakfast confident in themselves and in their actions—as well they should have. They had provided a wonderful example of how students who felt silenced could turn the tables and take advantage of a disrespectful and unacceptable effort to silence them.

O O O

Although no one theme dominated the Monday breakfasts, two persisted over the years. The theme most often repeated was about student concerns that the administration, the trustees, the president, or some unknown force was trying to remake Hampshire into a more traditional and conservative institution. The focus was often on me. Having spent nineteen years as an administrator at a traditional Ivy League institution, I was suspect. The students were always wondering if I was trying to change Hampshire into a Dartmouth College. They were never reluctant to challenge me or the trustees on this topic. The students viewed it as their responsibility to challenge any authority when it came to protecting what they felt was the distinctiveness of the college. It was tiring sometimes but almost always educational and affirming.

A second breakfast theme focused on the silencing issue that the Young Republicans had raised. Although not the usual breakfast topic, students did come with some regularity to talk about how they felt silenced in the classroom or within the institution as a whole. I was always interested in how students who had no problem challenging the institution and its authority figures could feel so much more cowed in the classroom where the faculty did not even give traditional letter grades. The answer, in the case of Hampshire, seemed clear. Student culture and student peer pressure were as much a force for silencing students as authority figures.

At one time or another certain alienated students talked to me about what it was like in the Hampshire culture to be in a minority with respect to "politically correct" issues such as abortion rights. They would tell me how they felt silenced because there was too little diversity of opinion, or a particular professor's teaching style was too dogmatic and insensitive. Many of these students were deeply religious, or staunchly conservative. Sometimes they were antiabortion or supportive of aggressive foreign policy positions abroad; or maybe they just had general political differences with the immediate community and/or the student body. They usually wanted to know what I was going to do about the silence that they felt had been imposed on them.

I would often begin, as I did above, by explaining that I was proud of the social justice focus of the college, but I was even more excited by its ability to attract students willing to be independent— a quality they exhibited simply by enrolling at Hampshire. I never dismissed their concerns and never told students they should just "suck it up" and keep going. Nevertheless, when they asked what I would do about the silencing that some experienced, I always responded as I did to the Young Republicans Club. I condemned any effort to silence them or their opinions, and then asked how they might turn those efforts to silence them into opportunities to amplify their voice. They did not always like my theory that their discomfort was really an opportunity, but I was always impressed with how many students responded with imaginative strategies. I was also impressed with how those who were doing the silencing responded when challenged.

Silencing always will be an issue because every institution has its own culture and orthodoxies. Some students, professors, and staff members will feel uncomfortable challenging implicit and explicit behaviors and opinions. Silencing and self-censorship will always exist at some level when difficult ideas are being discussed and intellectual inquiry is encouraged and actively pursued, regardless of whether or not positions are being taken. When professors, students, or institutions take certain positions, the ultimate challenge is to vigorously promote safe space so that dissenting minority opinions can be expressed. What all those conversations with students at Hampshire and abroad about silencing taught me is how aware students are that some form of "orthodoxy" always exists. Such awareness will not eliminate the negative effects of dominant orthodoxy, but it can limit them. Those in the minority on certain controversial views were discomforted and conscious of the challenges they faced. Their awareness of these challenges enhanced their education and stimulated their intellectual engagement.

I was never worried when students came to me asking how they could develop and articulate their own opinions if a professor was aggressively pushing a specific agenda—or, even worse, was ridiculing ideas that were opposed to his or her own. I knew their self-awareness of the context in which they were working and their interest in confronting the challenge signaled significant engagement. If their engagement could be supported, then learning (as opposed to frustration) could take place. Therefore, I usually responded with questions. How could they learn to assess and deal with the bias or ridicule from people they would encounter throughout their lives without direct experience in reacting to verbal challenges? How could they learn to filter out biases in order to develop their own views if they did not hear firsthand the passionate presentation of specific opposing opinions? How could they develop their capacity for critical evaluation if they were not placed in real situations where they had to exercise that ability? And how could they learn to transform ridicule, sarcasm, and negative energy directed at them into a harmless or even positive force if they did not have practical experience in doing so.

I explained that I had several interconnected goals. First, I wanted to help create an atmosphere on campus where such negative encounters were few and far between; but recognizing that nasty confrontations will arise on occasion, I was committed to helping students deal with them constructively for themselves and then for the community. Remarkably, I found that students were consistently willing to try and transform a negative situation into a positive one that would benefit them and the community at large.

The relationship between student and professor lies at the heart of all questions about learning and teaching. Formal tertiary education began as a form of apprenticeship, usually to a priest. In its least exploitative form, it provided genuine mentoring for the apprentice. As that relationship evolved into the current formal structures that separate teachers and students, progressive educational traditions countered with efforts to narrow the gap. Educators recognized the importance of that relationship for nurturing both the intellectual and personal development of the student. When universities talk of small classes, they are assuming that they make possible a closer student-faculty relationship.

When students complained about specific cases of being silenced, I took them with all seriousness. I would state explicitly to the student that while I suspected there was more than one perspective on the situation, I would base my response on what they had described. Silencing, if it occurred as described, undermined in a fundamental way what the teacher-student relationship should be about and what was needed to develop the student's critical thinking. I would then use the situation to coach the student on how they might have responded in order to transform the situation from a negative to a positive one.

I would begin that part of the conversation by asking how they had responded or reacted, exactly what he or she had done, and what had transpired after those actions. More often than not, the student would admit he or she had not responded, but had simply withdrawn without a confrontation. At that point, I would ask the student about any alternative strategies they could have followed. If the student could not think of any, I would propose some. What usually followed was an extended conversation about strategies for dealing with a professor who held to a specific opinion with arrogance, closed-mindedness, or whatever other negative mind-set one could imagine. I would urge students not to think of their own specific situation but to focus instead on abstract situations and how they might best respond. They should put themselves in the place of the professor. They would respond, sometimes slowly, to this effort to imagine alternative approaches. They would begin to imagine strategies for holding their ground without necessarily creating confrontation. More often than not, they also began to see how their original perception of the professor's behavior might not fully capture what was taking place. Once they got into the spirit of the exercise, I was often impressed with their imagination and their willingness to consider a specific argument or situation from different perspectives.

As different as each situation was, students usually ended up in the same place: they needed to get their professors to explore positions that countered the ones being advocated. To accomplish this, they would ask the professors to suggest the most persuasive counterarguments to their positions. Or the students would ask who the leading opponents of the professor's positions were and how would the professor respond to these views. In the end, students came to recognize that there were limits to what they could do unless they were willing to develop their own arguments and take some risks.

Students came to understand that ultimately they had to become comfortable with being uncomfortable. Some, but by no means all, students came to accept that they should engage rather than withdraw from difficult situations. They knew they needed to learn how to organize their own thoughts and gain more control over certain confrontational situations. They realized that they should welcome and use these uncomfortable situations as a way to strengthen their own ability to present a position. Of course, some students never accepted that approach. In those cases, I had to accept that Hampshire had failed on two counts. These students would leave Hampshire without developing a capacity to respond critically (but constructively) to disagreement or hostility. And we had failed as teachers to create a context where these individuals could develop this critical capacity.

The key to ameliorating those failures lies in creating a more inviting forum where students can confront opposing ideas, whether from peers or faculty, without withdrawing and without feeling overwhelmed and diminished. As educators, it is important that we help students to develop the capacity to challenge any encounter they feel is inappropriate—without being defeated by it. At the same time, we need to help faculty become more skillful in creating an environment in which they put forward their own opinions and arguments and, at the same time, invite students to challenge their positions. Most professors can and do create such an environment, but almost all professors will fail from to time with specific students. It is a never-ending challenge made more difficult by the range of individual maturity that exists in any class.

Although students often brought questions to my breakfasts about confronting strongly held positions, parents of current and prospective students were even more concerned about the community's openness to diverse opinions and about Hampshire's reputation for political correctness. They invariably asked questions about the subject at parents' and admission weekends. I never denied there was a problem. In fact, I urged that if they had a son or daughter who was more conservative than most of Hampshire's students, they would be doing me a great favor by encouraging their child to enroll at Hampshire.

I supported their concern and told them about some of the situations I faced while trying to encourage that diversity. I would use real-life examples, taken from students' actual experiences, to point out that Hampshire had many faculty and administrators who would help create space for students to voice unpopular opinions. But I also told them that as they acquired the courage to express their views, students had to be willing to take advice from peers and faculty members. Prospective students had to realize that being outspoken would not always be comfortable; but support would be available. I asserted that Hampshire did have a strong mission-based culture and that challenging it would not be easy. But I said that learning how to thrive in this sort of environment would be a valuable experience for the student, and they would end up with a first-class education in both what they had learned and how the had learned it. I would use different examples of how students who were willing to take risks often succeeded at Hampshire. Parents left reassured that we were a community that took inquiry seriously and that we valued diversity of opinion, even if perfectly proportioned ethnic and political diversity ultimately eluded us.

O O O

The impact of internationally diverse student bodies, as seen through the comments of AUBG students and the experiences of many college and university students outside the United States, can have a dramatic effect in training students to overcome both parochialism and passivity and become fully engaged in their education. The international diversity of AUBG helps the students put many different issues into broader perspective. Their international diversity has helped them create space for debate and for the exploration of what different conceptions of the "Other" mean. Many of the American-styled universities abroad that have this eclectic representation of nationalities offer important insights for U.S-based institutions: for example, they can learn to be more focused in teaching young people how to live together harmoniously. The presence of international students on American campuses has the same effect. Just the two-week visit of South African students to Hampshire, described in Chapter 4, affected how Hampshire students viewed U.S. race relations—a significant consequence of that visit. And, as noted above, that diversity enriches the education large urban universities and community colleges offer in the United States.

The enrichment does not come without thoughtful, intentional, and persistent effort. Bridging the divide produced by widely differing histories, cultures, and habits is a never-ending struggle. Each new incoming freshman class transforms the student body, and to some extent the institution, and brings with it both old and new tensions. Even with the heightened sense of difference that exists, the need to expand representation of and sensitivity toward minority groups at AUBG (one example is the Roma people in Bulgaria) remains a challenge. The students seemed to accept that need, along with the long-term effort that was needed to build more cross-cultural understanding in southern Europe.

The impact of international students at AUBG was aided immeasurably by their full support of the AUBG mission. A major part of the university's mission is to promote more constructive relationships among the nations in the Balkans region—a task that all accepted as urgent, given the region's long history of war, genocide, and repression of minority groups. The students took pride in that mission and saw their international diversity as essential to the school's mission. Their commitment to learning to live harmoniously with one another was structured and intentional. The students and the university understood that this commitment to accepting diversity did not happen simply by chance. This is a lesson most American institutions have not absorbed with regard to international students or our country's own minority groups.

AUBG's achievements have impressed me. I suspect that what the Asian University for Women will achieve in building a different, more positive sense of the "Other" will be equally impressive. We struggled at Hampshire to build multicultural, racial, and international diversity, and we never doubted that these were ultimately the most important areas to emphasize in striving for the ideal scholastic environment. This cultural diversity will lead to the fully formed intellectual diversity for which an engaged institution strives.

In attempting to obtain the desired diversity, we often made a point that our ultimate goal should be to become an international institution, like AUBG, rather than a U.S. institution offering international programs. The difference is profoundly important. When I left Hampshire we had established a number of high-quality and often unique international exchange programs in countries such as Cuba, Germany, the Tibetan exile community in India, and China. We also understood that these international programs did not constitute an international presence that would transform the culture of the institution. This transformation might never happen, but it was and still is our goal.

The experiences of both the American University in Bulgaria and Hampshire provide strong support for the emphasis that neutralists and all educators place on the importance of exposing students to diverse perspectives in tertiary education. The neutralists define diversity in terms of political perspectives and de-emphasize (and at times even attack) the effort to support cultural, ethnic, and international diversity. Multiculturalism is dismissed as the agenda of a particular political group (liberals, usually) rather than as a means for diversifying perspectives. They lament the "negativism" engendered in academic institutions whose lecturers highlight the failures in U.S. history, arguing that there should be a more balanced presentation. They do not accept that these "negative" perspectives might themselves be reality checks balancing the society's generalist, mainstream view of history. At its core, the neutralists seem to care less about neutrality and more about opposing the specific views of liberal democrats presiding in the classroom.

Tertiary education in the United States needs to develop more multicultural and international institutions where students learn in an environment that will allow them to see themselves and their history from the perspectives of others. Creating such an opportunity does not weaken or undermine the strengths of our own values. Rather, it creates a deeper understanding of our own values even as it prepares students to understand the different strengths, weaknesses, and challenges faced by every society. Critical thinking that is not informed with multicultural and multinational perspectives ultimately cannot meet the test of rigor explicit in the concept of critical thinking.

O O O

Leaving aside my concern about the narrowness of the diversity they seek, neutralists also underestimate the capacity of the students themselves. What I found at the American University of Bulgaria and at Hampshire was a wonderful reminder that young people are resilient, and they are not as prone to intimidation as the neutralists would have us believe. Students are very good at sizing up the motives, strengths, and weaknesses of their teachers. Every teacher lives with that knowledge, and it takes a special courage to subject yourself to regular interaction with students—especially in an engaged classroom setting.

The students who testified in the Pennsylvania hearings delivered the same message, including those students who felt that faculty could be biased and often act inappropriately. They did not seem intimidated, and they certainly had not been indoctrinated. Coming from very different institutions than AUBG or Hampshire, they delivered remarkably similar messages.

Rachel Carson, from the University of Pittsburgh, testified as follows:

> If professors must work under the constant threat of being reported for revealing one ideological bias or another, I fear that they will reveal nothing at all to their students. Future students won't have the opportunity to argue with their professors about the pros and cons of [the] social security overhaul, the overradicalization of the Sandinista Movement in Nicaragua in the 1980s, or the breadth of our rights to privacy guaranteed to us by the U.S. Constitution on our behalf. The best professors that I can have here at the University of Pittsburgh are also the ones with whom I've argued the most. I have never once been penalized for disagreeing with one of my professors.[2]

Carson went on to note that procedures were in place if a student felt discriminated against. She concluded:

> I think we have to ask ourselves if we are prepared to deal with the extent of the consequences that this resolution may have on Pennsylvania's academic climate. Would John Stuart Mill have written his treatise *On Liberty* if he thought that his students would turn him in as an ideologue? Would Mary Wollstonecraft have written *Thoughts on the Education of Daughters* or would professors nationwide show their students their power to participate in the political process by way of activism for civil rights in the 1960s? Not only is it not particularly possible, in my opinion,

to force our professors to shy away from everything unconventional, controversial, or simply subjective, but I find it downright undesirable as a student.... That's part of the learning experience and part of the academic experience to be exposed to any number of biases, ideologies, or even parts of philosophies so that we as students can make up our own minds about what we do and do not choose to agree with.[3]

Ms. Carson was in no danger of being indoctrinated.

Students from Millersville University were equally effective. Terry Christopher, a U.S. military veteran who began his education at Harrisburg Area Community College, stated explicitly that the faculty was open to disagreement and challenges from students. He described at length the disagreements he had with one professor who had made his political positions very clear. Christopher maintained that this individual was his best professor and that he never missed one of his classes. He then noted that in earlier testimony, someone had complained about a professor who had biased cartoons on his door, implying that the cartoons would discourage students from taking certain positions. Mr. Christopher explained that from the description and other comments made in previous testimony, he was sure he knew who that professor was. He concluded, "I'm going to his class as soon as I leave here; and he knows vehemently my political affiliation. I've shared it with him many times. He's shared his with me. And he's extremely liberal and I'm extremely conservative. However, like I said about [the Professor at Harrisburg Area Community College], that professor here is one of my favorite professors; and I feel free to express my opinion in his class. So far I'm getting an A."[4]

Donald R. Dodson, Jr., then a student at the Lancaster Branch of Harrisburg Area Community College who planned to transfer to Millersville in the fall, summarized most succinctly a repetitive note. He began his testimony with what always got the attention of the committee:

Did I always agree with what was being said? No. Did these discussions challenge my thinking? You bet. Did any of these discussions change my opinion on issues? Sure. Did I change my party affiliation because of these discussions? Certainly not.

In fact, the greatest degree of discomfort came not from my professors but from the students themselves. I have been in classes with self-proclaimed Nazis, Communists, and Libertarians. And religious fundamentalists. Some had pretty extreme views, as you can imagine.

In many cases the professor merely had to pose a question and the discussion would begin. The professor would serve more as a referee rather than some left-wing radical seeking to convert students to his political views as is too often portrayed in the media and politics.

At appropriate points he would clarify the actual facts of the issue and make comments keeping within the context of our discussion. In the end, we were free to draw our own conclusions on the issue.

After all, do we have so little faith in the ability of our youth to think critically? I have led young people in the battlefield in Iraq. And I have seen them in the classroom. They do question. They do challenge. So let them make that decision.

Don't underestimate their ability to draw their own conclusions. Trust them to determine from their own perspective what they wish to believe or not believe.

After all, finding a broader perspective and critically thinking about the issues is what college is all about. Placing any restrictions hinders that opportunity for free expression and discussion.[5]

The set of final hearings offered two more examples of why young people should be listened to and spoken with, instead of meeting with professors' insensitive condescension. Holly Otterbein, a student at Harrisburg Area Community College, urged the committee not to interfere:

> To limit what is being said in the classroom is to insult our intelligence as students. We are fully capable of addressing professors who we think are unfairly promoting their viewpoints and forcing the agreement of them. We do not need our lawmakers to determine whether Marx or Rand is better for us to digest, and we do not want our professors to teach under the fear of outside control. If this anxiety consumes our professors, we will lose exactly what the opposition is claiming to defend: a broad education where all viewpoints are presented.[6]

Anna Peak, a graduate student at Temple University, expressed a more strident position. She argued that those favoring this "bill" are less interested in having all views represented and more interested in having their own views represented. She noted that she worked as a teaching assistant for one of the proponents of the Academic Bill of Rights, and although he testified about the importance of having a multiplicity of views represented, in class his actions said otherwise. She said this professor

> actively encourages only comments that supported his views and actively discourage any comments that did not support his views.
>
> However, I find all such professors perfectly within their rights. They are, after all, allowed to profess. That is what the word means. It's where it comes from. It's the traditional mission going back to the Middle Ages, and it's their right as citizens in a country that protects freedom of speech.
>
> I personally find it much more useful to learn from those that feel free to passionately put forth their own views, whatever they may be, than from those who mouth preselected formulae, in accordance with certain boundaries or limits or what have you.
>
> Ultimately what is most important is not forcing every individual to say the same things or the same roster of things or to hit the right selections from a smorgasbord of views, but in making sure that the universities are places were groups of people gather, each individual one of whom is free to say what they believe.[7]

Students from AUBG, Hampshire, and the diverse campuses of the Pennsylvania state system all delivered a similar message: we can take care of ourselves. Worry less about us and more about more important questions. These students were self-selected representatives to be sure, but their experience contrasts with (and raises profound questions about why) others in democratic societies who have experienced tertiary education still can be turned into suicide bombers. Understanding what created such different outcomes is essential. It also is essential to understand why so few people at places such as Enron were unwilling to challenge the greed-fueled culture of their company and raise questions about what was happening. When liberal education fails, the costs can be very high.

Strengthening the capacity and willingness of students to challenge authority in appropriate and constructive ways remains an important goal with far-reaching consequences for any society. Comparative studies of the impact of liberal education on students in different settings and cultures would provide useful insight. American institutions, if nothing else, should be watching all of these international institutions very closely. There will be much to learn from them. First and foremost, we would learn why so many of them believe what the Bulgarian Minister of Education may have put best at the AUBG graduation in 2006: "Education is a better defense of freedom than standing armies."

Listening to students who have absorbed what a liberal arts education seeks to provide makes it possible to believe that education truly is a better defense of freedom than standing armies. Listening to students indoctrinated in hate has the opposite effect. But listening is always important, although it is often uncomfortable and even threatening. Listening is difficult even in the best of circumstances, and that probably explains why so many avoid it.

This book's last section focuses on listening and examines the engaged university from the perspective of a profoundly simple and often asked question: Is it doing enough? Expectation is ninety percent of education. What universities expect of students is important, but what students expect of universities is even more important. Young people who are learning to think critically, but usually without extensive, "practical" experience, often see problems in relatively black and white terms, with little nuance or complexity. They can be unforgiving in judging whether professors and the university are doing enough to promote an education true to the values they claim to be promoting. It is just as good that the students are unforgiving, for their expectations raise the bar for the university just as the university's expectations should raise the bar for the students.

PART III

The Engaged University

CHAPTER 9

What Is Enough?: Communities and Universities

All universities are engaged institutions. The essential question is not whether an institution is engaged, but whether it is engaged enough—a difficult and subjective question, but one that should not be ignored. At almost every Monday breakfast a student presented a problem that essentially involved what I came to call an "enough" problem. Whether framed as a question or, as was most often the case, an assertion, it involved a judgment about what was enough. You aren't doing enough? Hampshire is not committing enough resources? The administration isn't focused enough on the problem? At times, I felt myself wanting to retort with "Get real!" or perhaps something even sharper. I would control that urge by reminding myself of the value of students' impatience. They saw issues from a fresh perspective, not jaded by habit or inertia. Being free of responsibility, they could be simplistic—but often in a profound way.

Liberal education promotes self-reflection—the often-stated "examined life." An academic institution should do no less, and the "enough" question should be at the heart of that self-reflection. Is it engaged enough with its students to overcome the cultural inertia that inhibits their intellectual and personal maturation? Is it sufficiently engaged with the community to make a difference in overcoming at least some of what undermines the health of that community? Is it engaged enough to fulfill its mission? The students at Hampshire promoted that self-reflection constantly. It was a drumbeat. Fortunately, students around the world use that same drum. Their institutions' leaders should be beating this drum as well. But they do so far too infrequently.

Student impatience is a major part of the "naivete" of youth that Robert J. Bork railed against in *Slouching Toward Gomorrah*. Yet that impatience represents a significant part of the naïve idealism of youth that helps drive societies toward productive social change. He lamented the impatience. I welcomed it, in spite of the pressure this youthful impatience created. Tertiary education needs a more intense conversation about what is enough and when enough's enough. The Association of American Colleges and Universities' Greater Expectations report and program are both efforts to intensify that conversation. The neutralists, by focusing only on teaching critical thinking and avoiding issues pertaining to social change, simplify the challenge. It is not surprising so many trustees and even many faculty and administrators lean in their direction.

The "are-you-doing-enough" questions made many of my breakfasts uncomfortable because the answer was always yes and no. *Yes*, relative to resources and opportunities; *no*, with respect to needs and what should be done. Persuading students that such a seemingly equivocal answer was not simply waffling was always a challenge—and should have been. The pressure was good for Hampshire, and exploration of the "enough" questions provided a rich learning environment not only for students but for the entire community.

Student assertions that the "administration" is not doing enough are a strong antidote to inertia and complacency. At the American University in Bulgaria, the students focus on the multinational composition of the student body as being critical for creating the diversity of opinions they want. They carefully monitor the level of that diversity, confronting the administration whenever they think that the forces of homogeneity were threatening their diversity. Hampshire students raised the diversity question constantly, and it was the core cause of at least two extended sit-ins, one of which was on my watch. It was never a question of whether we were engaged. More appropriately, it was a question of whether we were engaged enough.

The students' vigilance also helped the college in many ways. One incident in particular stands out for me because it continues to shape my post-Hampshire life. At the very end of 1992, Arthur Serota, the aggressively energetic director of the Learning Tree, an NGO in Springfield, Massachusetts, made a startling request.[1] On the strength of his recommendation, he wanted Hampshire to admit into the quickly approaching spring term of that year the first four "graduates" from his program. They had just passed their GED exams, but he was convinced that getting them past the GED was not enough. These African American students were from underserved, economically depressed innercity neighborhoods, and Serota was worried that the streets might claim them if they waited to enroll at the beginning of the next academic year. Among the Five Colleges he chose Hampshire because Hampshire alumnus Sara Buttonweiser was on the Learning Tree board and Barbara Orr-Wise, Hampshire's Affirmative Action Officer, was a resident of Springfield. Both of these women knew the program well and supported it. Serota also thought Hampshire would understand the urgent needs of these students. And finally, as he told me quietly, he targeted Hampshire because he did not think the college was doing enough for the community, given its mission. He knew Hampshire students were pushing the college to do more with respect to diversity; and from what he had heard, he suspected I would agree with him. He had done his homework. I asked him for a couple of days to consider his request.

A few days later Serota and I met again, joined this time by Norma Baker, head of Northern Educational Services—another Springfield NGO that worked with underserved students. I told them, frankly, that we needed their help. At that point in the college's early development, Hampshire's African American student population was almost nonexistent; so I feared Hampshire lacked the critical mass to increase its diversity. And I readily acknowledged that Hampshire was not even meeting its own educational needs, let alone helping society meet the challenges it faced.

I felt strongly the students could contribute significantly to Hampshire. I was less confident that Hampshire was in a strong position to help them, given our lack of experience with this type of transition program. I warned these community representatives that there was a real danger rushing these students into the program so precipitously. If we create a transition-year program that fails, we could do real harm to the students, to the Learning Tree and Northern Educational Services, and to Hampshire itself. There would be no easy second chance. The transition would be difficult for any student enrolling in the middle of the school year—especially students who had finished their high school education outside mainstream channels. I knew Hampshire could not ignore those issues. We talked and we listened.

Mr. Serota and Ms. Baker made a compelling case for the students Serota recommended and urged that Hampshire take immediate action for the impact the potential success of these students would have on similar youths following them. In the end we decided that the "Are you doing enough?" challenge was compelling, so we invited the Learning Tree students to help Hampshire plan a transition-year program. In return for the students' assistance, Hampshire would enroll them for the coming semester at no cost; this way, they could get to know the college and be better equipped to advise Hampshire on diversity issues. They would be earning their way, not just receiving charity, which would give them a psychological edge. They would be partners in, not objects of, the effort to try and remedy Hampshire's previous diversity-related shortcomings. It was a difficult transition for everyone, but in the end, the experiment led to real progress.

That experiment became the James Baldwin Scholars Program, which continues to this day at Hampshire. It began officially in the fall by accepting students from a group recommended by Springfield community organizations and other NGOs; the offer was for one year of study fully funded by Hampshire. The students were deemed visiting students, or nonmatriculants, so they did not use eligibility for federal financial aid should they elect to attend another college after the transition year. We felt the program would be stronger if they were encouraged to look at other colleges in light of their experience at Hampshire. At the same time, if they applied to and were accepted by Hampshire, the work they had done in the transition year would count toward satisfying their degree requirements.

The strategy for that first year worked, although not without difficulties. Many elements contributed to the program's early success, but the most important elements were not only the decision to include students in the initial planning but also the partnership with the community agencies. In one particularly difficult meeting with Mr. Serota, Ms. Baker, and me, the transition-program students upbraided Hampshire for the problems with racism they encountered almost every day. They described the extra surveillance in the campus bookstore, the more focused attention the public safety officers gave to the students' friends who came to campus, and the vaguely dismissive comments from students about "the program," indignities that often occur when a homogenized community must face an "Other" for the first time. It was a sobering reminder of how far we had to go to learn to live together well and to build the kind of community to which we aspired. Hampshire was taking a positive step to reach out to the community; and the students, with more passion than diplomacy, were telling us, straightforwardly and accurately, that it was not enough, however well-meaning our intentions were. It was a tough message to be on the receiving end of.

In that first assessment meeting, the transition-year students had no trouble challenging authority. After all, they had been rebelling against authority much of their lives. That first meeting made clear the challenge everyone faced, a challenge that educators often face in all sorts of circumstances: Could Hampshire do enough to create a context in which these students felt safe and supported enough to constructively transform themselves as well as the college?

If that first meeting had simply involved the students addressing the college and the college responding, it would have been an extremely difficult conversation. Whatever I had said about the difficulties of starting a new program would have sounded defensive at best and probably insensitive at worst. Fortunately, I did not have to respond. Mr. Serota turned to me and forcefully stated that we (the "we" including the community agencies as well as

Hampshire) still had a lot of work to do in transforming our own organizations in addition to working with these students. He made it clear to the students that they were being heard. With considerable emotion, he then asked them if they thought they would be better off somewhere else; part of their role in helping to plan the program, he told them, was helping Hampshire learn how it could improve on its weaknesses. He told them that they had an incredible opportunity. He advised them not to focus primarily on Hampshire's failings but rather on their own individual academic growth. Their success would put to shame the racism they were encountering. Serota reminded them that this was the kind of racist behavior they would encounter almost anywhere—but without the nurturing and support that Hampshire was offering. The students heard him. They turned their attention to the academic help they felt they needed, and we began to work on those ideas.

Having a third party at the table who shared the same goals, had credibility, and would speak "truth to power" as well as to the students was invaluable. It focused attention on the issues and limited the tendency to make problems personal. Many of the meetings were tense, but the conversations ended up being constructive because the context made it possible to listen and not be defensive. Because we did listen, we succeeded in engaging and addressing both the students' and the college's problems. What could have been finger-pointing, "you are not doing enough" accusations against defensive "but we are doing enough" retorts, was transformed, by the tripartite arrangement, into a discussion where all agreed they had to do more. It ended with an understanding that we all shared common goals even if no one had yet done enough to meet those goals. These were some of the most profound conversations I experienced at Hampshire. I learned about listening and about what it meant to be engaged. In the process, we—the community, the college, and the students—had taken the first steps toward creating an educational program that exists to this day, has worked well for most students, and continues to improve.[2]

In squarely facing the issue of whether we were engaged in developing the diversity pipeline, the students, faculty, administration, and community understood the answer was still "no." Hampshire was working with specific schools. It was training science teachers in underprivileged communities; it was helping specific schools and programs in places like North Carolina and Arkansas; it had extensive programs in Holyoke and Springfield, Massachusetts. For a college with little endowment and with only 1,200 students, many felt the commitment was extensive. Although what we did was important for individual students, the college, and the communities with whom we worked, the students certainly did not hesitate to remind me it was not enough. The pressure of their questions about what *was* enough kept us looking for ways to engage more deeply and effectively. The pressure was not always welcome, but it helped spur our efforts to deal not only with issues of diversity but also with sustainable development, political action, and much more. Although the initiatives were neither consummately successful nor the flawed product of students' naïve expectations (the words Robert J. Bork quoted) the fact is that they often generated positive results and constructive action. Tertiary education needs more, not less, "vaulting ambition" from students, faculty, administrators, and boards of trustees.

As part of that questioning and searching process, I arranged to meet with Judith Griffin, president of the oldest and preeminent college-access program in the United States, A Better Chance, known to many as ABC. I found her to be a good listener who was truly engaged and willing to help Hampshire do more. She agreed to become a trustee. Ms. Griffin was concerned with the same questions as we were. What did it mean to be engaged? And was her institution engaged enough? She had concluded it was not. By the time Ms. Griffin joined the Hampshire board, A Better Chance was placing over four hundred students annually in independent schools and in well-financed public high schools, where they received the best possible preparation for college. These students often went on to attend the most prestigious universities in the United States. Oprah Winfrey declared it "her favorite charity." Yet every year Ms. Griffin ended up with another 1,200 wait-listed students for whom no financial support and, therefore, no place in an ABC-connected school existed. The program could not find places for all the individual students it was identifying as needy, and it certainly was not addressing the underlying problems in the communities from which the students were recruited.

Driven by that daily reminder of the waiting list, Judith Griffin developed a complementary program at A Better Chance called Pathways to College.[3] Pathways works with students in their own schools rather than sending them to schools with more rigorous academic programs outside their respective communities. Pathways works with schools in economically depressed communities, recruiting the twenty-five students from each grade deemed to have the most potential for collegiate success. Then they recruit six of the best teachers, as identified by the students and faculty in each school, to run the four-hour-per-week after-school program. Pathways pays these teachers, not the school board. So Pathways is free to select any teacher it thinks will be most effective as a leader.

Pathways provides the teachers with a research-based curriculum that focuses on having the students develop the skills and confidence needed for success both during and after college. In the words of the program's brochure, the reality is that "they must learn a new language and culture, not 'better' than the one they know, but one needed to optimize their potential for success in college and in their desired careers." Students visit businesses, cultural attractions, work on projects, and visit and meet with colleges— especially the partner colleges that support Pathways directly.

Pathways students, almost all of whom are students of color, become leaders in their schools and end up attending colleges and universities of the caliber of the University of Chicago and the other partner colleges. As the program grows, partner colleges will be able to put alumni on each local board who will then encourage students to consider their respective institutions. For the students, being solicited by highly selective colleges because of their intellectual and leadership potential is heady and affirming. And well it should be. Very few students in the United States, no matter what their race or economic background, hear from colleges in the early high school years unless they are athletes—an unfortunate signal from tertiary education that is not lost on high school students and that Pathways has the potential to alter.

In 2004, after ten years of being refined as a program within A Better Chance, Pathways became an independent not-for-profit headed by Griffin. It was organized as if it were a franchise operation. Each school-based program is locally funded either by the school district or by local community support, with the national office providing curricular materials, teacher training, and quality control. The franchise model makes it possible for Pathways to grow to whatever level is needed. Over a ten-year span the results in these two pilot programs have been extraordinary. Since Pathways became independent, ninety-nine percent of over two hundred students have gone on to nationally selective colleges, where they have been very successful. Of the two students who did not go to college, one entered the military to earn college support for the future and one did not have legal immigration status and was afraid to apply. But just as important as college access is the bond between students and teachers; working together, they become like a varsity sports team within their respective schools. The program creates a safe place for the students to be smart and they, in turn, create a culture in which it is actually *cool* to be smart. Peer pressure is a powerful influence on young adults—and the right kind of peer pressure can change the culture of a school for the better.

Pathways helps students, their high schools, and the college they attend. It employs a long-term strategy that emphasizes multi-institutional cooperation, underscored by the belief that the fastest way to reforming K-12 education in the United States is to give students a major role in that process. Unfortunately, Pathways is also struggling to grow. The program struggles because few people believe that students can change a school. It struggles because the adults in charge of schools are more concerned with their own personal power than with educating students. It struggles because even when the adults care, resources are still scarce. Finally, Pathways struggles because most universities are waiting to see if it will succeed rather than joining the effort and helping it succeed. Pathways founding partner colleges are an exception, having stepped forward with a spirit of leadership and social entrepreneurship: Smith, Dickinson, Ursinus, Occidental, Wheelock, and not surprisingly, Hampshire College, Wesleyan University (CT), and the University of Chicago.

In the final analysis, very few U.S. colleges and universities have experience working cooperatively with the same institutions they traditionally compete with for the brightest students. Collaborative competition is an unsettling, even alien, concept in spite of the fact that individual institutions acting alone cannot adequately address the critical diversity pipeline issues in the United States. For me it was one more reason why tertiary education in the United States needs a deeper conversation with itself and the community at large about what is enough when it comes to being an engaged university.

Measuring engagement requires comparing practice and the alignment of resources with the rhetoric of goals and ideals—the case made in the Association of American Universities and College's Greater Expectations document. Whether focusing on community, faculty, or student needs, measuring engagement requires comparing accomplishment and progress against what is actually needed, not just against improvements over current practice. However, engagement with the community may be the most difficult to evaluate. Universities committed to promoting civic engagement in their missions must begin by assessing how well they model the ability to listen to the community and whether they, as institutions, are addressing real needs directly through their actions and not just through the education they provide their students. Hundreds of institutions make that commitment successfully. But the next question, and one that students are usually willing to ask, is whether the institution is doing enough to make a difference in addressing those needs. Measured by the standard set by the international universities cited in this book, and considering the scant resources available to them and the urgent needs of their societies, U.S. universities are not sufficiently engaged with their communities. If the administrative leaders of these universities accept the premise that universities should be neutral, they will never be engaged at the level they should be. If our universities are to make a real difference in their communities, they first and foremost must accept the premise that as institutions they have a responsibility to make a significant difference in their respective communities, independent of the education they provide and the accomplishments of their graduates. That standard of engagement is a difficult one to meet, no doubt; but is mandatory if universities set out to model for its students the values it seeks to instill in them.

Unfortunately, few U.S. colleges and universities embrace that standard. Perhaps this is because colleges and universities are not listening to the public and their surrounding communities. They are insufficiently engaged in exploring and debating crucial issues of interest to the public at large. Academia's silence concerning the controversy in the United States over the teaching of evolution is but one example of how disengagement helps to build a major divide. The academy in general does not think creationism deserves a voice in the classroom, especially in science courses such as biology. Scientists do not address the issue because they are scientists, not theologians. Presidents and academic leaders do not think those who question evolution deserve serious responses, at least until they gain control of a local school board. The silence may be understandable, but it creates a vacuum that allows ideas that challenge the university's mission to grow. The leaders of tertiary education have a responsibility to respond rather than to be dismissive.

Our colleges and universities are showing an unhealthy streak of indifference nowadays. Indifference is a product of not listening well, of not trying to understand what is at stake. Consequences can be severe when this failure to listen occurs. In fact, blue-state inattentiveness is a theme Thomas Frank's groundbreaking book *What's the Matter with Kansas?* develops brilliantly and, at times, very humorously. He argues that the liberal establishment has ignored the voice of the general public; in the process, liberal leaders have lost the ability to communicate with that public. He also argues that the failure has become so consummate that even when liberal policy is clearly in the public's best interest, the message is not heard and definitely not accepted.[4]

Frank focuses more on how the "conservative noise machine" has manipulated the heartland by playing on the fears of the other: blacks, gays, immigrants, non-Christians—the wedge issues. He is right about their strategies, but I argue that the silence of university leaders—boards, faculty, and administrators—has helped create the opportunity for those wedge issues to gain as much traction as they achieve. And when conservatives claim that the university is out of touch with the mainstream, as was stated frequently in the Pennsylvania hearings, the claim becomes self-fulfilling because the academy is speaking with such a soft voice. When a student puts forth a "wrong" idea in class, most faculty members still feel an obligation to respond and to work with the student. Educational leaders should feel the same obligation to the public as they do to each individual student. It takes time and resources. Academic leaders are under tremendous pressure to respond to many different constituencies. Responding opens up the individual and the institution to attack, but it also provides opportunities for educating the public as well as one's own students. At the very least, the students would see more than one model of engagement. Over the long-term, inaction and silence can lead to great dangers.

○ ○ ○

The Pennsylvania hearings represented an unusual opportunity for public engagement and the kind of debate our society needs concerning education. I was surprised more by the low level of engagement from the institutional representatives than by the case the neutralists were making. Institutional representatives from the University of Pittsburgh, Temple University, Harrisburg Area Community College, Millersville University, and Montgomery County Junior College all testified and only one official, Vice President Garland of Millersville, really seemed fully engaged with the subject. He stated that there were certainly in-class incidents where students were upset about the opinions presented by faculty; but he thought the real issue should be how we deal with those concerns from students. He then gave his thoughts on what a college education should mean, and he came the closest of any of the witnesses to challenging the underlying assumption so many seemed to accept— that the university and the classroom should be neutral:

> Education is a challenging enterprise. It is much more than simply imparting information. It is about engaging students in and out of the classroom and helping them to expand their knowledge and skills to become critical thinkers and effective problem solvers. College and university campuses are vibrant institutions that rely on the exchange of ideas to stimulate intellectual growth as well as career preparedness.
>
> It is in this environment that students have the opportunity to learn about the world: about the world around them, and their place

within it. Universities help students to become thinkers and doers and to become advocates for causes in which they believe. Yes, we do want to teach students to be advocates—not for a specific cause, but for the causes they consider important. Active civic engagement is the essence of American democracy.

In this light, academic freedom is essential to enabling faculty and students to engage each other in lively and purposeful debate. Sometimes this means challenging each other's knowledge, assumptions and beliefs. It is important that the classroom remain an arena where open discussion not only is permitted but also is encouraged—where neither professor nor student feels restricted in his or her thoughts or words as they apply for the course.[5]

The institutional representatives had no obligation to challenge the premise of the hearings, and most did not. At the end of eight days of hearings spread over nine months, the concept that neutrality and balance in the classroom should be a universal standard remained an unchallenged assumption. Those who were in the best position to speak for their respective institutions and about the overall responsibilities of tertiary education spoke as if lawyers were sitting at their shoulders. They responded narrowly, not expansively, in their prepared testimony and in response to questions.

They had an opportunity to engage the public and they blew it. They may have felt that particular venue was not a good place to take on such a complicated issue. They may have believed themselves that they should be neutral. I cannot determine which motive dominated, but they are all disturbing.

In contrast to the presidents, deans, and provosts who testified, many academic figures, not necessarily representing an institutional point of view, did focus more on substantive educational issues. In so doing, they fulfilled a critical dimension of the engaged university: the responsibility to engage with the public about serious issues that the public as well as the academy deemed important. The substantive example they set helped salvage the productivity of the hearings.

Whether intended or not, the minimalist response creates a form of silence that the public often misinterprets as aloofness, disinterest, or outright disrespect. It can appear that academics are reluctant to take on larger issues—or, worse, that tertiary education considers itself above having to explain itself to the public. Each college operates autonomously, and each college experiences real pressure not to call attention to and become a target for one group or another. Competition for students and rankings, even among the most selective colleges, encourages caution and silence, certainly. This kind of competitiveness can make schools reluctant to be an engaged institution and interact with the public as well as the students on important social issues.

Although lamenting the quality of public discourse and the academy's role in it has become popular sport, determining how to enliven that discourse or who can lead this change is not so clear. Frank's *What's the Matter with Kansas?* cogently defines the problem, and that is a start. The neutralists, who criticize the academy for not including a sufficient diversity of views, are correct on this front, even if I believe their definition of diversity itself is rather narrow. However, the need is not just for a greater diversity of speakers on college campuses. The need is for a deeper, more meaningful dialogue between the academic community and the public. It will come only when the academic community puts a higher priority on generating public discourse. Universities' reward systems must support those who are willing to engage in public discourse; schools should not deny professors their rightful promotions because they are speaking out on controversial or popular issues as opposed to doing introverted library-bound research. The academy needs to restore the concept of the public intellectual and be willing to reward and defend such people if they bring seriousness, commitment, and substance to their presentations and observe the Principles of Discourse. The conversations that would evolve just might create a healthier society.

○ ○ ○

The consequences of silence may be seen in the academic community's slow response to individuals such as Ward Connally, who has tirelessly pushed his view that affirmative action is reverse discrimination. In a sense, inaction may have doomed affirmative action. Although the debate now continues, having been regalvanized by the controversy over the University of Michigan's suspect admissions policy, a lot of lost ground must be made up, as the statewide vote in Michigan against affirmative action indicates. The intensified conservatives leanings of the U.S. Supreme Court may doom any success in that arena.

I worry that the silence of the academy in the face of creationism and intelligent design is creating a vacuum about what is defined as science; a vacuum that has led the Bush administration in the United States to dismiss science in a manner not seen in this country since before World War II. Silence is a clear and present danger. These topics clearly have become political issues in America today, and they involve subjects of critical importance to the academy. Neutrality is silencing those who should be speaking out on these critical issues.[6]

As I have been fairly relentless in speaking out against the neutralists, part of my own past visited me recently in an unusual way. I stumbled upon a message that reinforced the importance of public dialogue and made this often abstract subject more concrete. A friend gave me a copy of Jeffrey Hart's newest book, *The Making of the American Conservative Mind:* The National Review *and Its Times.* This gift was given with some humor, since my friend knew that Jeffrey Hart and I agreed on very little: he was a tireless advisor and promoter of the very conservative *Dartmouth Review* as well as a nationally recognized columnist for the *National Review*. Hart was a professor of English at Dartmouth while I was there, and I invited him many times to guest-lecture in my course "Recent U.S. History: 1945 to the Present." Some of my history colleagues wondered why I wanted a professor of literature to lecture in a history course, especially one with whom I disagreed so strongly. The answer was simple. His analysis of the U.S. political scene was brilliant. No one in class doubted his bias, but he made clearer than anyone I knew the underlying strategies and dynamics of the election process and could explain in historical context the strategy of the Republican and Democratic parties as well as the role he was playing as an active public intellectual.

I found Hart's book to be a dramatic and insightful picture of what a deliberate effort to listen well and to respond clearly in political dialogue can accomplish.[7] Professor Hart described how a group of individuals—all of whom could be described as public intellectuals—set about to make conservative thought in the United States intellectually respectable. The academic community, liberal and conservative alike, could learn much from that history. Reading it was a poignant reminder for me that all professions have a responsibility to speak to the larger public and that education had better become more proficient or the public's respect for it will begin to decline as much as it has for other professions. This history of the *National Review* also demonstrated the importance of substance as opposed to public relations.

The *National Review* adopted a mission and took on the most difficult issues of the day in a very straightforward manner. Along with Hart, its major principals—individuals such as William F. Buckley, Jr., Hart, James Burnham, Willmoore Kendall, Russell Kirk, and Frank Meyer—set out to create an intellectually respectable conservative movement and modeled the behavior they encouraged. Like the Civil Liberties and Public Policy program at Hampshire, those founders of the *National Review* began with a hypothesis based on a well-articulated "biased" point of view. With a strong sense of mission, they were remarkably open, intensely argumentative, and often angst-ridden; they proceeded to make conservatism intellectually respectable, and in the process they helped lay the foundation for a political transformation in the United States. Although I disagreed with them from the beginning, and continue to disagree with most of their positions, I do respect the intellectual clarity and directness they pursued their goals with. I also respect the success they achieved in generating a national debate about who we were and where we were going as a nation.

The effort of David Horowitz's Students for Academic Freedom is another open and direct effort to engage the public and the academy in an important debate. Although I do respect the effort—and I hope this book conveys that respect as well as my disagreements with it—I consider it also a warning to the academy that it must engage with the public more rigorously, intensely, and openly. The work of writers such as Thomas Frank and Jeffrey Hart help to explain why this dialogue is needed and how far education has to go to reclaim its voice and place in important national debates. Unfortunately, what took place in the Pennsylvania hearings does not give me hope that the message has been heard. The tendency of tertiary educators to be dismissive of what they consider to be the product of either philistines or fringe groups simply confirms the sense of those groups that dissent is not tolerated in these professors' classrooms. Whatever the motives and no matter how outrageous the views, tertiary education should respond. It takes time and energy to do so; and with other pressing issues, few are inclined to join many of these debates. They are viewed as distractions. But silence, in the end, allows inaccurate perceptions and bad ideas to grow unchecked. The reluctance, inexperience, or simple lack of interest on the part of tertiary education leaders in taking on controversial issues compounds other deeper more complicated causes that challenge civil discourse.

Taking positions on major national issues will always anger someone, and that is why many are so cautious and reluctant to speak out. But caution, in the end, encourages the growing intolerance in the United States for out-of-the-mainstream views. Students rarely get excited when their respective college or university presidents speak out on national issues when they agree with the position taken; but students do get angry when the president takes a position with which they disagree. It is hard for a college or college president to ignore the low return on speaking out.

On the other hand, if colleges and universities did speak out and explain to the students the core values they were modeling, professors and administrative staff might create an expectation that this kind of behavior is the norm for their alma mater and its leaders. Alumni might even become less concerned with a specific position and more concerned with the moral courage displayed, the quality of the means used to display it, and the extent to which taking a stand exemplifies the Principles of Discourse. Academic leaders could even dream of a time when institutions' displays of moral courage inspire as much pride in students and alumni as the school's successful athletic teams often do.

College communities need to learn to recognize the value of the president and the university putting forward a strong opinion on a controversial subject and the moral courage such a position requires. What is the future of political and civil dialogue in our country if silence in elementary and secondary education is depriving students of the chance to learn how to disagree and still be friends? And what will happen if college students and alumni cannot learn to be proud of their universities even when they disagree with the decisions the school makes?

If institutions of higher learning do not provide models, commentators such as Don Imus, Rush Limbaugh, and Laura Ingraham—who violate the Principles of Discourse as a matter of strategy—will continue to dominate the airwaves with their inflammatory rhetoric. They accept that the ends (i.e., the advancement of conservative ideas) do justify the means, and they personalize disagreements. They attack the proponent of a view rather than the argument. Rush Limbaugh, to his credit, is very honest about what he does. His tactics improve ratings and, thus, his income. For him the ends do justify the means. Don Imus, another radio "shock jock," felt he was protected by his marketability and that he could say anything he wanted as long as he delivered high ratings. Unfortunately he was probably right, although in the end he was fired by NBC after his disparaging remark directed at the Rutgers women's basketball team. Of course, he will no doubt have found another lucrative outlet for his off-color commentary by the time this book comes out. In Imus's case, NBC only made its decision to fire Imus after advertisers began to pull out, which suggests that the substance of his commentary was not the real problem for the network. NBC was just as despicable an actor in that sorry story as Imus himself. When tempers cool, however, Imus is likely to get his microphone back.

There are specific costs in not speaking out and not taking challenges to key academic values seriously. Silence in response to the claims that the Students for Academic Freedom make, or a simple response that bias does not exist, reinforces alarming and very harmful assumptions upon which the charge is made. The neutralists see the problem primarily in terms of liberal and conservative politics. The problem is much larger. U.S. college students' lack of exposure to global perspectives is a more severe problem than their lack of exposure to a wide range of political perspectives. Those who focus on political bias regularly explain that one consequence of this bias was a negative revisionist portrayal of U.S. history. They are concerned that American values are now subordinate to multicultural and global issues. That theme expresses a long-standing theme in the culture wars that lies at the heart of the neutralists' concerns. They are concerned with which perspectives are being introduced, not just with the abstract concept of having diverse perspectives represented. Viewpoints in the classroom are becoming diverse, only in ways the neutralists actually condemn.

Another incident that took place in Pennsylvania at around the time of the academic freedom hearings underscores why I am alarmed about the academy's lack of engagement with the public. Largely under the radar of the national press, a newly elected school board in Upper St. Clair Township, an affluent suburb of Pittsburgh, Pennsylvania, voted at the beginning of 2006 to terminate one of the strongest international baccalaureate high school programs in the United States. They cited costs as the problem, but at hearings attended by hundreds of the school district's parents, the new board members referred to the program as "pro-Marxist," "anti-American," and "anti-Christian." When Pennsylvania Governor James Rendell offered to have the state pay for the program, the school board was not interested in his offer. Costs were definitely not the issue. It was international and, therefore, anti-American.

As alarming as the decision itself was, I was struck even more by the silence that followed. Tertiary education in the United States completely ignored the event. It was covered in local papers, but there was no comment from tertiary institutions or their associations. The silence was alarming because the issue itself is so important, because the silence encourages further attacks on principles critical to the academy, and because tertiary education failed to come to the defense of a group of teachers who had created a high school program recognized nationally for its quality and their students' access to the kind of quality education society needs. I worry this attack went unchallenged because too many were too preoccupied with issues closer to home to realize the urgent need for a diversity of international and multicultural perspectives in the classroom. The United States and, in many respects, the world will be irrevocably harmed if a majority (or even a large plurality) in the United States come to equate international, multicultural perspectives with anti-Americanism. This is happening in the minds of many conservatives, whether they are sitting on the Upper St. Clair Township school board or listening to conservative radio commentators. Tertiary education in this country does place a high priority on promoting internationalism. Still, I worry that our schools may not be doing enough.

The attack on the international baccalaureate program caught me by surprise, but I had no doubt about its importance and seriousness. It was one more sign that the world indeed was facing a major conflict taking place within all major cultures—not among them. It was a clash initiated by those in different societies who have turned their backs on the complexities of modernity and seek solace in provincialism and in the distorted simplifications of complex and intellectually rich cultural and religious traditions. These groups stereotype and scapegoat in order to dehumanize those they fear. They personalize disagreements and demonize those who would struggle to humanize modernization and manage complexity to achieve greater social justice. It is not just a single nation that is at risk—to co-opt a well know phrase in U.S. educational circles—but it is the world at risk. In that context, universities should feel compelled to engage the public at large and the communities around them on this subject.

Assessing whether a specific institution or tertiary education as a whole are sufficiently engaged with the community and the public is difficult. Trying to determine the sufficiency of faculty engagement with students and with the mission of the institution is even harder but more essential. Professors are the heart and mind of an academic institution, and they must listen to their students just as an institution must listen to its community. As the next chapter explores, this capacity to listen is the critical measure of the quality of engagement between professor and student just as it is between the university and its community.

CHAPTER 10

What Is Enough?:
The Role of
the Professor

Although the relationship with the larger community is an important measure of the engaged university, the penultimate measure is the intensity and quality of the faculty's engagement in the process of teaching and research. The controlling factor of the quality of those processes will be how well professors listen. Professors, like institutions, must listen well. A passion for knowledge and for people is necessary for effective research and teaching, but these qualities alone are not sufficient.

Engagement driven by caring for the well being of students and a passion to stimulate a love of learning and a spirit of inquiry makes education effective; and listening well is the key to transmitting that caring and passion constructively to the student. Listening well demands keen observation, knowledge, openness, and reflection. When advocacy and passion for an idea or a field of study inhibits the ability to listen, then the quality of engagement takes on its military sense. The student is at risk and education is threatened. On the other hand, if you listen well, you will come to know the mind of the person you listen to; you will become empathetic and stimulate the other's capacity for self-reflection by prompting a dialog with them, not just expecting them to absorb information passively. Great teachers are good listeners. They come to know the other person in a way that enables them to speak to that student in a way that helps the student hear and absorb what is being said. Listening well helps others to listen.

Education is as much about listening as it is about transmitting information. The experiences of two very different individuals living and working in very different times and places define what it means to listen well and what it means to be sufficiently engaged.

○ ○ ○

Eric Carle, the well-known picture-book artist, author of the classic children's book *The Very Hungry Caterpillar* and founder of the Eric Carle Picture Book Museum, located on the Hampshire College campus, once told me about the profound influence one of his teachers had on him. In 1944, as a young elementary school student, his parents had sent him to live in a small country town in Germany to avoid Allied bombing raids on that country's major cities. He loved to draw and make art; and he apparently showed enough talent to attract the attention of his art teacher, Friedrich Krauss. One day the teacher asked Eric to stop by his home because he had something he wanted to show him. During the visit, Mr. Krauss told Eric quietly that he was aware of Eric's talent and knew that Eric had a passion for art. He then took from a hiding place a group of banned books depicting the work of German expressionist artists and said, "I want to show you what real art is, not what these Nazi charlatans say it is." Seventy years later Eric Carle still speaks of his excitement and amazement at what he saw and how much it affected all that was to follow in his work.

Here was a teacher so passionate about his subject and so engaged with his students that he was willing to risk his job, if not his life, to open up a world he believed this very special young person needed to see. By Eric Carle's own admissions, the impact was profound. Years later, through the publication of *The Very Hungry Caterpillar, Brown Bear, Brown Bear,* and dozens of Carle's other picture books, that "tendentious," engaged teacher is still impacting thousands of young people the world over. He has set for me one almost impossible standard for answering the question, "What is enough?"

○ ○ ○

The life story of Professor Diane Bell offers another compelling example of the value of an engaged approach to teaching and the immense and needed impact such teaching has on students and the communities outside the university. Professor Bell, an Australian anthropologist, began her academic career in Australia, taught in the United States, and has since returned to Australia. She served as a trustee of Hampshire College for twelve years (which is how I came to know of her work), was the Henry Luce Professor of Women's Studies and Anthropology at Holy Cross University, and later was chair of women's studies at George Washington University.

When Professor Bell walks into the classroom, she cannot be neutral. For her to do so would require hiding a life spent living what she teaches and teaching what she has lived. Her career illustrates what it means to teach individuals to think critically, to challenge authority and convention, to advocate, engage, and be open to disagreement simultaneously. She has lived what she has taught in a way that eliminates the false barriers between academia and the "real" world and between neutrality and advocacy. Diane Bell was and is still an artist: the classroom, her research, her writing as a scholar and a novelist, and her nonacademic advocacy for social justice are her modes of creative expression. As she always reminded me: "I like to think academia is the real world." She's right.

It is not possible to separate the roles Diane Bell has played, for each influences the others: college trustee, teacher, scholar, advocate, advisor, and friend of my wife's and mine. Her scholarship, teaching, and advocacy are integrated into a whole much greater than the sum of its parts. When she advocates, she teaches. When she teaches, she uses her advocacy to challenge assumptions and expects to be challenged and critiqued. When she is in research mode, she becomes an advocate for the logic used to amass data that bring to life her research and conclusions. Many have challenged her personally and professionally throughout her career and she has turned those occasions, some of which were painful and debilitating, into learning opportunities for her students, her critics, and herself. Her career, like the actions of those four students in North Carolina, reminds us why educating students to challenge authority in constructive and appropriate ways is essential to sustaining a healthy democratic society and must be an integral part of liberal education.

Diane Bell was born in Melbourne, Victoria, Australia, in 1943. She did well in math and science, but left high school with a "leaving certificate." She did not complete the sixth form required to go on to college because she was counseled that there was no place for girls in science and that teaching was more appropriate. In 1961 she attended Frankston Teacher's College, expanding her interests from math and science to art, literature, and music, and she earned a certificate as a primary school teacher. She taught at the primary school level from 1961 to 1967, and this experience formed the basis for all of her teaching that followed. Teaching, Bell says, is a "constantly shifting terrain" that truly requires lifelong learning. Her classes were filled with students who were not interested in the subject, who were a challenge to control and discipline, and who certainly were not socially motivated to stay in school. She transformed students, as she put it, by becoming a "performer" who orchestrated a different approach to knowledge for her students. Art, music, literature, and science became an integrated, synthesized whole. Using an interdisciplinary approach most uncommon in the 1960s, she had the students dance, sing, and paint in English class as a way of learning language. She would join in as a character in the plays they wrote. Through this curriculum, she helped them discover their life goals and dreams. She was captivated by the developmental aspect of teaching, and created her own style of connecting to and caring about her students. Later, at the college level, in large courses she would sometimes take the microphone and run up and down the aisles of the raked lecture hall asking students questions like a talk show host and get them to talk to each other. "What do you think the author is saying? I think the person sitting next to you has a different idea? Can you explain how you came to different conclusions having read the same texts? You have read the texts?" It certainly was a way of engaging the students, and, more important, it was a way of distinguishing between opinion and belief, which she found American students were always happy to share (and were fed on TV shows) from evidence-based reasoning.

Diane Bell definitely brought the experience and skills she learned as a primary school teacher to her college teaching, and she has always respected those who teach at the primary level, accepting them certainly as her intellectual equal if not beyond. Given the disdain of "higher education" toward K-12 education is the greatest problem faced by K-12 education in the United States, Professor Bell's experience has profound meaning in itself, independent of the value of her example for my argument that teaching students how to challenge authority in appropriate and constructive ways is a core goal for educators at all levels.

In 1965 Diane Bell married, and she temporarily stopped teaching upon the birth of her first child in 1967. She reentered the academic world when she realized that marriage and childrearing were not going to be her entire life; she knew she needed intellectual stimulation beyond the domestic domain, which was a decision that may have contributed to the breakup of her marriage that followed. She set out to complete the sixth form of high school by studying at night. Taking the national exams and earning special distinction, she gained admission to Monash University. But the scholarship that her academic distinction should have earned her was denied; at the age of twenty-seven, she was considered to be too old to be offered an academic scholarship.

At Monash, she had to argue her way into already-full courses, such as anthropology, because of age discrimination; but she did so well in her first year that she received a Commonwealth scholarship, a scholarship awarded by the federal department of education and the only award available at the university level. In 1975 she graduated with honors, which was an unusual accomplishment in Australia at that time for a single mother with two children. She received an appointment as Vacation Scholar in Anthropology from the Research School of Pacific Studies of the Australian National University. The Vacation scholarship is an award specific to the ANU that was awarded over the summer vacation for graduate students who had a project they could pursue over the vacation— they were fiercely competitive. She got one when she was still an undergraduate, and with it she did the research for her honors thesis. After graduating from Monash later that year, this award was followed by a postgraduate fellowship at the Australian National University. There she earned a PhD in social anthropology in 1981, having not only conducted fieldwork with Aboriginal groups but also living among these groups as well. Having her children with her contributed significantly to the trusting relationship she created with the Aboriginal communities with whom she lived. That trust became key to all that followed.

Developments in Australian national policy toward Aboriginal people during this period had shaped Professor Bell's career choice of social anthropology and fieldwork. In 1967 a constitutional referendum in Australia, supported by a 90 percent majority in a nation where voting is a legal obligation and where a majority in each state must pass constitutional referenda, dramatically altered the status of the Aborigines and Torres Strait Islanders. It became compulsory that they be included in the census, a requirement that had not been included in the country's original constitution. The federal government also gained a concurrent right with the states to legislate for the Aborigines, the word "for" becoming the pivotal word, in later disputes. At the time there was a nationwide assumption that the word "for" meant "for the benefit" of the Aborigines and giving the federal government that right was to protect the Aborigines from the actions of individual states. This interpretation was later to be challenged in 1998 when "for" came to be interpreted as "with respect to" and thus not necessarily for the benefit of the Aborigines.

In 1972 Gough Whitlam became prime minister and the Labor Government embarked on a major revolution in national policy, including withdrawal of Australian troops from Vietnam and the creation of the Woodward Commission to determine how land rights for Aboriginals would be recognized—not *if* they should be recognized. The government also eliminated fees for university attendance. It was a major transformation. At this time, the official government policy for the Aborigines became one of self-determination.

This societal and legal transformation occurred when Diane Bell was at Monash University. At that time, she was challenging the university administration by occupying the sports center during a vacation period; in this venue, she had begun running a daycare center for children. The vice chancellor responded by telling her that "universities were not made for people like her." Her riposte was, "They will have to change."[1]

In 1975 what is often termed a "constitutional coup" occurred in Australia when the governor general, at the request of the minority Conservative Party (called the Liberal Party), not the prime minister, prorogued Parliament, thereby forcing an election in both houses of Parliament. The Liberal Party won the elections, and one of the first acts of the government was to pass the new Aboriginal Land Rights Legislation in 1976. This happened just as Diane Bell was entering the field to study Aboriginal women's religious beliefs and practices, work that resulted in the publication of *Daughters of the Dreaming*, in 1983. It was a seminal work on Aboriginal culture and is still in print.

The Land Rights Act dramatically altered the direction of national policy toward the Aborigines. Although it did set policy toward how land claims could be filed, it placed serious limitations on the process. The act was to be applied only to unalienated crown lands in the Northern Territories, and it eliminated as a basis for a claim the need for land (a basis conceived by the Labor government that had initiated the original legislation). Instead, the claim had to be based on the more restrictive standard that claimants prove they were descendants of a group that had exercised primary spiritual responsibility for the land and remained attached to it. As Diane Bell significantly noted, it generated lots of work for lawyers and anthropologists.

During Bell's time in the field, when Aboriginal land councils were established in Alice Springs and Darwin, Aborigines began to enter the university system. At the same time a national lobby on behalf of Aboriginal rights consolidated and strengthened, as did a strong backlash from mining and development companies. By the 1980s the rhetoric in Australian politics had shifted from Aborigines' rights to discourse that questioned why the Aborigines people were getting something that other Australians were not.

Returning from the field while still a graduate student, Diane Bell began to advise Justice John Toohey, who was then serving as the Aboriginal land commissioner and later was elevated to the Australian High Court, on the appropriateness of land-claim evidence and the context in which that evidence was developed; she also met with all parties involved on the same issues. In advising the court on the relevance and validity of evidence, she was playing an ombudsperson-type role, a role facilitated by her fieldwork with Aborigines in the areas subject to claim. To be sure, many individuals and groups contesting claims did not see her as a "neutral" party, but those who looked past the conclusions she was presenting realized that listening to her astute commentary could be valuable in strengthening their case.

Diane Bell had walked into a storm with no calm eye. Between 1978 and 1984 she authored thirty-four reports and studies relating to land-claims cases under the Land Rights Act, in the process becoming one of the most knowledgeable individuals in Australia on Aboriginal culture—not to mention one of the foremost experts on legal and evidentiary issues involved in claims cases. Her original scholarship, in effect, was the basis for the formulation and implementation of this public policy.

While connected with the academy during this period, she also was outside of it, giving evidence to Senate Committees, writing reports on matters of public policy, and developing materials for use in primary schools. In 1980 she coauthored *Law: The Old and the New*, with Pam Ditton, a lawyer working for Aboriginal Legal Aid in Alice Springs, Northern Territory. In 1982 she went into private practice as a consulting anthropologist, forming Diane Bell and Associates. She pursued this practice for a full year and then part time through 1988, holding several adjunct or part-time academic appointments during the same period.

In 1986, having never held a full-time academic appointment, she was appointed full professor at Deakin University and became the founding director of its Centre for Australian Studies. At the time, she was the only woman in the professoriate at Deakin. In addition to providing leadership for a new academic center, she had to struggle with a pronounced bias against women. In the end, she succeeded in building a strong program with a national and international reputation, although she noted that she "never did learn to make tea and coffee the way my male colleagues expected."

The reputation of her work at Deakin eventually led to a commission from the Australian Bicentennial Authority to write a book on women in Australia, and *Generations: Grandmothers, Mothers and Daughters* was published in 1987. That work and her international reputation led to a fellowship in the United States and to her appointment in 1988 as a Henry R. Luce Professor of Religion, Economic Development and Social Justice at Holy Cross College in Worcester, Massachusetts. She held that position until 1999 when she became a professor of anthropology and women's studies and the director of women's studies at George Washington University, in Washington, D.C. She held this position until she retired in June of 2005, the same year I retired.

Whether inside or outside the academy in Australia or the United States, Diane Bell's scholarship was the basis for an outspoken advocacy for the "truth," or the reality she had discovered in her work. When she entered the academy full time, the idea that she would be neutral with respect to major questions in her field about Aboriginal culture was a concept that had no meaning. She had already held strong public positions based on her research and had advocated for policies that confirmed the conclusions she had reached in that research. In fact, her research had become controversial in and of itself. She could not be neutral, but she could model for her colleagues, her students, and the public what it meant to pursue truth as a scholar and what the Principles of Discourse actually meant for scholarship and teaching in general. The controversy and its resulting conflicts were intense, and the public ramifications were significant.

Bell and a small group of Australian women anthropologists argued that in Aboriginal societies there was a parallel world of women's knowledge known only to women within those communities and that this knowledge could only be shared with other women; thus, this realm had gone unnoticed and unknown to male anthropologists. The argument sent shock waves through the anthropology profession in Australia. And there were some extreme responses from male academics and even some women who were obviously comfortable with men in the role of "making culture" and women in the role of "making babies." The dispute was not limited to the academy however, for the issue had profound importance for land-claim cases. The parallel world of women's knowledge included sacred sites known to and protected by women. Since the Aboriginal and Torres Straits Heritage Protection Act of 1984 and the Land Rights Act of 1976, both protected sacred sites, the acceptance or rejection of an entire layer of knowledge shared only among women had profound implications for these laws' implementation and greatly increased the public policy ramifications of Bell and her colleagues' argument.

Because of her public advocacy on many issues, her opinions would inevitably emerge in classroom discussions. She could not go into the classroom and be neutral with respect to specific policies, many of which arose out of her research and her experience as a woman breaking gender barriers in the academy. She was proudly and logically a feminist scholar—but not "feminist" in the sense those who would disparage the term would have it mean. She was a feminist because of what she saw, experienced, and tried to interpret throughout her life. And her brand of feminism came from her conviction that one has to resist injustice wherever it may be: at home, abroad, in the family, in politics, in the workplace, or the academy. As an educator, she used her conclusions to clue students in on the reasoning processes that led to her conclusions, and she urged them to judge the evidence and the process for themselves. She not only welcomed challenges but also insisted that the rigor of a challenger's analysis meet the standard she tried to set in her own work. By modeling for students what she expected of them, she gave them guidance and an open invitation to challenge her views.

For example, during her tenure at Holy Cross (a Catholic college) she often met students who took the position that abortion was murder—a position she openly disagreed with. But she would not tell these students they were wrong. Rather, she would push the students to ask the kinds of probing questions she had asked as an anthropologist. She would ask these students why they thought abortion was murder and would ask them if all killing was to be condemned. That would lead to a conversation about when and if taking a human life was permissible and why the church had condemned some forms of killing and not others. She asked when and why the church concluded that life began at inception, or even earlier, and what led the church to construct certain inviolable positions and then later change them. She used the example of Galileo being in trouble with the Catholic Church for teaching that the Earth revolved around the sun. Today that position is obviously not controversial. In short, she would ask the student to think more clearly about the assumption underlying his or her position, to carefully consider how arguments and knowledge itself are constructed, and why one position dominates and another does not. Then she might ask what the truly inviolate universal principles are that transcend time and place.

In such a context, her rigor could intimidate. Given the sharpness of her mind and the depth of her courage, most would be foolhardy not to feel awed, if not outright intimidated. Students who cared about their grades more than their education certainly would think twice about taking one of her challenging courses. But giving students those choices is what education has to be about. Many who disagreed with her position did accept the challenge and the overwhelming majority of that group ended up feeling great respect for her rigor, integrity, and commitment.

Professor Bell's career illustrates why the assumption that a strong and openly held position could possibly generate a wrong does not mean a wrong has definitely occurred or will occur. Individuals who value scholarship and have devoted a lifetime to it are likely to be passionate about the subject and their work; but that passion is a combination of a deep interest in the subject and a deep commitment to the process of critical examination, analysis, and questioning. Questioning often can generate discomfort, and one of the goals of liberal education is to increase the tolerance for and willingness to question what appear to be irrefutable positions. Not all positions will be or should be refuted, but individuals—professors and students alike—have to be willing to suspend the construction of opinions in order to examine new evidence. But suspending a belief to consider new evidence is not the same as neutrality.

Intense disputes occur when individuals are unwilling to suspend their beliefs in order to entertain new evidence. In Professor Bell's classroom, students who accepted the challenge for personal growth reasons found a caring and supportive atmosphere even as they were pushed to rethink every assumed certainty they had brought to class. The goal was to have the student build a stronger foundation of values and beliefs that could stand up to the challenges of time, circumstances, and those who disagreed with them. She excelled in the art of helping students grow, mature, and become excited by the world of ideas.

Professor Bell's work on women's knowledge in Aboriginal cultures became so controversial and intense that it gave her a rare opportunity to model all of the values and skills she hoped to instill in her students. In essence, Professor Bell had to publicly model for her students the very principles she was demanding of them in class.

After Bell left Australia, the dispute over Aboriginal land claims culminated in what would be called the "Hindmarsh Island" case. But she willingly participated in it because of her passion for the process of inquiry, her confidence in the quality of her scholarship and field research, and her sense of commitment to those she worked with. The Hindmarsh Island case is well known in Australia but not in the rest of the world. However, it should be well known worldwide for all that it involved and can teach about the essence of education. Developers and government officials in South Australia wanted to build a bridge from a Mainland town call Goolwa to a little island nestled in the mouth of the River Murray. A group of Ngarrindjeri Aboriginal women objected because the construction of the bridge would intrude on land and waters that were sacred to Aboriginal women. There was great exasperation among developers, which led to a strenuous objection to the argument that knowledge and practices known only to Aboriginal women could block the development projects they were supporting. They sought to counter this with expert advice from other anthropologists, including those in the South Australian government, who could find in the archival records no evidence of restrictions based on Aboriginal women's knowledge.

The matter came to national attention in 1995 when the federal minister for Aboriginal affairs agreed to place a twenty-five-year ban on development of the site; but that decision was set aside on a technicality. Then it eventually came before the South Australia Land Commission, which found the claimants to be "fabricators," assuming that because there was no written record of the women's beliefs and that not all women knew the story, it could not be a legitimate claim. In December of 1995 and January 1996 Diane Bell joined the case, presenting evidence from her fieldwork that was published in the 1998 book *Ngarrinjeri Wurruwarrin: A World That Is, Was, and Will Be.* Of course, since money and power were at stake, the case became very bitter. There were angry accusations and charges made by those who rejected the Aboriginal women's claims and dismissed the opinions of the women anthropologists who supported these claims. A larger group of male anthropologists accused these Aboriginal women of lying and fabricating stories and said the pro-Aboriginal women anthropologists had been hoaxed.

In 2002 Australian Supreme Court Justice John von Doussa found the Aboriginal women to be credible witnesses and supported their claim. Von Doussa explained why he did not side with Iris Stevens, the South Australia Royal Commissioner on the "anthropology" of the case:

> On the anthropological evidence, I have serious concerns about the objectivity of Dr. Clarke [of the South Australia Museum] and the opinions he has given in evidence. His personal diaries on which he has been extensively cross-examined disclose that he is and has, from the time his first declaration [under the Heritage legislation] was made, been resistant to considering the possibility that his spontaneous assessment that Dr. Fergie's [the woman anthropologist who filed the first report that claimed the site was sacred to women] opinion is wrong is itself incorrect. He formed that opinion before he had read the reports of either Dr. Fergie or Professor Saunders [the lawyer who heard the first application under the Act], and within hours of learning of the declaration [by the Minister for Aboriginal Affairs]. His diaries show that he was the originator of the fabrication theory, and that he thereafter embarked on a course to undermine and discredit Dr. Fergie and her opinion, at times attributing blame for the fabrication to Dr. Fergie, Mr. Hemming [a pro-Ngarrindjeri Museum researcher who left his job under the strain of the accusations] and Dr. Draper [an independent pro-Ngarrandjeri consultant]. When the Royal Commission was announced, he claims to have taken a role and provided information that influenced the course of the Royal

Commission in a way that I consider lacks professional objectivity and was inappropriate. I am not satisfied that Dr. Clarke has fairly and objectively considered whether the reasoning and interpretation of research materials relied upon by others may leave open the possibility that his opinion is wrong. I prefer the views of Mr. Hemming, Dr. Draper, and Professor Bell. I am not persuaded by the applicants' submissions that their opinions are not reasonably based on the research and other materials on which they have relied. On the opinions of Professor Bell, Dr. Draper, and Mr. Hemming, I find that the restricted women's business identified in the reports of Dr. Fergie and Dr. Saunders is not such that it should be rejected on the ground of inconsistency with known historical and ethnographic material. On the contrary, I accept their evidence that there is a measure of support to be found in that material for the existence of restricted women's knowledge of the kind identified in the Fergie and Saunders reports.[2]

In the end, the issues of scholarship involved in the specific Hindmarsh Island case were swept away by the Liberal government. They passed the Hindmarsh Island Act, which amended the federal Heritage Act, making it possible to protect sacred Aboriginal sites anywhere in Australia except on Hindmarsh Island. Now the bridge is being built. And Aboriginal sacred lands are being sacrificed. As foretold by the women fighting to protect the site, Aboriginal women did sicken and die.

Professor Bell, simply on the grounds of her research, had become an advocate for the quality of that research and its relevance to critical national issues and legal cases. However, that extended controversy overlapped with others. The issue of Aboriginal rights in Australia, like Native American rights in the United States, is a protracted struggle for justice. Diane Bell's research was continuously drawn into that struggle as she tried to present to both the scholarly and lay public a picture of Aboriginal life and customs.

What affects me most about Diane Bell and Friedrich Krauss is the intensity of their commitment to what is "real" and truthful. I respect not only their willingness to share their passions with others but also their willingness to risk extreme personal discomfort. Their impact is stunning. Young people respond to such engagement because they can sense its authenticity. I know nothing more about

Friedrich Krauss than the story Eric Carle relayed to me. On the other hand, I worked with Diane Bell for years and can testify to the intensity of her engagement as a trustee, a scholar, and a teacher. Her colleagues knew she cared about ideas and they respected her opinions, even though their own views may have differed from hers. That intensity of engagement and the authentic voice she developed, which advocated the importance of scholarship and critical thinking, distinguished her as an effective teacher and scholar.

Those who favor so-called neutrality and the presentation of "balanced" views would not challenge Diane Bell's right to defend her research. They would question whether her classroom lectures on a particular controversy were attempts at indoctrinating her students. She always outlined the controversy in question and its opposing viewpoints, but she could not do so in a way that appeared to be neutral, balanced, or evenhanded. Partly it was not in her nature; but more to the point, her students would have known that any attempts she made to be neutral were not genuine. What she always did was to invite students to disagree with her and challenge her opinions. She assured them that she would return the challenge if she thought their logic or analysis was flawed. In effect, she told them that their arguments would be taken seriously if they took the questions seriously and respected her enough to argue against her interpretations. To challenge her required preparation and I suspect many were intimidated by the prospect of doing so—not because she would penalize them but because it was hard work refuting her well-informed positions.

Bell brilliantly exhibited the sort of professional standards that take the students' opinions seriously but require the student to meet the same professional standards for inquiry, evidence, and analysis. It does not mean that all opinions are respected equally. It means that an effort to meet the standards is respected, even if the effort fails. Assertions without any effort to meet the standards of inquiry do not have to be respected. Students often miss that distinction.

○ ○ ○

Respecting different opinions and interpretations while disagreeing with them requires a common ground based on how inquiry must take place. In law, there are rules of evidence and accepted procedures and rights. Eliminate that common ground and there can be no justice. The same is true for education. The central question is not whether professors espouse positions in class directly related to the material, but whether the professor adheres to the Principles of Discourse and values openness, civility, and disagreement. There is no question that there are times when guidelines and standards are not followed, just as there are times when accepted procedural principles are not followed in the legal system. In the legal system, such procedural lapses lead to injustice. In education, such failings lead to an incomplete education and, on occasion, to injustice as well. In both settings, silence can be dangerous and, ultimately, dishonest.

These portraits define the artistry and the courage it takes to be a successful teacher who is sufficiently engaged. The success or failure of teachers to be true artists rests on their ability to interact with the student in a way that respects the student even when disagreeing with that student. Whether they take a stand on controversial issues or not should not determine how they interact with students. But how they interact with students will determine whether engagement or neutrality impacts the learning and growth of the student in a positive or negative way. Professor Bell's lifetime of teaching and scholarship defines what would be lost if all teachers felt compelled to be neutral.

The critical word in the previous sentence is "all." Not every engaged professor needs to be as deeply involved in political and social issues as Professor Bell was. A deep engagement with and passion for a chosen field sends its own valuable lessons to students about the importance of ideas. What great teachers have in common, however, is that they listen well; and by engaging with their students, this often means teachers are listening to them and respecting them, no matter where they stand on any particular issue. These engaged teachers create an atmosphere where it is safe to ask questions and where it is okay to be uncomfortable. If educational institutions cannot create such an open atmosphere, the societies they serve will also fail to do so. It is a necessity.

Whatever their teaching style, educators share a common desire to see their students positively engage with the material being presented. The quality of that engagement, in turn, is affected by the quality of the engagement between the teacher and the student. The neutralists and those who accept more extreme activism acknowledge the importance of this relationship between faculty and students. The key difference lies in what kind of student they assume they are teaching.

The central debate in the Pennsylvania hearings, concerning the proper role of the faculty and how to teach critical thinking, were two very different and often unstated views of students. Those arguing for the neutral university saw university students as impressionable tabula rasas on which the faculty could inscribe their own views or any prejudices they wished. They were inheritors of the Bork line of reasoning about the naïve idealism and impressionableness of youth. On the other hand, those arguing that faculty bias was not a problem also did not focus on the students. Hardly anyone discussed the role of students; their silence, unfortunately, implied a rejection of what I have nearly always found to be the case. If encouraged, students are seldom silent and often cannot be silenced. They are naturally curious and eager for dialog. Their growth into intellectually mature and thoughtful contributors to society rests as much as anything on the ability and willingness of adults to challenge them and to listen. The Pennsylvania hearings were supposed to be all about the students; but the students' needs were not given the same kind of analysis devoted to assertions about how professors should behave in the classroom. The final chapter returns to this blind spot in the debate, arguing that students need to be challenged, not protected.

CHAPTER 11

Conclusion: Listen to Students

All academic institutions engage their students. Far fewer, however, listen to them. An institution's willingness to listen means taking students seriously and seeing them as contributors and actors in their education, not simply as passive objects of education. Institutions must respect students, inviting their participation and taking their contributions seriously. Doing so will give students more self-confidence and, in turn, they will contribute more to their scholastic environment.

When selling the quality of education they provide, universities cite the faculty, class sizes, student-faculty ratios, the number of seminars, independent work, and various measures indicating the number of successful graduates. The student-faculty ratios and close student-faculty relationships, in effect, are surrogates for the concept of engagement. Those promoting the university and potential students for the most part assume that if the classes are small, engagement occurs. Monitoring or measuring the quality of that engagement, however, is rare. Thinking about the quality and intensity of student-faculty engagement requires asking essential questions about how individual students learn and what students, not just faculty, can contribute to the process of education. It is the answers to these questions that should be the basis for evaluating advising systems, pedagogy, and the entire educational program.

When I arrived at Hampshire in 1989 I had to confront these essential questions in ways I never had to previously, since Hampshire offered a negotiated, rather than either a prescribed or an elective, education. More important, I realized that the general public had very little understanding of the educational implications of any of these options for guiding students in the choices they make.

The critical difference between free choice, prescription, and negotiation lies in the nature of the conversation between students and faculty that each approach generates. In the standard format of U.S. tertiary education, the student and the advisor go through a process of matching a student's interests with available courses and college requirements. It is usually a matter of checking off categories and making the resulting schedule as interesting and as useful as possible to the student. In a negotiated education, the process resembles what happens in graduate school. The process begins with identifying the questions the student wants to ask and then an explanation of what lies behind the questions. Only then does the conversation turn to courses, research, and possible activities like internships that will illuminate the central questions the student wants to address. A student's scholarly inquisitiveness drives his or her education; there are no boundaries except those the students place on themselves. However, professors do have to agree to the plan. They judge the rigor and clarity of the student's central focus of study and whether their research plans contain the necessary scope and depth.

Negotiation is a part of every educational program in every university. The key is whether students are offered the opportunity to negotiate about their education or simply about a set of courses. Open negotiation is at the core of many honors programs and even a few freshman programs. At the undergraduate level in the United States access to this type of negotiation is usually limited to a few students or to a student's final year. But when students are expected to negotiate their own education, the institution's entire culture changes. What is radical about the handful of institutions such as

Hampshire, Evergreen, and Marlboro is that they use what is actually a graduate-school model for undergraduates—a model that applies to all students, not just a few. In effect, they are arguing that the "honors" approach, emphasizing negotiation and student ownership of their education (with professors as partners in that ownership, of course), creates a more transforming experience for the student, regardless of the students' ability or interests. These colleges and universities do not assume every student is an honors student, but they do assume that creating the expectation of honors work and providing the opportunity will help each student grow more than in a traditional system. I found this to be true at Hampshire, not because the nature of the engagement between faculty and student was different than what I had experienced at Dartmouth, but because every student and every faculty member at Hampshire was expected to "engage" with high intensity. The intensity was not always achieved, but it was far more than when the system expected this engagement from only a select few students.

The negotiation process places a high premium on both listening and engagement. Not only does it make close student-faculty relationships mandatory—no progress can be made without that closeness—it also shapes the purpose of that closeness and places a premium on listening and provides an incentive to learn to listen well. Unfortunately, the contract system cannot guarantee that all students or faculty will learn to listen effectively, but the system does create favorable conditions for progress in the art of listening— far more than could be achieved in either a prescribed or free-choice system.

Creating the expectation that students are to be partners in the educational process, and assuming they will bring valuable insights to it, had a liberating impact on all involved. Faculty members bring depth of knowledge and experience, while students bring the power of their fresh, unconventional worldviews. The mix is creatively explosive and can generate a level of engagement with knowledge and with peers that energizes everyone. For me, it offered a new standard of what engagement and listening meant. As I taught and served on divisional committees, I found the experience to be the most challenging and rewarding teaching I had ever done. I was offered an entirely new perspective on what listening to students really meant.

I soon began to understand that the expectations created by a negotiated educational program provide the energy and liberation that made the Monday breakfasts so intense and valuable to me and, I hope, to the students as well. It is crucial to understand the value of treating students as partners in their education, rather than the presumptive way they were dealt with in the Pennsylvania hearings. Although the debate was about their academic freedom, they were treated more as secondary citizens. Students did testify in the Pennsylvania hearings but usually the line of questioning directed at students reflected a low level of interest in what they had to say. The legislators merely tolerated the students, and they were certainly not engaged, even though the students presented some of the most relevant and moving testimony.

Although I am being critical, I do recognize and give credit to the Pennsylvania Committee that they invited students to testify. The committee, however, could have structured the hearings to focus more on the students. They could have asked the student governments on each campus to hold their own hearings or a conference on the same subjects and provide a summary of results to the committee. That process alone would have done far more to educate the students about their rights than anything the legislature actually accomplished; and this approach may have engaged the entire community in a far more intense conversation about academic freedom. The Select Committee also could have taken the student-generated information and asked academics, administrators, and concerned organizations (such as Students for Academic Freedom) to comment on what students had said. If the Select Committee had chosen such an approach, there would have been a threefold impact on the outcome. First, a legislature that had actually asked the students about problems that affected them directly would have grabbed the public's attention. Since the issue at hand was whether the students' academic freedom was at risk, giving more emphasis on the students' thoughts would have made sense. Second, the process of engaging students with their institution would have educated them about the value of academic freedom and alerted them to problems that might have existed, the remedies available, and how they could assert their rights if they needed to. Finally, by focusing more on the students, the legislature would have gotten a far better sense of students' perceptions of the issues and what was actually happening in the classroom. Perceptions are a critical aspect here.

Either the Select Committee or the universities involved could have initiated this very different approach. None of these entities did, however, which was probably because of their habitual indifference to students' views in cases where hot-button, controversial issues are concerned. If the committee or universities had initiated a more student-friendly approach, they would have created a teachable moment of far greater power than what took place. In the process, they might have effected a fourth and even more important result: bringing conservative and liberal students together to work on bridging a particular political divide that hindered campus-wide social progress. This way, the quality of dialogue on campus and between the campus and the public at large could have been improved. In the process, the legislators may have discovered that the public and the legislature do not need to protect the students. Students need to be engaged. That engagement, in the end, is the best way to teach the citizens of any country how to challenge authority in appropriate and constructive ways. If this principle had been instilled, I suspect more students may have voted as well.

Listening to students was a key factor in what I considered to be my most successful educational initiatives as president of Hampshire. The Voting Conference was one such event and the James Baldwin Scholars Program was another. The students identified key areas of concern early and accurately. And by making them partners in their own education, they reacted to faculty failures very differently than I suspect they would have had they been treated as mere objects. I came to realize at Hampshire that when I had a seemingly unsolvable problem or was confronted with a difficult challenge, the best strategy was to involve students. The creativity unleashed with that student-faculty engagement is exhilarating. And although involving students almost always required much more work and time commitments, the results had much greater impact and provided much more satisfaction for both students and faculty members. Students were responsible for the greatest highs I experienced over my entire educational career and yet the formula was so simple: ask students serious questions and their answers will often prove to be the most insightful advisement an educator could ask for.

○ ○ ○

In 1991, when Lee Brown, then commissioner of the New York City police department, and I planned the first of the Hampshire Urban Conferences described earlier, he was reluctant to include students in the conference. We were including the heads of the major departments, such as health, human services, education, economic development, and social services in ten major U.S. cities; he felt the program already was complicated enough without adding any generational differences. He said no. At first I was reluctant to challenge him on this matter; but I did begin to design a different approach that would accomplish the same goal.

All of the participants came to the conference without knowing what was planned. They did know that many U.S. cities were in crisis and they recognized the importance of people such as Lee Brown and William Bratton, then police commissioner of Boston and now, as I write this book, police commissioner of Los Angeles. The conference began with a dinner and no reception. The participants were divided into ten groups with no two representatives from the same city or profession in the same group. The task of each group was to take a two-page description and accompanying map of a fictitious, economically depressed city created by Hampshire and write a foundation proposal. The proposal would support their group's plan of how to use four city blocks, located in the most problematic part of the city, to begin a citywide revitalization process. Two Hampshire students were at each table, not as "participants," but rather to keep flip charts detailing the ideas developed at each table and to help prepare each table's proposal. The proposals were to be typed overnight and put into a notebook. Over the next two days, the groups would examine the ideas and assumptions underlying each proposal to see if they could develop a set of common ideas and principles for building healthy urban communities. As we predicted, within thirty minutes of the start of the working session, everyone had accepted the students as full participants. At the end of the conference, Lee Brown stood up and said that the past two days had been some of the most important in his professional life because the students had been present. And he graciously acknowledged and thanked Hampshire for ignoring his "order" to me that they not be included. With no specific expertise but many different backgrounds and experience, the students had contributed in a small but important way to building community-policing initiatives in the United States.

The American Bar Association's Council on Racial and Ethnic Justice, on which I served as vice chair, understood and welcomed student voices. In 1999 the council organized a national conference on affirmative action that university undergraduate students were invited to. Over sixty students attended, joined by over two hundred judges, lawyers, and professionals affiliated with the justice system. Charles Smith, Justice of the Washington State Supreme Court, had helped recruit a large number of these judges, especially from the national bar associations of color.

The students participated in all conference sessions and were asked to take on one additional and distinctive group assignment: drafting a so-called Declaration of Interdependence. They were encouraged to write whatever they felt needed to be said and to present the declaration at the conference conclusion. The conclusion was scheduled for the Saturday afternoon of a long holiday weekend. Still, no one left early. Two hundred judges and lawyers, not accustomed to waiting for others, waited patiently for the students, who were frantically finishing their declaration. The students arrived thirty minutes late, having sent continual messages that they were almost finished. When the students entered the room, the judges gave them a standing ovation because of what the students' participation had already added to the conference over the previous two days.

After the students read their declaration, the judges asked two hours of questions about every imaginable subject affecting the lives of young people in the United States and especially the lives of young people of color. The next day, noting that judicial ethics bans judges from making demands, the judges "asked" that the council organize such a conference every two years. The council has held three such conferences since then, and the response is always the same: it is a brilliant idea to include students. As a final note, the council held its third national conference in New Orleans in November 2006 and has prepared a final report that calls on emergency planners and responders to formally engage young people in the planning process and in response strategies. Young people were the most invisible group in New Orleans' disaster plan and in the response to what happened during and after Hurricane Katrina. The council concluded that the most effective response to that invisibility is to engage them in the process of helping the community rather than simply seeing them as a group to be helped.[1]

What I have learned from students over my forty years in education is simple and direct. If you ask them real questions and ask them to help you solve real problems rather than simply tell them what the answer is, they will respond with a level of energy, insight, and commitment that is astoundingly constructive. More important, the process of listening to students eliminates cynicism, increases voting and civic engagement, and improves the health of the society. Other cases highlight the same point.

A prominent citizen in a New England state, who had just been asked by the governor to co-chair a noninvestigative, nonjudicial statewide ethics commission, once asked me, "What should I do; what does such an ethics commission do?" We pondered the problem at length, wondering whether the commission was supposed to proclaim the importance of ethics, speak out about ethical lapses that had come to light, or do something more concrete. However, if they were not investigating specific cases, we could not figure out what that concrete action would be. Finally, I told him that when I was stumped on such matters I would solicit the students' opinions and get them involved in a meaningful way. He asked me to explain, so I began to think out loud: *The best way to get students involved is to ask them meaningful questions.* For example, the commission could ask the students what they thought the appropriate ethical standards for all public officials should be.

I suggested that the commission might ask every school in the state to have social studies students write a code of ethics for state employees—principles they felt should guide all state employees, from police officers and firefighters to economic-development and family-support workers. The commission could then host regional "conventions" that individual schools would bring their drafts to, and through a convention-like process, they would draft and adopt a single document. The commission could then have the students repeat the process in a statewide convention. At the end of that process, the students could even lobby the legislature to adopt the document in the form of a pledge that every person hired by the state would sign.

I explained that I had no idea what might develop from such an effort, or if the state legislature would even accept what was put forward. But at the end of the process almost every family in the state with children (and many without them) and all of the members of the legislature would have given much thought to the subject of ethics. He asked me to put those ideas in a formal proposal. I did so, and my understanding is that the draft was submitted to the governor almost two years ago. There has been no response so far. Persuading people to involve students and to ask students serious questions (for which complex answers are needed) is always difficult, even if it seems so obviously logical.

Students can transform entire schools, as the Pathways to College program has demonstrated. Students can help address other educational challenges as well. I have argued throughout this book that exposure to a multiplicity of cultural and international perspectives is essential. In the United States, creating the necessary diversity is an immense challenge, especially for underfunded institutions that cannot attract international students with extensive scholarship aid and schools that do not have the enrollment levels and/or resources to send many students abroad. The faculty, no matter what their chosen field or their own knowledge and experience, cannot introduce enough diversity in their course material to create the needed international awareness; and more often than not, the professors do not have sufficient knowledge and experience with multicultural issues themselves. On the other hand, if these same institutions created the expectation that every student in every course introduce, in some form, a perspective or question about material drawn from or relating to a different culture, the collective effort could be positively transformative for everyone. It would create an extraordinary level of diverse perspectives embracing all kinds of political and nonpolitical contexts.

The concept of diverse perspectives would become far more complex and interesting than the simplistic dichotomy of conservative and liberal. Such an expectation would have the added advantage of helping students integrate their study-abroad experiences into all of their work and would help international and noninternational students find more ways to work together and to get to know each other on a deeper level than is currently taking place on most campuses.

Even students in the sciences might find it interesting, not because there is a Chinese perspective on calculus but because they might want to know, for example, who studied calculus in China and when, or to know something about pre-medical education in South Africa or India. The intellectual power of the students would be harnessed to generate engagement and enrich the pluralism of views to which each student and faculty member was exposed.

What I am proposing here will seem simplistic and naïve to many, including many educators. It is neither. Students want to be taken seriously; and when they are, they become serious. Young people already recognize that developing a global perspective will be a valuable asset for whatever career they chose. The older generation is failing them by not giving them enough opportunity to develop that perspective.

Educators and citizens alike fail our students when we do not set high enough expectations. We fail our students when we allow a school board to close a successful and challenging International Baccalaureate program that the students themselves want. Tertiary education did not do enough then, and does not do enough now, when it remains silent as politicians and pundits spend their time arguing about whether English should be made the official language of the United States, as is happening as I review the copyediting of this manuscript.

Instead of silence we should listen and respond to our students, who are telling us they want both to be challenged and prepared for *their* future, not their parents' past. As one student asked in one of my last breakfasts at Hampshire, "Why shouldn't it be national policy that every student speak English and one other language?" Imagine what would happen if such a goal were adopted nationally. Suddenly all of those children of immigrants who are struggling in school with English and therefore are deemed a liability because they bring test scores down would become assets. They would be fluent in one language and more than likely way ahead of their classmates in learning a second language, in their case, English. Overnight they would become the advantaged students and would have an advantage in the college application process. Discussions about bilingual education would take on a whole new meaning.

Such a dream may be naïve and idealistic, but today's students just might surprise the older generation if it provided the resources. The investment could be justified on economic grounds to be sure, but national defense always seems to be more persuasive. Imagine where we would be in the war on terrorism if the United States had a population that was bilingual and trilingual like so many other nations, and if the U.S. had made the preservation of the ability to speak one's birth language a national priority, rather than dismissing it as something to be lost as quickly as possible. There would certainly be many more Arabic-speaking citizens. The real point, however, is that tertiary education should be a strong voice in the conversations taking place about language competences. It should engage in the debate, and it should invite the students themselves to be part of that debate. In so many ways we need to listen to our students.

○ ○ ○

As I was completing this book, I had the opportunity to visit Vilnius, Lithuania, for a day and was able to spend three hours talking with students from the European Humanities University who had read a summary of this book's main themes. I began the session by expressing my admiration for the choices they had made and the courage they were exhibiting in pursuit of their education. To a person, they were surprised by my praise. Their responses, in turn, surprised me, as they explained, "What choice? We had no choice. We had to leave to get an education."

Although they acknowledged that they were challenging authority, they did not see themselves as doing anything out of the ordinary. They simply wanted a "real" education. They knew that traditional education in Belarus was about absorbing a specific view and not about developing critical thinking. Even though some did not have the full support of their families, and although they knew that their actions might subject their families to pressure from the Belarus KGB, they did not see themselves as having done something worthy of admiration. They were engaged in their education so deeply they did not see how exceptional they were. I left hoping that someday the current government in Belarus would listen to them or, better yet, that some day these free-thinking students would be part of that government.

Unfortunately, getting the government to listen to them is a distant hope at the moment. Lukashenko continues to be afraid of the university and constantly berates it. The Belarus secret police continue to harass Belarus EHU students and their families. In June of 2007 the state-owned news agency BELTA, the "mouthpiece" of Belarus authorities, ran a story on its Web site about EHU, entitled "University for Political Brainwashing."

The article describes support for the university as part of a conspiracy between the European Union and the United States to embarrass Belarus. The article's author attacks the students themselves. They are accused of not having "any special aspiration for study" and of having "low motivation to obtain knowledge." They "abuse alcohol," organize "overnight debauches," and violate public order. At the conclusion, the author summarizes the authorities' complaints about the university:

> The real objectives of EHU are spreading destructive propaganda among Belarusian students, creating conditions for destabilization of the social and political situation in Belarus, and increasing the number of radically-minded young people who act in the interests of foreign subversive centers. The EHU operations are aimed at damaging the interests of the Republic of Belarus in the political, humanitarian, and information fields, and are also used by foreign

secret services and related organizations and individuals in carrying out illegal activities against our country.[2]

The Belarus students at the European Humanities University may need protection—but not from biased faculty. As I listened to these students talk about education, I knew I had come full circle. I was in the presence of students who, like the four students in North Carolina almost fifty years before, understood clearly what education should be about and were not afraid to challenge authority in appropriate and constructive ways in order to achieve socially beneficial goals. The parallels seemed overwhelming as we discussed the themes of this book. The North Carolina A &T students had to challenge authority to establish and make others understand and accept the dignity their education was giving them. The EHU students had to challenge authority in order to gain an education that would give them dignity. Many in the world face similar situations. In these two cases, the concept of neutrality in education itself is not neutral and certainly is not acceptable. It should not be acceptable in any democracy nor in any country interested in being a healthy society.

Notes

Foreword

1. *Newsweek* (January 9, 2006), 37.
2. Sizer, T. R., and N. F. Sizer, *The Students Are Watching: Schools and the Moral Contract* (Boston: Beacon Press, 1999).

Chapter 1: Origins: Educating a College President

1. Robert Bork, *Slouching Toward Gomorrah: Modern Liberalism and American Decline* (New York, 1996), 328.
2. Ibid., 4–6.
3. For an alternative view of the causes of "moral decline" see Callahan, D. *The Cheating Culture* (2003). In the spirit of full disclosure, David Callahan is an alumnus of Hampshire College.
4. Bork, 86.
5. Ibid., 87.
6. Ibid., 88.
7. Ibid., 154.
8. Ibid., 230.
9. Ibid., 250.
10. Ibid., 251.
11. Ibid., 272–276.
12. Another way to view these connections is to look at the geographical dispersal of the colleges themselves as this concept of education moved westward from Oxford and Cambridge to Harvard and Yale Colleges and then farther westward into the hinterland of the U.S., with the founding colleges such as Dartmouth, Amherst, Williams, Kenyon, Oberlin, Macalester, Reed, and the Claremont Colleges.
13. The core of this definition comes from a 1962 speech given by Theodore Greene, a Yale University Professor of Philosophy at New Asia College, now part of the Chinese University of Hong Kong. I was teaching in the English department as a Yale-China Fellow at the time.
14. In the United States, small liberal arts colleges like Oberlin, Amherst, Smith, Wellesley, Macalester, and literally hundreds more created living/learning communities in which the classroom and the living experience became one and the individual and the communal selves could be developed simultaneously and in an integrated manner.
15. For a more nuanced and moving discussion of the meaning of liberal education, I would recommend, among other titles, James O. Friedman's elegant book, *Liberal Education and the Public Interest* (2003). Iowa City: University of Iowa Press.

Chapter 2: The Engaged University vs. the Neutral University

1. Report of the Select Committee on Academic Freedom in Higher Education Pursuant to House Resolution 177. November 21, 2006, 3–4.

2. Ibid.

3. Balch described NAS as "a membership organization of professors, academic administrators and graduate students committed to strengthening standards, open market place of ideas, and, in general, higher education improvement." Ibid.

4. Transcripts of public hearings of Select Committee on Academic Freedom in Higher Education Pursuant to House Resolution 177 (November 9, 2005), 9–10. (This and all of the other quotations taken from the Pennsylvania hearings, unless otherwise noted, come from court transcripts of oral testimony and are not always grammatically or syntactically correct. Throughout the book I have not added "sic" because it would interrupt the flow of that sense of oral dialogue.)

5. Ibid., 14.

6. Ibid., 30.

7. Ibid., 40.

8. Ibid., 78.

9. Ibid., 83–84.

10. Ibid., 19.

11. Ibid., 19–21. The article by Cass Sunstein to which Balch is referring is "The Law Group Polarization."

12. Theodore Sizer, whose work was cited earlier in the preface, founded the Coalition of Essential Schools, a secondary-school reform effort in the United States. The curriculum in these schools encouraged students to identify, reflect upon, and attempt to answer the essential questions in a field, a problem, or a text.

13. Balch, *op. cit.*, 10.

14. See Neal, A. P., and D'Avanzo, C., eds., *Student Active Science: Models of Innovation in College Science Teaching* (Toronto: Saunders College Publishing, 1997), which explores the topic in detail with respect to science teaching and that includes an article I cowrote with Nancy Kelly placing active learning in a macro context.

Chapter 3: Protecting vs. Challenging Students

1. Students for Academic Freedom is an offshoot of another Horowitz-headed organization, the Center for the Study of Popular Culture. As such, SAF is only one of several causes that Horowitz has advanced over time. One of the most recent, as this book goes to press, is his charge about what he calls "Islamo-fascists" on college campuses. While his activities suggest that he has his own agenda and that he is as concerned with the content of positions as he is with simply having a diversity of views expressed, I will only address Horowitz as a spokesperson for SAF and as an advocate of that plea for diverse perspectives and university neutrality. I will leave to others to sort out what is a more complex interpretation of his other goals and intellectual interests.

2. Students for Academic Freedom, Academic Bill of Rights. (www.studentsforaca demicfreedom.org).

3. Ibid.

4. David Horowitz, Pennsylvania hearings (January 10, 2006), 142. The official transcript leaves out the phrase "social justice" after the word "advocates," but it is included in the written testimony Professor Horowitz submitted to the committee and shared with the author.

5. Report of the Select Committee on Academics in Higher Education Pursuant to House Resolution 177, November 21, 2006.

6. A. D. Neal, Pennsylvania hearings (January 10, 2006), 55.

7. Ibid., 58.

8. Mike Ratliff, Pennsylvania hearings (March 22, 2006), 214.

9. Ibid., 214.

10. Ibid., pp. 216–217. (It should be noted that as this work is in production, I am a Senior Fellow of the Association of American Colleges and Universities (AAC&U) and think highly of the leadership AAC&U and its president, Carol Schneider, have provided to education in America.)

11. Ibid., 219.

Chapter 4: The University of Natal: Modeling the Behavior We Expect from Students

1. For the University of Cape Town struggle see Saunders, S., *Vice-Chancellor on a Tightrope* (Cape Town: David Phillips).

2. Among the trustees were several who held very strong positions for and against divestment. The president, Adele Simmons, held a PhD in African Studies and was in touch with leading figures in South Africa, including Bishop Tutu and Helen Suzman. As she explained to me in reviewing this section of the book, "People in South Africa who wanted to change the system were not all in agreement that divestment was the right thing, arguing that the jobs that might be lost as U.S. firms pulled out could have a divesting impact in the African community. . . . It was not so clear at the time that this was the right way to help Africans who were trying to promote change. In retrospect it is much clearer."

Chapter 5: The European Humanities University: Challenging Authority Abroad and at Home

1. Letter from the rector, www.data.minsk.by.edu

2. Mission Statement, European Humanities University, http://www.data.minsk .by/ehu

3. "Chronicles of the Conflict," European Humanities University brochure.

4. Conversation with Anatoly Mikhailov, November 27, 2006, at a dinner honoring the university hosted by its International Advisory Committee at the Oriental Club in London.

5. "Chronicles of the Conflict."

6. Ibid.

7. Ibid.

8. EHU Web page.

9. I was not able to acquire the tape but I am confident that the sense of the statement is correct.

Chapter 6: The Asian University for Women: Charting a New Course and Living Up to Expectations

1. Someday U.S. for-profit educational institutions may be an equally distinguished third leg, although most likely with a very different set of missions that might in turn help not-for-profit educational institutions understand more clearly what makes them unique.

2. American Council on Education's Statement on Academic Freedom and Diversity of Perspectives taken from the Web site: www.acenet.edu.

3. Interview with Kamal Ahmed in Cambridge, MA, May 2006.

4. Ibid.

5. Plan of operations, Asian University for Women, Chittagong, Bangladesh, May 2005.

6. The board of directors includes, in addition to Kamal Ahmad: board vice chair, president and CEO, Asian University for Women Support Foundation; Vivian Lowery Derryck: senior vice president of the Academy for Educational Development, former assistant administrator for Africa at the U.S. Agency for International Development; Stephen J. Friedman: Dean of Pace University School of Law, former senior partner, Debevoise & Plimpton LLP, former chairman, Overseas Development Council; Hanna H. Gray: President Emerita, Harry Pratt Judson Distinguished Service Professor Emerita of History, University of Chicago; Jeffrey S. Lehman: former president and professor of law, Cornell University, former Dean of the University of Michigan Law School; Kathy M. Matsui: managing director and chief Japan strategist; codirector of Pan Asian Investment Research, Goldman Sachs (Japan) Ltd.; William H. Newton-Smith: fellow and tutor in philosophy, Balliol College, Oxford University, chair, Higher Education Subboard, Open Society Institute; Henry Rosovsky: Lewis P. and Linda L. Geyser University Professor Emeritus and former Dean of the Faculty of Arts & Sciences, Harvard University.

7. Ibid.

8. Ibid.

9. Association of American Colleges and Universities (2002). Greater Expectations National Panel Report, Washington, D.C., 33–34.

10. Since the Michigan case decision, Lee Bollinger has become president of Columbia University where he, at the time of finishing this manuscript, was embroiled in controversy evolving from the president of Iran, Mahmoud Ahmadinejad, speaking on campus. Bollinger's introduction of Iran's president was strongly hostile. A group of Columbia faculty members later criticized Bollinger for the tone of the introduction, arguing that he used "the language of war." In response, as reported in the *New York Times* (November 14, 2007: A21), Bollinger stated that he believes "it is crucial for university presidents to speak out on important issues." A second statement by another group of faculty members supported his actions. Since the Michigan case decision, Marvin Krislov has become president of Oberlin College, a small liberal arts college with a long and highly respected history of institutional activism.

11. The mission statement for St. John's College is presented as the mission for liberal education: "Such education seeks to free men and women from the tyrannies of unexamined opinions and inherited prejudices. It also endeavors to enable them to make intelligent, free choices concerning the ends and means of

both public and private life. At St. John's, freedom is pursued mainly through thoughtful conversation about great books of the Western tradition. The books that are at the heart of learning at St. John's stand among the original sources of our intellectual tradition. They are timeless and timely; they not only illuminate the persisting questions of human existence, but also have great relevance to contemporary problems. They change our minds, move our hearts, and touch our spirits."

Chapter 7: Singapore Management University: Teaching Critical Thinking and Why Teachers Teach

1. Office of Corporate Communications, *SMU: The New Educational Environment*, Singapore, 2006, 12.
2. While Singapore is one of the very few, if not the only, cases globally where a basically authoritarian, nondemocratic government has established, as a matter of official government policy, a liberal arts institution. What happens here may have important lessons for independent liberal arts institutions in countries like Russia, Pakistan, or Saudi Arabia, where democratic institutions are under threat or only just emerging.
3. *SMU: Educational Environment*, 22.
4. Ibid., 15.

Chapter 8: The American University in Bulgaria: Speaking to Authority

1. Speech by Deyan Vassilve at the American University in Bulgaria, fifteenth anniversary celebration in Blagoevgrad, October 13, 2006.
2. Rachel Carson, Pennsylvania hearings (November 10, 2005), 166–167.
3. Ibid., 167–168.
4. D. R. Dodson, Jr., Pennsylvania hearings (March 22, 2006), 127.
5. T. Christopher, Pennsylvania hearings (March 22, 2006), 127–128.
6. H. Otterbein, Pennsylvania hearings (May 31, 2006), 120.
7. A. Peak, Pennsylvania hearings (May 31, 2006), 140–141.

Chapter 9: What Is Enough?: Communities and Universities

1. The Learning Tree helps high school dropouts regain focus and earn the General Equivalence Diploma (GED) as a way of completing their high school education.
2. See Fernandez, Y. M., *Navigating Bridges and Barriers: A Case Study of the James Baldwin Scholars Program*, unpublished PhD dissertation, Graduate School of the University of Massachusetts, Amherst, Massachusetts (2007). The study documents the program's successes and the challenges the students have faced. While the founders are no longer involved and changes have been made, it continues to succeed to the extent that it does because individuals like its current director, Madeleine Marquez, continue to do what is most important: be deeply engaged with the students and listen to them.
3. I have served on the board of Pathways to College, and when I retired as president of Hampshire, I left the Pathways board and became a consultant.
4. Thomas Frank, *What's the Matter with Kansas: How Conservatives Won the Heart of America* (New York, NY: Henry Holt and Company, 2004).

5. P. H. Garland, Pennsylvania hearings (May 31, 2006), 10–11.

6. Another example of the "slow" response of academia came as I was finishing this manuscript. It was not until the summer of 2007 that the American Association of University Professors came out with an extensive critique of the efforts of groups like Students for Academic Freedom to pass legislation about what is happening in classrooms. It is a well-thought-out critique addressing and refuting the four major claims of the neutralists, which are: 1) instructors "indoctrinate" rather than educate; 2) instructors fail to fairly present conflicting views on contentious subjects, thereby depriving students of educationally essential "diversity" or "balance"; 3) instructors are intolerant of students' religious, political or socioeconomic views, thereby creating a hostile atmosphere inimical to learning; and 4) instructors persistently interject material, especially of a political or ideological character, irrelevant to the subject of instruction. Although the response came late for this book, if not for the debate, it does address some of the key educational issues; however, it also remains silent on whether the university should be neutral. Horowitz responded to *Inside Higher Education* and said there was no mention of a problem with professors violating the academic freedom of students, and he was correct. See also American Association of University Professors, "Freedom in the Classroom," 2007 (Authored by subcommittee composed of Mathew W. Finkin (Law), University of Illinois at Urbana-Champaign, chair; Robert C. Post (Law), Yale University; Carey Nelson (English), University of Illinois at Urbana-Champaign; Ernst Benjamin (Political Science), Washington, D.C.; Eric Combest, staff. The full document is available on the AAUP Web site, www.aaup.edu.

7. Hart, J. (2005), *The Making of the American Conservative Mind: National Review and Its Times.* Wilmington DE: ISI Books.

Chapter 10: What Is Enough?: The Role of the Professor

1. The material about Diane Bell came from a two-day interview with her in Norwich, Vermont, U.S.A., from material she provided at that time and from working with her as a trustee of Hampshire College for twelve years.

2. Hindmarsh Case, 2001: paragraph 373.

Chapter 11: Conclusion: Listen to Students

1. American Bar Association's Council on Ethnic and Racial Justice (2007), "Making the Invisible Visible": A New Approach to Disaster Planning and Response: Chicago. www.abanet.org/randejustice.

2. Original Russian text of the June 8, 2007, article by Victor Lougach is available at http://www.belta.by/ou/actual/comments?i=159907. The English translation was provided by the rector's office, European Humanities University.

Bibliography

Association of American Colleges and Universities, *Greater Expectations*.

Bellah, R., et. al., *The Good Society*. New York: Random House, Vintage Books, 1992.

Bellah, R., et. al., *Habits of the Heart*. New York: Harper & Row, Perennial Library, 1985.

Bell, D., *Ngarrwndjeri Wurruwarrin: A World That Is, Was, and Will Be*. North Melbourne, Victoria, Australia: Spinifex Press, 1998.

Bok, D., *Our Underachieving Colleges*. Princeton, NJ: Princeton University Press, 2005.

Bork, R. H., *Slouching Toward Gomorrah: Modern Liberalism and American Decline*. New York: Regan Books/Harper Collins, 1996.

Callahan, D., *The Cheating Culture*. New York: Harcourt, Inc., 2004.

Fernandez, Y. M., *Navigating Bridges and Barriers: A Case Study of the James Baldwin Scholars Program*. Unpublished PhD dissertation, Graduate School of the University of Massachusetts, Amherst, Massachusetts, 2007.

Florida, R., *Rise of the Creative Class*. New York: Basic Books, 2002.

Frank, T., *What's the Matter with Kansas?* New York: Henry Holt, 2004.

Freedman, J. O., *Liberal Education and the Public Interest*. Iowa City: University of Iowa Press, 2003.

Freeman, J. O., *Idealism and Liberal Education*. Ann Arbor: University of Michigan Press, 2000.

Giamatti, A. B., *A Free and Ordered Space: The Real World of the University*. New York: W.W. Norton & Co., 1990.

Hart, J., *The Making of the American Conservative Mind: National Review and Its Times*. Wilmington, DE: ISI Books, 2005.

Hampshire College. The only major book on Hampshire is the founding document: *The Making of a College*, not currently in print. Current information about the college can be found on its Web page: www.hampshire.edu.

Neal, A. P., and D'Avanzo, C., eds., *Student-Active Science: Models of Innovation in College Science Teaching*. New York: Sunders College Publishing, 1997.

Office of Corporate Communications, *SMU: The New Educational Environment*. Singapore, 2006.

Pennsylvania House of Representatives Select Committee on Academic Freedom (2005–06), official transcripts of Public Hearings. Harrisburg, PA.

Saunders, S., *Vice-Chancellor on a Tightrope*. Cape Town, South Africa: David Phillips, 2000.

Sizer, T. R., and Sizer, N. F., *The Children Are Watching: Schools and the Moral Contract*. Boston: Beacon Press, 1999.

Further Reading

Teach Them to Challenge Authority, as an argument and a memoir, embraces a lifetime of reading and influences, particular to me but not necessarily useful to those in other countries interested in the major themes of this book. Whatever longer list I could provide would not necessarily speak to those living in places like South Asia, the European Union, South Africa, or Australia, all specifically referenced in the book; nor in the many other places not mentioned, such as Pakistan, Saudi Arabia, or China, where nascent efforts to build a liberal arts tradition exist; nor in Latin America, where the university, not necessarily embracing the liberal arts tradition, has been for decades a major source for challenging authoritarian or corrupt governments. There will be many valuable sources in those regions with which I have no familiarity. Readers from those regions seeking further background on the subjects covered in this book should do subject searches focused on the major themes of this book: the purposes of education, the nature of liberal education, the characteristics of healthy societies, theories of learning and personal development, and public education policy. Exploring those themes in such local contexts, if nothing else, will test my own argument that liberal education is universal education, relevant to, even if not welcome in, any specific society.

Index